SUMMATION OF SERIES

COLLECTED BY

L. B. W. JOLLEY, M.A. (Cantab.), M.I.E.E.

Second Revised Edition

DOVER PUBLICATIONS, INC.

NEW YORK

Library of Congress Catalog Card Number: 61-65274

International Standard Book Number: 0-486-60023-8
Manufactured in the United States of America
Dover Publications, Inc.
180 Varick Street
New York, N. Y. 10014

PREFACE TO DOVER EDITION

A SECOND edition published in the United States of America provides an opportunity for including many new series with an increase of more than 50 per cent over the original number. It has also been possible to rearrange the series in a more reasonable form.

Some corrections have been received from readers, and useful suggestions have been made by them for the present arrangement. These are gratefully acknowledged, and it will be of great assistance for future editions if readers will communicate their ideas for further expansion.

In using this collection himself, the author has experienced difficulty in tracing certain series, and there does not seem any solution excepting a complete search through all the series given. For example, certain series including inverse products appear in different parts of the book, and, if a search is to be avoided, a complete rearrangement combined with excessive duplication would be necessary. It does not seem possible, as in the case of a collection of integrals, to arrange them in a completely rational manner. Any suggestion in this direction would be specially welcome.

Among the new series included are some of those developed by Glaisher in many publications, notably the *Quarterly Journal of Mathematics*. Basing his series on Bernoulli functions, Glaisher evolved a number of coefficients which apparently simplify the appearance of the series. In this present collection, only a few are given, and the original articles should be consulted if the reader wishes to investigate them further.

The author wishes to acknowledge permission by the London Scientific Computing Service to publish tables from the *Index of Mathematical Tables* by Fletcher, Miller, and Rosenhead—an

152307

exceedingly useful book for any engaged in work on applied mathematics; and also to thank Mrs. H. M. Cooper for her excellent work in typing a difficult manuscript.

L. B. W. JOLLEY

623 Upper Richmond Road West,
Richmond, Surrey, 1960

PREFACE TO FIRST EDITION

FOR a long time past there has been a need for a collection of series into one small volume for easy reference together with a bibliography indicating at least one of the textbooks to which reference could be made in case of doubt as to accuracy or to the method by which the series was arrived at.

The 700-odd series in this collection (with the exception of a few which have been specially prepared) are not new, and represent only the labour of extracting the material from the many textbooks on algebra, trigonometry, calculus and the like. Yet such a collection will, it is felt, be of considerable benefit to those engaged in the solution of technical problems, and will save a great deal of time in searching for the required result.

Criticism may be offered on the grounds that the inclusion of easy algebraical summations is unnecessary, but they have been inserted for a very definite purpose. For example, a series of inverse products may have for its sum an expression which is simple to find; but on the other hand, the solution may entail a complicated expression involving the integration or differentiation of other series. For this reason the arrangement of the series has been difficult, and overlapping is unavoidable in certain instances. To overcome this difficulty, the series have been set forth in as pictorial a manner as possible, so that the form of the individual terms can be readily seen.

On this account also, the inclusion of such series as are evolved for elliptic integrals, Bessel functions and the like has been restricted, perhaps to too great an extent; but reference to standard works is usually essential in such cases, and practically only such references are included.

The final column refers to the bibliography at the beginning of the book, and here again it has been quite impossible for obvious reasons to provide for all the references.

One of the most useful works, if it is desired to pursue any one particular problem further, is the *Smithsonian Tables*.

The scope of many of the series can be greatly enlarged by differentiation or integration of some of the forms given, and in the case of an integrated series, the constant of integration must be obtained by suitable methods.   Infinite products are often of value in obtaining new series by taking logarithms and by differentiating or integrating subsequently.

In many cases it has been impossible in this small volume to comment on the limits or assumptions made in any particular summation; particularly is this the case with oscillating series: and in case of doubt it is always safer to refer to a textbook, and to bear in mind that this collection is supplementary to, and not in place of, the usual mathematical books.

Special attention is drawn in cases of difficult summations to the General and Special Forms (pages 216–225).

In all cases logh denotes the logarithm to the Napierian base, in accordance with modern practice.

Finally, any additions or corrections would be welcomed for embodiment in subsequent editions.

L. B. W. JOLLEY

Fairdene, Sheen Road,
Richmond, Surrey, 1925

CONTENTS

BIBLIOGRAPHY

Indicating Letter	Author	Title and Publisher
A†	T. J. Bromwich	*Introduction to the Theory of Infinite Series*, London: Macmillan Co., 1926.
B	L. L. Smail	*Elements of the Theory of Infinite Processes*, New York: McGraw-Hill Book Co., 1923.
C	G. Chrystal	*Algebra, An Elementary Text Book for the Higher Classes of Secondary Schools*, New York: Dover Publications, Inc., 1961.
D	Levett and Davison	*Plane Trigonometry*, New York: Macmillan Co., 1892.
E	S. L. Loney	*Plane Trigonometry* (Parts I and II), Cambridge: Cambridge University Press, 1900.
F	H. S. Hall and S. R. Knight	*Higher Algebra*, London: Macmillan Co., 1899.
G	E. T. Whittaker and G. Robinson	*Calculus of Observations*, Glasgow: Blackie and Son, 1937.
H	H. Lamb	*Infinitesimal Calculus*, Cambridge: Cambridge University Press, 1921.
J	L. Todhunter	*Integral Calculus*, London: Macmillan Co., 1880.
K	C. P. Steinmetz	*Engineering Mathematics*, New York: McGraw-Hill Book Co., 1911.
L	J. Edwards	*Differential Calculus for Beginners*, London: Macmillan Co., 1899.
M	J. Edwards	*Integral Calculus for Beginners*, London: Macmillan Co., 1898.
N	G. S. Carr	*Synopsis of Pure Mathematics*, London: Hodgson, 1886.

† In the text, the numbers preceding the *Reference* letter refer to the volume of the work cited; the numbers following the *Reference* letter refer to pages.

xi

Indicating Letter	Author	Title and Publisher
O	E. W. Hobson	*A Treatise on Plane Trigonometry*, New York: Dover Publications, Inc., 1957.
P		*Encyclopaedia Britannica*, 11th edition.
Q	E. T. Whittaker and G. N. Watson	*Modern Analysis*, Cambridge: Cambridge University Press, 1920.
R	E. Goursat	*A Course in Mathematical Analysis*, Vol. 1, New York: Dover Publications, Inc., 1959.
T	E. P. Adams	*Smithsonian Mathematical Formulae*, Washington: Smithsonian Institute, 1922.
U	W. E. Byerly	*Fourier's Series*, New York: Dover Publications, Inc., 1959.
W	G. Boole	*Calculus of Finite Differences*, New York: Dover, 1960.
X	A. Eagle	*Fourier's Theorem*, New York: Longmans Green and Co., 1925.
Y	J. Edwards	*Differential Calculus*, London: Macmillan Co., 1938.
Z	J. Edwards	*Integral Calculus*, Vols. I and II, London: Macmillan Co., 1922.
AA	K. Knopp	*Theory and Applications of Infinite Series*, Glasgow: Blackie and Son, 1928.
AB	H. S. Carslaw	*Fourier's Series and Integrals*, New York: Dover Publications, Inc., 1950.
AC	Fletcher, Miller, and Rosenhead	*Index of Mathematical Tables*, London: Scientific Computing Service, 1946.
AD	E. Jahnke and F. Emde	*Tables of Functions*, New York: Dover Publications, Inc., 1945.
AE	J. W. L. Glaisher	*Quarterly Journal of Mathematics*, Vol. 29, 1898.
AE.I.	J. W. L. Glaisher	*Quarterly Journal of Mathematics*, Vol. 28, 1896.
AG	E. W. Hobson	*The Theory of Functions of a Real Variable*, Vol. II, New York: Dover Publications, Inc., 1957.

SUMMATION OF SERIES

Series No.

I. Arithmetical Progression

(1) $a + (a + d) + (a + 2d) + \ldots n$ terms

II. Geometrical Progression

(2) $a + ar + ar^2 + \ldots n$ terms

(3) $a + ar + ar^2 + \ldots \infty$

(4) $1 + ax + a^2x^2 + a^3x^3 + \ldots \infty$

III. Arithmetical and Geometrical Progression

(5) $a + (a + d)r + (a + 2d)r^2 + \ldots n$ terms

(6) $a + (a + d)r + (a + 2d)r^2 + \ldots \infty$

(7) $1 + 2x + 3x^2 + 4x^3 + \ldots \infty$

(8) $1 + \dfrac{4}{5} + \dfrac{7}{5^2} + \dfrac{10}{5^3} + \ldots n$ terms

(9) $1 + \dfrac{2}{2} + \dfrac{3}{2^2} + \dfrac{4}{2^3} + \ldots n$ terms

(10) $1 + \dfrac{3}{2} + \dfrac{5}{4} + \dfrac{7}{8} + \ldots \infty$

(11) $1 + 3x + 6x^2 + 10x^3 + \ldots \infty$

† See footnote to Bibliography.

$$= \frac{n}{2}\{2a + (n-1)d\} = \frac{n}{2}(a + l) \quad \text{where } l = \text{last term} \qquad \text{F. 29}$$

$$= a\frac{(r^n - 1)}{r - 1} \qquad \text{F. 39}$$

$$= \frac{a}{1 - r} \quad \text{where } r < 1 \qquad \text{F. 40}$$

$$= \frac{1}{1 - ax} \quad \text{where } ax < 1 \qquad \text{F. 158}$$

$$= \frac{a}{1 - r} + \frac{dr(1 - r^{n-1})}{(1 - r)^2} - \frac{\{a + (n-1)d\}r^n}{1 - r} \qquad \text{F. 44}$$

$$= \frac{a}{1 - r} + \frac{dr}{(1 - r)^2} \quad \text{where } r < 1 \qquad \text{F. 44}$$

$$= \frac{1}{(1 - x)^2} \quad \text{where } x < 1 \qquad \text{F. 44}$$

$$= \frac{35}{16} - \frac{12n + 7}{16 \cdot 5^{n-1}} \qquad \text{F. 45}$$

$$= 4 - \frac{1}{2^{n-2}} - \frac{n}{2^{n-1}} \qquad \text{F. 45}$$

$$= 6 \qquad \text{F. 45}$$

$$= \frac{1}{(1 - x)^3} \quad \text{where } x < 1 \qquad \text{F. 45}$$

Series No.

(12) $x(x + y) + x^2(x^2 + y^2) + x^3(x^3 + y^3) + \ldots n$ terms

(13) $\dfrac{2}{3} + \dfrac{3}{3^2} + \dfrac{2}{3^3} + \dfrac{3}{3^4} + \dfrac{2}{3^5} + \ldots \infty$

(14) $\dfrac{4}{7} - \dfrac{5}{7^2} + \dfrac{4}{7^3} - \dfrac{5}{7^4} + \ldots \infty$

(15) $1^2 + \dfrac{3^2}{2} + \dfrac{5^2}{2^2} + \dfrac{7^2}{2^3} + \ldots n$ terms

(16) $1 + 3x + 5x^2 + \ldots + (2n - 1)x^{n-1}$

IV. Powers of Natural Numbers

(17) $\displaystyle\sum_{x=1}^{x=n} x^p$

(18) $1 + 2 + 3 + 4 + \ldots n$

(19) $1^2 + 2^2 + 3^2 + 4^2 + \ldots n^2$

(20) $1^3 + 2^3 + 3^3 + 4^3 + \ldots n^3$

(21) $1^4 + 2^4 + 3^4 + 4^4 + \ldots n^4$

$$= \frac{x^2(x^{2n} - 1)}{x^2 - 1} + \frac{xy(x^n y^n - 1)}{xy - 1}$$

F. 46

$$= \frac{9}{8}$$

F. 46

$$= \frac{23}{48}$$

F. 46

$$= 34 - (4n^2 + 12n + 17)\frac{1}{2^{n-1}}$$

$$= \frac{1 + x - (2n + 1)x^n + (2n - 1)x^{n+1}}{(1 - x)^2}$$

$$= \frac{n^{p+1}}{p + 1} + \frac{n^p}{2} + \frac{1}{2}\binom{p}{1} B_1 n^{p-1} - \frac{1}{4}\binom{p}{3} B_2 n^{p-3}$$

$$+ \frac{1}{6}\binom{p}{5} B_3 n^{n-5} - \ldots \quad \text{where } \binom{p}{n} \text{ are the binomial coefficients}$$

and B_n are Bernoulli numbers, see No. (1129). The series ends with the term in n if p is even, and with the term in n^2 if p is odd.

T. 27

$$= \frac{n(n + 1)}{2}$$

F. 50

$$= \frac{n(n + 1)(2n + 1)}{6}$$

F. 50

$$= \left\{\frac{n(n + 1)}{2}\right\}^2$$

F. 51

$$= \frac{1}{30} n(n + 1)(2n + 1)(3n^2 + 3n - 1)$$

F. 256

Series No.

(22) $1^5 + 2^5 + 3^5 + 4^5 + \ldots n^5$

(23) $1^6 + 2^6 + 3^6 + 4^6 + \ldots n^6$

(24) $1^7 + 2^7 + 3^7 + 4^7 + \ldots n^7$

(25) $1^2 + 3^2 + 5^2 + 7^2 + \ldots n$ terms

(26) $1^3 + 3^3 + 5^3 + 7^3 + \ldots n$ terms

(27) $1^3 + (1.5)^3 + 2^3 + (2.5)^3 + \ldots \left(\dfrac{n+1}{2}\right)^3$

(28) $2^2 + 4^2 + 6^2 + 8^2 + \ldots n$ terms

(29) $1^2 \cdot 2^1 + 2^2 \cdot 2^2 + 3^2 \cdot 2^3 + \ldots n$ terms

(30) $1 \cdot 2^2 + 2 \cdot 3^2 + 3 \cdot 4^2 + \ldots n$ terms

(31) $(n^2 - 1^2) + 2(n^2 - 2^2) + 3(n^2 - 3^2) + \ldots n$ terms

(32) $\displaystyle\sum_{1}^{n} (2n - 1)^2$

(33) $\displaystyle\sum_{1}^{n} (2n - 1)^3$

(34) $\displaystyle\sum_{1}^{n} (x^n + n)(x^n - n)$

(35) $\displaystyle\sum_{1}^{n} (x^n + y^n)(x^n - y^n)$

(36) $\displaystyle\sum_{1}^{n} \left(x^n - \dfrac{1}{x^n}\right)\left(y^n - \dfrac{1}{y^n}\right)$

$$= \frac{n^6}{6} + \frac{n^5}{2} + \frac{5n^4}{12} - \frac{n^2}{12}$$
F. 337

$$= \frac{n^7}{7} + \frac{n^6}{2} + \frac{n^5}{2} - \frac{n^3}{6} + \frac{n}{42}$$
F. 338

$$= \frac{n^8}{8} + \frac{n^7}{2} + \frac{7n^6}{12} - \frac{7n^4}{24} + \frac{n^2}{12}$$
F. 338

$$= \frac{1}{3} n(4n^2 - 1)$$
F. 256

$$= n^2(2n^2 - 1)$$
F. 256

$$= \frac{1}{8} \left\{ \frac{(n + 1)(n + 2)}{2} \right\}^2 - \frac{1}{8}$$

$$= \frac{2n(n + 1)(2n + 1)}{3}$$

$$= 2^n\{2n^2 - 4n + 6\} - 6$$

$$= \frac{1}{12} n(n + 1)(n + 2)(3n + 5)$$
F. 256

$$= \frac{1}{4} n^2(n^2 - 1)$$
F. 323

$$= \frac{1}{3} n(2n - 1)(2n + 1)$$

$$= n^2(2n^2 - 1)$$

$$= \frac{x^2(x^{2n} - 1)}{x^2 - 1} - \frac{1}{6} n(n + 1)(2n + 1)$$

$$= \frac{x^2(x^{2n} - 1)}{x^2 - 1} - \frac{y^2(y^{2n} - 1)}{y^2 - 1}$$

$$= \frac{\{(xy)^n - 1\}\{(xy)^{n+1} + 1\}}{(xy)^n(xy - 1)} - \frac{\left\{ \left(\frac{x}{y}\right)^n - 1 \right\}\left\{ \left(\frac{x}{y}\right)^{n+1} + 1 \right\}\frac{y}{n}}{\left(\frac{x}{y}\right)^n \left(1 - \frac{y}{x}\right)}$$

Series No.

(37) $\displaystyle\sum_1^n \frac{x^{n+1} - y^{n+1}}{x - y}$

(38) $\displaystyle\sum_1^n (a_0 n^r + a_1 n^{r-1} + \ldots a_r)$

See No. (17)

(39) $\displaystyle\sum_1^\infty x^n$

(40) $\displaystyle\sum_1^\infty n x^n$

(41) $\displaystyle\sum_1^n (1 + 2 + 3 \ldots + n) x^{n-1}$

V. Products of Natural Numbers

(42) To find the sum of *n* terms of a series, each term of which is composed of *r* factors in arithmetical progression, the first factors of the several terms being in the same arithmetical progression: Write down the *n*th term, affix the next factor at the end, divide by the number of factors thus increased, and by the common difference, and add a constant.

(43) $1 \cdot 3 \cdot 5 + 3 \cdot 5 \cdot 7 + 5 \cdot 7 \cdot 9 + \ldots n$ terms

(44) $1 \cdot 2 + 2 \cdot 3 + 3 \cdot 4 \ldots n$ terms

(45) $2 \cdot 5 + 5 \cdot 8 + 8 \cdot 11 + \ldots n$ terms

(46) $2 \cdot 2 + 4 \cdot 4 + 7 \cdot 8 + 11 \cdot 16 + 16 \cdot 32 \ldots n$ terms

(47) $1 \cdot 2 \cdot 3 + 2 \cdot 3 \cdot 4 + 3 \cdot 4 \cdot 5 \ldots n$ terms

(48) $1 \cdot 2 \cdot 3 \cdot 4 + 2 \cdot 3 \cdot 4 \cdot 5 + \ldots n$ terms

$$= \frac{x^2(1 - x^n)}{(x - y)(1 - x)} - \frac{y^2(1 - y^n)}{(x - y)(1 - y)}$$

$$= \{a_0 b_r + a_1 b_{r-1} + \ldots + a_r n\}$$
$$b_r = 1^r + 2^r + 3^r + \ldots n^r$$

$$= \frac{x}{1 - x} \quad \text{where } x < 1$$

$$= \frac{x}{(1 - x)^2} \quad \text{where } x < 1$$

$$= \frac{1 - x^n}{(1 - x)^3} - \frac{n(n + 3)x^n}{2(1 - x)^2} + \frac{n(n + 1)x^{n+1}}{2(1 - x)^2}$$

F. 314

$$= \frac{(2n - 1)(2n + 1)(2n + 3)(2n + 5)}{4 \cdot 2} + \frac{15}{8}$$

$$= n(2n^3 + 8n^2 + 7n - 2)$$ F. 315

$$= \frac{n(n + 1)(n + 2)}{3}$$ F. 52

$$= n(3n^2 + 6n + 1)$$ F. 318

$$= (n^2 - n + 4)2^n - 4$$ F. 333

$$= \frac{1}{4} n(n + 1)(n + 2)(n + 3)$$ F. 322

$$= \frac{1}{5} n(n + 1)(n + 2)(n + 3)(n + 4)$$ F. 322

Series No.

(49) $1 \cdot 4 \cdot 7 + 4 \cdot 7 \cdot 10 + 7 \cdot 10 \cdot 13 + \ldots n$ terms

(50) $1 \cdot 4 \cdot 7 + 2 \cdot 5 \cdot 8 + 3 \cdot 6 \cdot 9 + \ldots n$ terms

(51) $1 \cdot 5 \cdot 9 + 2 \cdot 6 \cdot 10 + 3 \cdot 7 \cdot 11 + \ldots n$ terms

(52) $6 \cdot 9 + 12 \cdot 21 + 20 \cdot 37 + 30 \cdot 57 + \ldots n$ terms
   nth term is $(n + 1)(n + 2)(2n^2 + 6n + 1)$

(53) $2 \cdot 2 + 6 \cdot 4 + 12 \cdot 8 + 20 \cdot 16 + 30 \cdot 32 + \ldots n$ terms
   nth term is $n(n + 1)2^n$

(54) $1 \cdot 3 \cdot 2^2 + 2 \cdot 4 \cdot 3^2 + 3 \cdot 5 \cdot 4^2 + \ldots n$ terms

(55) $\displaystyle\sum_1^n (p - n)(q - n)$

(56) $\displaystyle\sum_1^n \frac{m(m + 1) \ldots (m + n - 1)}{n!}$

(57) $\displaystyle\sum_1^n \frac{b(b + 1)(b + 2) \ldots (b + n - 1)}{a(a + 1)(a + 2) \ldots (a + n - 1)}$

(58) $\dfrac{1^2 \cdot x}{2 \cdot 3} + \dfrac{2^2 \cdot x^2}{3 \cdot 4} \ldots n$ terms

   This series is integrable if $x = 4$.

(59) $\displaystyle\sum_1^n \frac{n^2 4^n}{(n + 1)(n + 2)}$

$$= \frac{1}{12} (3n - 2)(3n + 1)(3n + 4)(3n + 7) + \frac{56}{12}$$ F. 322

$$= \frac{1}{4} n(n + 1)(n + 6)(n + 7)$$ F. 322

$$= \frac{1}{4} n(n + 1)(n + 8)(n + 9)$$ F. 322

$$= \frac{2}{5} n(n + 1)(n + 2)(n + 3)(n + 4)$$

$$+ \frac{1}{3} (n + 1)(n + 2)(n + 3) - 2$$ F. 331

$$= (n^2 - n + 2)2^{n+1} - 4$$ F. 332

$$= \frac{1}{10} n(n + 1)(n + 2)(n + 3)(2n + 3)$$ F. 323

$$= \frac{n(n + 1)}{6} \{(2n + 1) - 3(p + q)\} + npq$$

$$= \frac{(m + 1)(m + 2)\ldots(m + 1 + n - 1)}{n!} - 1$$ C. 200

$$= \frac{(m + n)!}{m! \, n!} - 1$$

$$= \frac{b(b + 1)(b + 2)\ldots(b + n)}{(b + 1 - a)a(a + 1)(a + 2)\ldots(a + n - 1)} - \frac{b}{b + 1 - a}$$

T. 28

$$= \sum_{1}^{n} \frac{n^2 x^n}{(n + 1)(n + 2)}$$ W. 58

$$= \frac{4^{n+1}}{3} \cdot \frac{n - 1}{n + 2} + \frac{2}{3}$$ W. 58

Series No.

VI. Figurate and Polygonal Numbers

(60) Figurate numbers—

1	1	1	1	1	1 ...
1	2	3	4	5	6 ...
1	3	6	10	15	21 ...
1	4	10	20	35	56 ...
1	5	15	35	70	126 ...

The sum to n terms of the rth order

(61) Method of Differences—

One Series is 12   40   90   168   280   432 ...
1st Diff.   28   50   78   112   152 ...
2nd Diff.   22   28   34   40 ...
3rd Diff.   6   6   6 ...
4th Diff.   0   0

The nth term is   The sum

$$12 + 28(n - 1) + \frac{22(n - 1)(n - 2)}{2!}$$

$$+ \frac{6(n - 1)(n - 2)(n - 3)}{3!}$$

(62) $4 + 14 + 30 + 52 + 80 + 114 + \ldots n$ terms

(63) $8 + 26 + 54 + 92 + 140 + 198 + \ldots n$ terms

(64) $9 + 16 + 29 + 54 + \ldots n$ terms

(65) $4 + 13 + 35 + 94 + 262 + \ldots n$ terms

(66) $2 + 12 + 36 + 80 + 150 + 252 + \ldots n$ terms

$$= \frac{1}{r!} n(n + 1)(n + 2)\ldots(n + r - 1) \qquad\qquad \text{F. 320}$$

$$= 12n + \frac{28n(n - 1)}{2!} + \frac{22n(n - 1)(n - 2)}{3!}$$

$$+ \frac{6n(n - 1)(n - 2)(n - 3)}{4!}$$

$$= \frac{1}{12} n(n + 1)(3n^2 + 23n + 46) \qquad\qquad \text{F. 326}$$

$$= n(n + 1)^2 \qquad\qquad \text{F. 332}$$

$$= \frac{1}{3} n(n + 1)(5n + 7) \qquad\qquad \text{F. 332}$$

$$= 6(2^n - 1) + \frac{1}{2} n(n + 5) \qquad\qquad \text{F. 333}$$

$$= \frac{3}{2} (3^n - 1) + \frac{1}{6} n(n + 1)(n + 5) - n \qquad\qquad \text{F. 333}$$

$$= \frac{1}{12} n(n + 1)(n + 2)(3n + 1) \qquad\qquad \text{F. 332}$$

Series No.

(67) $30 + 144 + 420 + 960 + 1890 + \ldots n$ terms

(68) $2 + 5 + 13 + 35 + \ldots n$ terms

(69) $2 + 7x + 25x^2 + 91x^3 + \ldots n$ terms

VII. Inverse Natural Numbers

(70) $$\sum_{1}^{n} \frac{1}{n} = C + \log h\, n + \frac{1}{2n} - \frac{a_2}{n(n + 1)}$$
$$- \frac{a_3}{n(n + 1)(n + 2)} - \ldots$$

Also $1 + \dfrac{1}{2} + \ldots + \dfrac{1}{n}$

(71) $1 - \dfrac{1}{2} + \dfrac{1}{3} - \dfrac{1}{4} + \dfrac{1}{5} - \ldots \infty$

(72) $1 - \dfrac{1}{2} - \dfrac{1}{3} + \dfrac{1}{4} + \dfrac{1}{5} - \ldots \infty$

(73) $\left(1 - \dfrac{1}{2} - \dfrac{1}{4}\right) + \left(\dfrac{1}{3} - \dfrac{1}{6} - \dfrac{1}{8}\right) + \left(\dfrac{1}{5} - \dfrac{1}{10} - \dfrac{1}{12}\right) + \ldots \infty$

(74) $\dfrac{5}{1 \cdot 2 \cdot 3} + \dfrac{14}{4 \cdot 5 \cdot 6} + \ldots \infty$

(75) $2\left(1 - \dfrac{1}{2} + \dfrac{1}{3} - \dfrac{1}{4} + \dfrac{1}{5} - \ldots \infty\right)$
$$= 8\left(\dfrac{1}{1 \cdot 2 \cdot 3} + \dfrac{1}{5 \cdot 6 \cdot 7} + \dfrac{1}{9 \cdot 10 \cdot 11} + \ldots \infty\right)$$

$$= \frac{1}{20} n(n + 1)(n + 2)(n + 3)(4n + 21)$$

F. 332

$$= \frac{1}{2} (3^n - 1) + 2^n - 1$$

F. 272

$$= \frac{1 - 4^n x^n}{1 - 4x} + \frac{1 - 3^n x^n}{1 - 3x}$$

F. 272

where $C = $ Euler's constant, see No. (1132),

$$a_2 = \frac{1}{12} \quad a_3 = \frac{1}{12} \quad a_4 = \frac{19}{120} \quad a_5 = \frac{9}{20}$$

and $a_k = \dfrac{1}{k} \displaystyle\int_0^1 x(1 - x)(2 - x)\ldots(k - 1 - x)\, dx$

T. 27

$= 7.48547$ where $n = 1000$

A. 325

$= 14.39273$ where $n = 10^6$

$= $ logh 2

F. 195

$$= 0.43882 = \frac{\pi}{4} - \frac{1}{2} \text{logh } 2$$

H. 475

$$= \frac{1}{2} \text{logh } 2$$

C. 252

$$= \sum_{1}^{\infty} \frac{9n - 4}{(3n - 2)(3n - 1)(3n)} = \text{logh } 3$$

C. 253

$= $ logh 4

C. 252

(76) $1 + \dfrac{1}{3} - \dfrac{1}{5} - \dfrac{1}{7} + \dfrac{1}{9} + \dfrac{1}{11} - \dots \infty$

(77) $1 - \dfrac{1}{3} + \dfrac{1}{5} - \dfrac{1}{7} + \dfrac{1}{9} - \dots \infty$

$$= 1 - 2\left[\dfrac{1}{3\cdot 5} + \dfrac{1}{7\cdot 9} + \dfrac{1}{11\cdot 13} + \dots \infty\right]$$

(78) $1 - \dfrac{1}{7} + \dfrac{1}{9} - \dfrac{1}{15} + \dfrac{1}{17} - \dots \infty$

(79) $1 - \dfrac{1}{4} + \dfrac{1}{7} - \dfrac{1}{10} + \dots \infty$

(80) $\dfrac{1}{2} - \dfrac{1}{5} + \dfrac{1}{8} - \dfrac{1}{11} + \dots \infty$

(81) $1 - \dfrac{1}{2} + \dfrac{1}{4} - \dfrac{1}{5} + \dfrac{1}{7} - \dfrac{1}{8} + \dots \infty$

(82) $1 - \dfrac{1}{5} + \dfrac{1}{9} - \dfrac{1}{13} + \dots \infty$

(83) $1 - \dfrac{1}{5} - \dfrac{1}{7} + \dfrac{1}{11} + \dfrac{1}{13} - \dfrac{1}{17} - \dfrac{1}{19} + \dots \infty$

(84) $1 - \dfrac{1}{5} + \dfrac{1}{7} - \dfrac{1}{11} + \dfrac{1}{13} - \dfrac{1}{17} + \dots \infty$

(85) $1 - \dfrac{1}{2}\cdot\dfrac{1}{3} + \dfrac{1\cdot 3}{2\cdot 4}\cdot\dfrac{1}{5} - \dots \infty$

(86) $1 - \dfrac{1}{3} + \dfrac{1\cdot 2}{3\cdot 5} - \dfrac{1\cdot 2\cdot 3}{3\cdot 5\cdot 7} + \dots \infty$

(87) $\displaystyle\sum_{1}^{n} \dfrac{1}{2n - 1}$

$$= \frac{\pi}{2\sqrt{2}}$$

C. 335

$$= \frac{\pi}{4}$$

E. 109

$$= \frac{\pi}{8}(1 + \sqrt{2})$$

M. 132

$$= \frac{1}{3}\left(\frac{\pi}{\sqrt{3}} + \log h \, 2\right)$$

A. 189

$$= \frac{1}{3}\left(\frac{\pi}{\sqrt{3}} - \log h \, 2\right)$$

A. 189

$$= \frac{\pi}{3\sqrt{3}}$$

27 P. 281

$$= \frac{1}{4\sqrt{2}}[\pi + 2 \log h \, (\sqrt{2} + 1)]$$

A. 190

$$= \frac{1}{\sqrt{3}} \log h \, (2 + \sqrt{3})$$

AB. 166

$$= \frac{\pi}{2\sqrt{3}}$$

A. 528

$$= \log h \, (1 + \sqrt{2})$$

Y. 90

$$= \frac{2}{\sqrt{3}} \log h \left(\frac{1 + \sqrt{3}}{\sqrt{2}}\right)$$

Y. 90

$$= \frac{1}{2}(C + \log h \, n) + \log h \, 2 + \frac{B_1}{8n^2} - \frac{(2^3 - 1)B_2}{64n^4} + \ldots$$

For C see No. (1132) and for B_n see No. (1129)   A. 325

Series No.

(88) $\dfrac{x}{1+x} + \dfrac{2x^2}{1+x^2} + \dfrac{4x^4}{1+x^4} \cdots \infty$

(89) $\dfrac{x}{1-x^2} + \dfrac{x^2}{1-x^4} + \dfrac{x^4}{1-x^8} + \ldots n$ terms

(90) $\dfrac{x}{1-x^2} + \dfrac{x^2}{1-x^4} + \dfrac{x^4}{1-x^8} + \ldots \infty$

(91) $\dfrac{1}{x+1} + \dfrac{2}{x^2+1} + \dfrac{4}{x^4+1} \cdots \infty$

(92) $\dfrac{1-2x}{1-x+x^2} + \dfrac{2x-4x^3}{1-x^2+x^4} + \dfrac{4x^3-8x^7}{1-x^4+x^8} + \ldots \infty$

(93) $\epsilon \left[\dfrac{1}{x} - \dfrac{1}{1!}\dfrac{1}{x+1} + \dfrac{1}{2!}\cdot\dfrac{1}{x+2} - \dfrac{1}{3!}\dfrac{1}{x+3} + \ldots \infty \right]$

(94) $\dfrac{1}{3}\,\mathcal{S}_2 - \dfrac{1}{5}\,\mathcal{S}_4 + \dfrac{1}{7}\,\mathcal{S}_6 - \ldots \infty$

(95) $\dfrac{1}{2}\cdot\left(\dfrac{2x}{1+x^2}\right) + \dfrac{1}{2\cdot4}\left(\dfrac{2x}{1+x^2}\right)^3 + \dfrac{1\cdot3}{2\cdot4\cdot6}\left(\dfrac{2x}{1+x^2}\right)^5 + \ldots \infty$

(96) $\displaystyle\sum_1^\infty 2x\left\{\dfrac{1}{n^2}\,\epsilon^A - \dfrac{1}{(n+1)^2}\,\epsilon^B\right\}$

$\qquad A = -\dfrac{x^2}{n^2} \quad B = \dfrac{x^2}{(n+1)^2} \quad C = -x^2$

VIII. Exponential and Logarithmic Series

(97) $1 + ax + \dfrac{a^2x^2}{2!} + \dfrac{a^3x^3}{3!} + \ldots \infty$

(98) $1 + x \log h\, a + \dfrac{(x \log h\, a)^2}{2!} + \ldots \infty$

(99) $x - \dfrac{x^2}{2} + \dfrac{x^3}{3} - \ldots \infty = x(1-x) + \tfrac{1}{2}x^2(1-x^2) + \ldots \infty$

$= \dfrac{x}{1-x}$ where $(x^2 < 1)$ — T. 118

$= \dfrac{1}{1-x} - \dfrac{1}{1-x^n}$ — A. 24

$= \dfrac{x}{1-x}$ where $x^2 < 1$, and

$= -\dfrac{1}{x-1}$ where $x > 1$ — T. 118

$= \dfrac{1}{x-1}$ where $x^2 > 1$ — T. 118

$= \dfrac{1+2x}{1+x+x^2}$ where $x < 1$ — Y. 54

$= \dfrac{1}{x} + \dfrac{1}{x(x+1)} + \dfrac{1}{x(x+1)(x+2)} + \ldots \infty$ — A. 102

$= \dfrac{\pi \log h\, 2}{8}$ where $S_{2n} = 1 + \dfrac{1}{2} + \dfrac{1}{3} + \ldots + \dfrac{1}{2n}$ — A. 192

$= x$ where $|x| < 1$ — Q. 132

$= 2x\epsilon^c$

AB. 167

$= \epsilon^{ax}$ — F. 188

$= a^x$ — F. 188

$= \log h\,(1+x)$ where $x < 1$ — F. 191

Series No.

(100) $- x - \dfrac{x^2}{2} - \dfrac{x^3}{3} - \ldots \infty$

(101) $1 + 2^3 + \dfrac{3^3}{2!} + \dfrac{4^3}{3!} + \dfrac{5^3}{4!} + \ldots \infty$

(102) $\dfrac{1}{2} - \dfrac{1}{2 \cdot 2^2} + \dfrac{1}{3 \cdot 2^3} - \dfrac{1}{4 \cdot 2^4} + \ldots \infty$

(103) $2\left\{\dfrac{1}{3!} + \dfrac{2}{5!} + \dfrac{3}{7!} + \ldots \infty\right\}$

(104) $\displaystyle\sum_{1}^{\infty} \dfrac{1}{n(4n^2 - 1)^2}$

(105) $(x - 1) - \dfrac{1}{2}(x - 1)^2 + \dfrac{1}{3}(x - 1)^3 - \ldots \infty$

(106) $\dfrac{2}{1} + \dfrac{3}{2!} + \dfrac{6}{3!} + \dfrac{11}{4!} + \dfrac{18}{5!} + \ldots \infty$

(107) $\epsilon \left(1 + x + \dfrac{2}{2!}x^2 + \dfrac{5}{3!}x^3 + \dfrac{15}{4!}x^4 + \ldots \infty\right)$

(108) $1 + 2x + \dfrac{2^2 - 1}{2!} \cdot x^2 + \dfrac{3^2 - 1}{3!} \cdot \dfrac{x^3}{2} + \ldots \infty$

(109) $1 + \dfrac{2x^2}{2!} - \dfrac{x^3}{3!} + \dfrac{7x^4}{4!} - \dfrac{23x^5}{5!} + \dfrac{121x^6}{6!} - \ldots \infty$

(110) $2\left\{\dfrac{x^2}{2} - \dfrac{1}{3}\left(1 + \dfrac{1}{2}\right)x^3 + \dfrac{1}{4}\left(1 + \dfrac{1}{2} + \dfrac{1}{3}\right)x^4 - \ldots \infty\right\}$

(111) $2\left\{\dfrac{x^2}{2} + \dfrac{1}{3}\left(1 + \dfrac{1}{2}\right)x^3 + \dfrac{1}{4}\left(1 + \dfrac{1}{2} + \dfrac{1}{3}\right)x^4 + \ldots \infty\right\}$

(112) $x^2 + \left(1 - \dfrac{1}{2} + \dfrac{1}{3}\right)\dfrac{x^4}{2} + \left(1 - \dfrac{1}{2} + \dfrac{1}{3} - \dfrac{1}{4} + \dfrac{1}{5}\right)\dfrac{x^6}{3} + \ldots \infty$

(113) $x^2 + \left(1 - \dfrac{1}{3} + \dfrac{1}{5}\right)\dfrac{x^6}{3} + \left(1 - \dfrac{1}{3} + \dfrac{1}{5} - \dfrac{1}{7} + \dfrac{1}{9}\right)\dfrac{x^{10}}{5} + \ldots \infty$

$= \operatorname{logh} (1 - x)$ where $x < 1$ F. 191

$= 15\epsilon$ F. 339

$= \operatorname{logh} 3 - \operatorname{logh} 2$ F. 195

$= \epsilon^{-1}$ F. 196

$= \dfrac{3}{2} - 2 \operatorname{logh} 2$ C. 253

$= \operatorname{logh} x$ where $0 < x \leqslant 2$ T. 124

$= 3(\epsilon - 1)$ F. 338

$= \epsilon^{\epsilon^x}$ T. 126

$= (1 + x)\epsilon^x$ F. 338

$= \epsilon^x - \operatorname{logh} (1 + x)$ F. 338

$= \{\operatorname{logh} (1 + x)\}^2$ where $x < 1$ F. 191

$= [\operatorname{logh} (1 - x)]^2$ A. 191

$= - \operatorname{logh} (1 + x) \cdot \operatorname{logh} (1 - x)$ A. 191

$= \dfrac{1}{2} (\tan^{-1} x) \operatorname{logh} \dfrac{1 + x}{1 - x}$ A. 191

Series No.

(114) $\epsilon^{-\pi} + \epsilon^{-9\pi} + \epsilon^{-25\pi} + \ldots \infty$

(115) $\sum a_n \theta^n$

(116) $1 - \dfrac{1}{2}\left(1 + \dfrac{1}{2}\right) + \dfrac{1}{3}\left(1 + \dfrac{1}{2} + \dfrac{1}{3}\right) - \ldots \infty$

(117) $\displaystyle\sum_{1}^{\infty} \dfrac{1}{nx^n}$

(118) $\displaystyle\sum_{1}^{\infty} \dfrac{x^n}{n}$

(119) $\displaystyle\sum_{1}^{\infty} \dfrac{x^n}{n!}$

(120) $\displaystyle\sum_{1}^{\infty} \dfrac{x^n}{n(n+1)}$

(121) $x + \left(1 + \dfrac{1}{2}\right)x^2 + \left(1 + \dfrac{1}{2} + \dfrac{1}{3}\right)x^3 + \ldots \infty$

(122) $\displaystyle\sum_{1}^{\infty} \dfrac{(n-1)x^n}{(n+2)n!}$

(123) $\displaystyle\sum_{1}^{\infty} \dfrac{(1^3 + 2^3 + 3^3 + \ldots n^3)}{n!} x^n$

(124) $\displaystyle\sum_{1}^{\infty} \dfrac{1}{x^2 + n^2}$

(125) $\displaystyle\sum_{1}^{\infty} (-1)^n \dfrac{1}{x^2 + n^2}$

$$= \frac{(2^{1/4} - 1)\Gamma(\tfrac{1}{4})}{2^{11/4}\pi^{3/4}}$$

$\Gamma(\tfrac{1}{4})$ $= 3.6256$ T. 144

$= \epsilon^A$ where $A = \epsilon^\theta$ and a_{n+1}

$$= \left(a_n + a_{n-1} + \ldots \frac{a_{n-2}}{2!} + \ldots \frac{a_0}{n!} \right) \frac{1}{n+1}$$ Y. 111

$$= \frac{\pi^2}{12} - \frac{1}{2}(\mathrm{logh}\ 2)^2$$ A. 520

$$= \mathrm{logh}\ \frac{x}{x-1}$$ H. 460

$$= \mathrm{logh}\ \frac{1}{1-x} \quad \text{where } x < 1$$

$$= \epsilon^x - 1$$

$$= 1 - \left(\frac{1}{x} - 1 \right) \mathrm{logh}\ \frac{1}{1-x}$$ F. 338

$$= \frac{1}{1-x}\ \mathrm{logh}\ \frac{1}{1-x} \quad \text{where } x < 1$$

$$= \frac{\{(x^2 - 3x + 3)\epsilon^x - \tfrac{1}{2}x^2 - 3\}}{x^2}$$ C. 236

$$= \epsilon^x \left(x + \frac{7}{2}x^2 + 2x^3 + \frac{1}{4}x^4 \right)$$ C. 235

$$= \frac{\pi}{2x} \cdot \frac{\epsilon^{\pi x} + \epsilon^{-\pi x}}{\epsilon^{\pi x} - \epsilon^{-\pi x}} - \frac{1}{2x^2}$$ T. 135

$$= \frac{\pi}{x} \cdot \frac{1}{\epsilon^{\pi x} - \epsilon^{-\pi x}} - \frac{1}{2x^2}$$ T. 135

Series No.

(126) $\dfrac{1}{2n} + \dfrac{1}{n+1} + \dfrac{1}{n+2} + \ldots \dfrac{1}{m-1} + \dfrac{1}{2m}$

$$- \frac{1}{12}\left(\frac{1}{n^2} - \frac{1}{m^2}\right) + \frac{1}{120}\left(\frac{1}{n^4} - \frac{1}{m^4}\right) - \frac{1}{252}\left(\frac{1}{n^6} - \frac{1}{m^6}\right)$$

$$+ \frac{1}{240}\left(\frac{1}{n^8} - \frac{1}{m^8}\right) + \ldots \infty$$

(127) $\dfrac{1}{2}\operatorname{logh} n + \operatorname{logh}(n+1) + \ldots + \operatorname{logh}(m-1)$

$$+ \frac{1}{2}\operatorname{logh} m - \frac{1}{12}\left(\frac{1}{m} - \frac{1}{n}\right) + \frac{1}{360}\left(\frac{1}{m^3} - \frac{1}{n^3}\right)$$

$$- \frac{1}{1260}\left(\frac{1}{m^5} - \frac{1}{n^5}\right) + \ldots \infty$$

(128) $\displaystyle\sum_{1}^{\infty}\left[n\operatorname{logh}\left(\frac{2n+1}{2n-1}\right) - 1\right]$

(129) $x - \dfrac{2}{3}x^3 + \dfrac{2\cdot4}{3\cdot5}x^5 + \ldots \infty$

(130) $1 + (x\epsilon^{-x}) + \dfrac{3}{2!}(x\epsilon^{-x})^2 + \dfrac{4^2}{3!}(x\epsilon^{-x})^3 + \dfrac{5^3}{4!}(x\epsilon^{-x})^4 + \ldots \infty$

$$= 1 + \sum_{1}^{\infty} \frac{(n+1)^{n-1}}{n!}(x\epsilon^{-x})^n$$

(131) $\dfrac{x^3}{1\cdot3} + \dfrac{x^5}{3\cdot5} + \dfrac{x^7}{5\cdot7} + \ldots \infty$ (if convergent)

(132)† $1 - 2(2-1)B_1\dfrac{x^2}{2} + 2(2^3-1)B_2\dfrac{x^4}{4!}$

$$- 2(2^5-1)B_3\frac{x^6}{6!} + \ldots \infty$$

(133)† $1 + 2ax + (2a)^2\left\{B_2\left(\dfrac{1}{2} + x\right) + \dfrac{1}{2}B_1\right\} + \dfrac{(2a)^3}{2!}B_2\left(\dfrac{1}{2} + x\right)$

$$+ \frac{(2a)^4}{3!}\left\{B_4\left(\frac{1}{2} + x\right) - \frac{1}{4}B_2\right\} + \ldots \infty$$

† For values of $B_n(x)$, see No. (1146).

$= \operatorname{logh} \dfrac{m}{n}$ where m and n integers   X. 141

$= m \operatorname{logh} \dfrac{m}{\epsilon} - n \operatorname{logh} \dfrac{n}{\epsilon}$ where m and n integers   X. 141

$= \dfrac{1}{2}(1 - \operatorname{logh} 2)$ A. 526

$= \dfrac{1}{\sqrt{1 + x^2}} \operatorname{logh}\{x + \sqrt{1 + x^2}\}$ where $|x| \leqslant 1$ A. 197

$= \epsilon^x$ Y. 456

$= \dfrac{x^2 - 1}{4} \operatorname{logh} \dfrac{1 + x}{1 - x} + \dfrac{x}{2}$ 1Z. 165

$= \dfrac{2x}{\epsilon^x - \epsilon^{-x}}$ AE. 12

$= \dfrac{2a\epsilon^{2ax}}{\epsilon^a - \epsilon^{-a}}$ AE. 14

Series No.

(134)† $\frac{1}{2} + xB_2\left(\frac{1}{2}\right) + \frac{x^3}{3!}B_4\left(\frac{1}{2}\right) + \frac{x^5}{5!}B_6\left(\frac{1}{2}\right) + \ldots \infty$

(135)† $\frac{1}{3} + 3xB_2\left(\frac{1}{3}\right) + \frac{(3x)^2}{2!}B_3\left(\frac{1}{3}\right) + \frac{(3x)^3}{3!}B_4\left(\frac{1}{3}\right) + \ldots \infty$

(136)† $\frac{1}{6} + 6xB_2\left(\frac{1}{6}\right) + \frac{(6x)^2}{2!}B_3\left(\frac{1}{6}\right) + \ldots \infty$

(137) $x - \left(1 + \frac{1}{2}\right)x^2 + \left(1 + \frac{1}{2} + \frac{1}{3}\right)x^3$

$\qquad - \left(1 + \frac{1}{2} + \frac{1}{3} + \frac{1}{4}\right)x^4 + \ldots \infty$

(138) $x - \frac{1}{2}\cdot\frac{x^3}{3} + \frac{1\cdot 3}{2\cdot 4}\cdot\frac{x^5}{5} - \ldots \infty$

(139) $\log h\, 2 + \frac{1\cdot 1}{2\cdot 2}x^2 - \frac{1\cdot 1\cdot 3}{2\cdot 4\cdot 4}x^4 + \frac{1\cdot 1\cdot 3\cdot 5}{2\cdot 4\cdot 6\cdot 6}x^6 - \ldots \infty$

(140) $1 - \frac{x}{2} - \frac{x^2}{12} - \frac{x^3}{24} - \ldots \infty = \int_0^1 (1-x)^t\, dt$

(141) $x + \frac{x^3}{3} - \frac{2}{3}\cdot\frac{x^5}{5} + \frac{2\cdot 4}{3\cdot 5}\cdot\frac{x^7}{7} - \ldots \infty$

(142) $x - \frac{2}{3}x^3 + \frac{2\cdot 4}{3\cdot 5}x^5 + \ldots \infty$

(143) $\frac{x^2}{2} - \frac{2}{3}\cdot\frac{x^4}{4} + \frac{2\cdot 4}{3\cdot 5}\cdot\frac{x^6}{6} + \ldots \infty$

(144) $-x + \frac{x^2}{2} + \frac{2x^3}{3} + \frac{x^4}{4} - \frac{x^5}{5} - \frac{x^6}{3} - \frac{x^7}{7} + \frac{x^8}{8} + \ldots \infty$

(145) $\frac{x^2}{2} + \frac{2x^3}{3} + \frac{3x^4}{4} + \ldots \infty$

† For values of $B_n(x)$, see No. (1146).

$$= \frac{1}{\epsilon^{x/2} + 1}$$

$$= \frac{1}{1 + e^x + \epsilon^{2x}}$$

$$= \frac{1}{1 + \epsilon^x + \epsilon^{2x} + \epsilon^{3x} + \epsilon^{4x} + \epsilon^{5x}}$$

$$= \frac{\log h (1 + x)}{1 + x}$$

$$= \log h (x + \sqrt{1 + x^2}) \quad \text{where } -1 \leqslant x \leqslant 1$$

$$= \log h (1 + \sqrt{1 + x^2}) \quad \text{where } x^2 < 1$$

$$= \frac{x}{\log h \dfrac{1}{1 - x}}$$

$$= \sqrt{1 + x^2} \log h \{x + \sqrt{1 + x^2}\}$$

$$= \frac{1}{\sqrt{1 + x^2}} \log h \{x + \sqrt{1 + x^2}\} \quad \text{where } x < 1$$

$$= \frac{1}{2} \{\log h (x + \sqrt{1 + x^2})\}^2$$

$$= \log h (1 - x + x^2)$$

$$= \frac{x}{1 - x} + \log h (1 - x) \quad \text{where } x < 1$$

Series No.

(146) $\log h\, 2 + \dfrac{x}{2} + \dfrac{x^2}{8} - \dfrac{x^4}{192} - \ldots \infty$

(147)† $\dfrac{x}{2} - B_1(2^2 - 1)\dfrac{x^2}{2!} - B_2(2^4 - 1)\dfrac{x^4}{4!}$

$$- B_3(2^6 - 1)\dfrac{x^6}{6!} - \ldots \infty$$

(148)† $2\left\{ B_1(2^2 - 1)\dfrac{x}{2!} - B_2(2^4 - 1)\dfrac{x^3}{4!} + B_3(2^6 - 1)\dfrac{x^5}{6!} - \ldots \infty \right\}$

(149) $\dfrac{x}{1\cdot 2} + \dfrac{x^2}{2\cdot 3} + \dfrac{x^3}{3\cdot 4} + \ldots \infty$

(150) $x + \dfrac{x^5}{5!} + \dfrac{x^9}{9!} + \ldots \infty$

(151)‡ $\log h\, 2 + \log h\, 3 + \ldots \log h\,(n - 1) + \dfrac{1}{2}\log h\, n$

(This series is not convergent.)

(152)‡ $1 - \dfrac{x}{2} + \dfrac{B_1{}^*}{2!}x^2 - \dfrac{B_3{}^*}{4!}x^4 + \dfrac{B_5{}^*}{6!}x^6 + \ldots \infty$

(153) $1 + \dfrac{x}{2} - \dfrac{1}{12}x^2 + \dfrac{1}{24}x^3 - \dfrac{19}{720}x^4 + \ldots \infty$

(154) $1 + \dfrac{x^2}{2\cdot 3} - \dfrac{x^4}{4\cdot 5} + \dfrac{x^6}{6\cdot 7} + \ldots \infty = 1 + \displaystyle\sum_{1}^{\infty} \dfrac{x^{2n}(-1)^{n-1}}{2n(2n + 1)}$

(155) $x^3 + x^4 + \dfrac{x^5}{2} + \ldots \infty$

(156) $\dfrac{x^r}{r!} - {}_rP_1\dfrac{x^{r+1}}{(r + 1)!} + {}_{r+1}P_2\dfrac{x^{r+2}}{(r + 2)!} - \ldots \infty$

† For B_1, B_2, etc., see No. (1129).
‡ For values of B_1 and $B_1{}^*$, etc., see No. (1129).

$= \log h \, (1 + \epsilon^x)$ H. 498

$= \dfrac{x}{\epsilon^x + 1}$ N. 1543

$= \dfrac{\epsilon^x - 1}{\epsilon^x + 1}$ N. 1544

$= 1 + \dfrac{1 - x}{x} \log h \, (1 - x)$ F. 338

$= \dfrac{1}{4} \left(\epsilon^x - \epsilon^{-x} - j\epsilon^{jx} + j\epsilon^{-jx} \right)$ where $j = \sqrt{-1}$ F. 338

$= \dfrac{1}{2} \log h \, (2\pi) + n \log h \, n - n$

$\quad + \dfrac{B_1}{1 \cdot 2 \cdot n} - \dfrac{B_2}{3 \cdot 4 \cdot n^3} + \ldots + \dfrac{(-1)^{r-1} B_r}{(2r - 1) \cdot 2r \cdot n^{2r-1}} \ldots$ 1P. 612

$= \dfrac{x}{\epsilon^x - 1}$ 2Z. 123

$= \dfrac{x}{\log h \, (1 + x)}$ W. 243

$= \dfrac{1}{x} \tan^{-1} x + \dfrac{1}{2} \log h \, (1 + x^2)$

$= \log h \, (1 + x^3 \epsilon^x)$ Y. 80

$= \dfrac{[\log h \, (1 + x)]^r}{r!}$ where $_r P_k$ is the sum of all products k at a time, of the first r natural numbers Y. 80

(157) $\dfrac{x}{2} - \dfrac{x^2}{24} + \dfrac{x^4}{2880} - \dots \infty$

(158) $x + \dfrac{x^2}{2} + \dfrac{x^3}{3} + \dfrac{x^4}{4} - \dfrac{4x^5}{5} + \dfrac{x^6}{6} + \dots \infty$

(159) Reversion of Series.

$$y = x - b_1 x^2 - b_2 x^3 - b_3 x^4 - \dots \infty$$

can become

$$x = y + C_1 y^2 + C_2 y^3 + C_3 y^4 + \dots \infty$$

if

C_1

C_2

C_3

C_4

C_5

C_6

C_7

See Van Orstrand (*Phil. Mag.* **19**: 366.1910) for coefficients up to C_{12}.

(160) $1 - \dfrac{1}{2(n+1)} - \dfrac{1}{2 \cdot 3(n+1)^2} - \dfrac{1}{3 \cdot 4(n+1)^3} - \dots \infty$

(161) $1 + \dfrac{2^3}{2!} + \dfrac{3^3}{3!} + \dfrac{4^3}{4!} + \dots \infty$

(162) $\dfrac{1}{n^2} + \dfrac{1}{2n^4} + \dfrac{1}{3n^6} + \dots \infty$

(163) $\dfrac{1}{n} + \dfrac{1}{2n^2} + \dfrac{1}{3n^3} + \dots \infty$

$$= \log h \frac{x \epsilon^x}{\epsilon^x - 1}$$

$$= \log h (1 + x + x^2 + x^3 + x^4)$$

$$= b_1$$

$$= b_2 + 2b_1{}^2$$

$$= b_3 + 5b_1 b_2 + 5b_1{}^3$$

$$= b_4 + 6b_1 b_3 + 3b_2{}^2 + 21b_1{}^2 b_2 + 14b_1{}^4$$

$$= b_5 + 7(b_1 b_4 + b_2 b_3) + 28(b_1{}^2 b_3 + b_1 b_2{}^2) + 84b_1{}^3 b_2 + 42b_1{}^5$$

$$= b_6 + 4(2b_1 b_5 + 2b_2 b_4 + b_3{}^2) + 12(3b_1{}^2 b_4 + 6b_1 b_2 b_3 + b_2{}^3$$
$$+ \ 60(2b_1{}^3 b_3 + 3b_1{}^2 b_2{}^2) + 330b_1{}^4 b_2 + 132b_1{}^6$$

$$= b_7 + 9(b_1 b_6 + b_2 b_5 + b_3 b_4)$$
$$+ \ 45(b_1{}^2 b_5 + b_1 b_3{}^2 + b_2{}^2 b_3 + 2b_1 b_2 b_4)$$
$$+ \ 165(b_1{}^3 b_4 + b_1 b_2{}^3 + 3b_1{}^2 b_2 b_3)$$
$$+ \ 495(b_1{}^4 b_3 + 2b_1{}^3 b_2{}^2) + 1287b_1{}^5 b_2 + 429b_1{}^7$$

$$= \log h \left\{ 1 + \frac{1}{n} \right\}^n$$

$$= 5\epsilon$$

$$= 2 \log h \, n - \log h \, (n + 1) - \log h \, (n - 1)$$

$$= \log h \frac{n}{n - 1}$$

Series No.

(164) $-\dfrac{x}{2} + \dfrac{5}{24} x^2 - \dfrac{1}{8} x^3 + \dfrac{251}{2880} x^4 - \ldots \infty$

IX. Binomials.   See also No. (1102).

(165) $x^n + nx^{n-1}a + \dfrac{n(n-1)}{2!} x^{n-2}a^2 + \ldots + a^n$

(166) $1 + \dfrac{1}{2} x^2 + \dfrac{1\cdot3}{2\cdot4} x^4 + \ldots \infty$

(167) $2 + \dfrac{5}{3\cdot2!} + \dfrac{5\cdot7}{3^2\cdot3!} + \dfrac{5\cdot7\cdot9}{3^3\cdot4!} + \ldots \infty$

(168) $1 - \dfrac{1}{2}\cdot\dfrac{1}{2} + \dfrac{1\cdot3}{2\cdot4}\cdot\dfrac{1}{2^2} - \dfrac{1\cdot3\cdot5}{2\cdot4\cdot6}\cdot\dfrac{1}{2^3} + \ldots \infty$

(169) $1 + \dfrac{3}{4} + \dfrac{3\cdot5}{4\cdot8} + \dfrac{3\cdot5\cdot7}{4\cdot8\cdot12} + \ldots \infty$

(170) $1 + \dfrac{1}{2} x - \dfrac{1\cdot3}{2\cdot4} x^2 - \dfrac{1\cdot3\cdot5}{2\cdot4\cdot6} x^3 + \dfrac{1\cdot3\cdot5\cdot7}{2\cdot4\cdot6\cdot8} x^4 + \ldots \infty$

(171) $1 - \dfrac{1}{2} x - \dfrac{1\cdot3}{2\cdot4} x^2 + \dfrac{1\cdot3\cdot5}{2\cdot4\cdot6} x^3 + \dfrac{1\cdot3\cdot5\cdot7}{2\cdot4\cdot6\cdot8} x^4 - \ldots \infty$

(The above two series are useful in forming certain trigonometrical series.)

(172) $\dfrac{1}{3} x + \dfrac{1\cdot4}{3\cdot6} 2^2x^2 + \dfrac{1\cdot4\cdot7}{3\cdot6\cdot9} 3^2x^3 + \ldots \infty$

(173) $1 - x + x^2 - x^3 + \ldots \infty$

(174) $1 - 2x + 3x^2 - 4x^3 + \ldots \infty$

(175) $1 + \dfrac{1}{2} x - \dfrac{1\cdot1}{2\cdot4} x^2 + \dfrac{1\cdot1\cdot3}{2\cdot4\cdot6} x^3 - \dfrac{1\cdot1\cdot3\cdot5}{2\cdot4\cdot6\cdot8} x^4 + \ldots \infty$

(176) $1 - \dfrac{1}{2} x + \dfrac{1\cdot3}{2\cdot4} x^2 - \dfrac{1\cdot3\cdot5}{2\cdot4\cdot6} x^3 + \dfrac{1\cdot3\cdot5\cdot7}{2\cdot4\cdot6\cdot8} x^4 - \ldots \infty$

$$= \text{logh } \{\text{logh } (1 + x)^{1/x}\}$$ Y. 107

$$= (x + a)^n$$

$$= \frac{1}{\sqrt{1 - x^2}}$$ H. 468

$$= 3\sqrt{3}$$ F. 167

$$= \sqrt{2/3}$$ F. 168

$$= \sqrt{8}$$ F. 168

$$= \sqrt{\frac{\sqrt{1 + x^2} + x}{1 + x^2}}$$

$$= \sqrt{\frac{\sqrt{1 + x^2} - x}{1 + x^2}}$$

$$= \frac{x(x + 3)}{9(1 - x)^{7/3}}$$

$$= (1 + x)^{-1}$$ T. 117

$$= (1 + x)^{-2}$$ T. 117

$$= \sqrt{1 + x}$$ T. 117

$$= \frac{1}{\sqrt{1 + x}}$$ T. 117

Series No.

(177) $1 + \dfrac{1}{3}x - \dfrac{1 \cdot 2}{3 \cdot 6}x^2 + \dfrac{1 \cdot 2 \cdot 5}{3 \cdot 6 \cdot 9}x^3 - \dfrac{1 \cdot 2 \cdot 5 \cdot 8}{3 \cdot 6 \cdot 9 \cdot 12}x^4 + \ldots \infty$

(178) $1 - \dfrac{1}{3}x + \dfrac{1 \cdot 4}{3 \cdot 6}x^2 - \dfrac{1 \cdot 4 \cdot 7}{3 \cdot 6 \cdot 9}x^3 + \dfrac{1 \cdot 4 \cdot 7 \cdot 10}{3 \cdot 6 \cdot 9 \cdot 12}x^4 - \ldots \infty$

(179) $1 + \dfrac{3}{2}x + \dfrac{3 \cdot 1}{2 \cdot 4}x^2 - \dfrac{3 \cdot 1 \cdot 1}{2 \cdot 4 \cdot 6}x^3 + \dfrac{3 \cdot 1 \cdot 1 \cdot 3}{2 \cdot 4 \cdot 6 \cdot 8}x^4 - \ldots \infty$

(180) $1 - \dfrac{3}{2}x + \dfrac{3 \cdot 5}{2 \cdot 4}x^2 - \dfrac{3 \cdot 5 \cdot 7}{2 \cdot 4 \cdot 6}x^3 + \ldots \infty$

(181) $1 + \dfrac{1}{4}x - \dfrac{3}{32}x^2 + \dfrac{7}{128}x^3 - \dfrac{77}{2048}x^4 + \ldots \infty$

(182) $1 - \dfrac{1}{4}x + \dfrac{5}{32}x^2 - \dfrac{15}{128}x^3 + \dfrac{195}{2048}x^4 - \ldots \infty$

(183) $1 + \dfrac{1}{5}x - \dfrac{2}{25}x^2 + \dfrac{6}{125}x^3 - \dfrac{21}{625}x^4 + \ldots \infty$

(184) $1 - \dfrac{1}{5}x + \dfrac{3}{25}x^2 - \dfrac{11}{125}x^3 + \dfrac{44}{625}x^4 - \ldots \infty$

(185) $1 + \dfrac{1}{6}x - \dfrac{5}{72}x^2 + \dfrac{55}{1296}x^3 - \dfrac{935}{31104}x^4 + \ldots \infty$

(186) $1 - \dfrac{1}{6}x + \dfrac{7}{72}x^2 - \dfrac{91}{1296}x^3 + \dfrac{1729}{31104}x^4 - \ldots \infty$

(187) $1 + n\left(\dfrac{x}{4}\right) + \dfrac{n(n-3)}{2!}\left(\dfrac{x}{4}\right)^2$
$$+ \dfrac{n(n-4)(n-5)}{3!}\left(\dfrac{x}{4}\right)^3 + \ldots \infty$$

(188) $1 + \dfrac{n^2}{2!}x^2 + \dfrac{n^2(n^2 - 2^2)}{4!}x^4 + \dfrac{n^2(n^2 - 2^2)(n^2 - 4^2)}{6!}x^6 + \ldots$
$$+ \dfrac{n}{1!}x + \dfrac{n(n^2 - 1^2)}{3!}x^3 + \dfrac{n(n^2 - 1^2)(n^2 - 3^2)}{5!}x^5 + \ldots \infty$$

$= (1 + x)^{1/3}$ T. 117

$= (1 + x)^{-1/3}$ T. 117

$= (1 + x)^{3/2}$ T. 117

$= (1 + x)^{-3/2}$ T. 117

$= (1 + x)^{1/4}$ T. 117

$= (1 + x)^{-1/4}$ T. 117

$= (1 + x)^{1/5}$ T. 118

$= (1 + x)^{-1/5}$ T. 118

$= (1 + x)^{1/6}$ T. 118

$= (1 + x)^{-1/6}$ T. 118

$= \dfrac{1}{2^n} \{1 + \sqrt{1 + x}\}^n$ where $x^2 < 1$ and n is any real number

                                                      T. 118

$= \{x + \sqrt{1 + x^2}\}^n$ where $x^2 < 1$ T. 118

Series No.

(189) $\displaystyle {}_mC_n = \frac{m(m-1)(m-2)\ldots(m-n+1)}{n!}$

(190) $1 + {}_mC_1 x + \ldots {}_mC_n x^n + \ldots {}_mC_m x^m$

(191) $\displaystyle {}_{m_1}C_n + {}_{m_2}C_1 \cdot {}_{m_1}C_{n-1} + {}_{m_2}C_2 \cdot {}_{m_1}C_{n-2} + {}_{m_2}C_n$

(192) $1 + {}_mC_1 + {}_mC_2 + \ldots {}_mC_n + \ldots$

(193) $1 - {}_mC_1 + {}_mC_2 \ldots (-1)^n {}_mC_n + \ldots$

(194) $1 \cdot {}_mC_1 + 2 \cdot {}_mC_2 x + \ldots n \cdot {}_mC_n x^{m-1} + \ldots$

(195) $\displaystyle m(m-1) + \frac{m(m-1)(m-2)}{1!} + \ldots$
$$+ \frac{m(m-1)\ldots(m-r+1)}{(r-2)!} + \ldots$$

(196) $\displaystyle 1 + m + \frac{m(m+1)}{2!} + \ldots + \frac{m(m+1)\ldots(m+r-1)}{r!}$

(197) $\displaystyle 2^n \left\{ x^n + \frac{n}{1 \cdot 2^2} x^{n-2}y^2 + \frac{n(n-3)}{2!2^4} x^{n-4}y^4 + \ldots \right.$
$$\left. + \frac{n(n-r-1)(n-r-2)\ldots(n-2r+1)}{r!2^{2r}} x^{n-2r}y^{2r} + \ldots \right\}$$

(198) $2^n(x^2 + y^2)^{1/2}$
$$\times \left\{ x^{n-1} + \frac{n-2}{1!2^2} x^{n-3}y^2 + \frac{(n-3)(n-4)}{2!2^4} x^{n-5}y^4 + \ldots \right.$$
$$\left. + \frac{(n-r-1)(n-r-2)\ldots(n-2r)}{r!2^{2r}} x^{n-2r-1}y^{2r} + \ldots \right\}$$

(199) $1 - {}_mC_1 + {}_mC_2 - \ldots (-1)^n {}_mC_n$

(200) $\displaystyle {}_nC_1 - \frac{1}{2} {}_nC_2 + \frac{1}{3} {}_nC_3 - \ldots$

C. 186

$= (1 + x)^m$ C. 186

$= {}_{m_1+m_2}C_n$ C. 189

$= 2^m$ where $m > -1$ C. 191

$= 0$ where m is positive C. 191

$= m(1 + x)^{m-1}$ C. 197

$= m(m - 1)2^{m-2}$ where $m \nless 1$ C. 200

$= \dfrac{(m + r)!}{m!r!}$ where r is a positive integer C. 200

$= (x + \sqrt{x^2 + y^2})^n + \{x - \sqrt{x^2 + y^2}\}^n$ where n is a positive
integer C. 204

$= \{x + \sqrt{x^2 + y^2}\}^n - \{x - \sqrt{x^2 + y^2}\}^n$ where n is a positive
integer C. 205

$= (-1)^n {}_{m-1}C_n$ where n is a positive integer C. 210

$= 1 + \dfrac{1}{2} + \ldots \dfrac{1}{n}$ C. 212

Series No.

X. Simple Inverse Products

(201)†   To find the sum of n terms of a series, each term of which is composed of the reciprocal of the product of r factors in arithmetical progression, the first factors of the several terms being in the same arithmetical progression: Write down the nth term, strike off a factor from the beginning, divide by the number of factors so diminished, and by the common difference change the sign and add a constant.

(202) $\dfrac{1}{1.2.3.4} + \dfrac{1}{2.3.4.5} + \ldots n$ terms

(203) $\dfrac{3}{1.2.4} + \dfrac{4}{2.3.5} + \dfrac{5}{3.4.6} + \ldots n$ terms

(204) $\dfrac{1}{1 \cdot 2} + \dfrac{1}{2 \cdot 3} + \dfrac{1}{3 \cdot 4} + \ldots n$ terms

$$+ \ldots \infty$$

(205) $\dfrac{1}{1 \cdot 3} + \dfrac{1}{3 \cdot 5} + \dfrac{1}{5 \cdot 7} + \ldots n$ terms

(206) $\dfrac{1}{2 \cdot 3} + \dfrac{2}{3 \cdot 4} \cdot 2 + \dfrac{3}{4 \cdot 5} \cdot 2^2 + \ldots n$ terms

(207) $\dfrac{2}{1 \cdot 3 \cdot 4} + \dfrac{3}{2 \cdot 4 \cdot 5} + \ldots n$ terms

(208) $\dfrac{1}{1 \cdot 4} + \dfrac{1}{4 \cdot 7} + \dfrac{1}{7 \cdot 10} + \ldots n$ terms

$$+ \ldots \infty = \sum_{1}^{\infty} \frac{1}{(3n-2)(3n+1)}$$

† In some cases the nth term can by partial fractions be resolved into the standard form when this rule can apply.

F. 316

$$= \frac{1}{18} - \frac{1}{3(n + 1)(n + 2)(n + 3)}$$

F. 317

$$= \frac{29}{36} - \frac{1}{n + 3} - \frac{3}{2(n + 2)(n + 3)} - \frac{4}{3(n + 1)(n + 2)(n + 3)}$$

F. 317

$$= \frac{n}{n + 1}$$

F. 322

$$= 1$$

$$= \frac{n}{2n + 1}$$

$$= \frac{2^n}{n + 2} - \frac{1}{2}$$

$$= \frac{17}{36} - \frac{6n^2 + 21n + 17}{6(n + 1)(n + 2)(n + 3)}$$

$$= \frac{n}{3n + 1}$$

$$= \frac{1}{3}$$

F. 322

Series No.

(209) $\dfrac{1}{1\cdot 3\cdot 5} + \dfrac{1}{3\cdot 5\cdot 7} + \dfrac{1}{5\cdot 7\cdot 9} + \ldots n$ terms

$+ \ldots \infty$

(210) $\dfrac{1}{1\cdot 4\cdot 7} + \dfrac{1}{4\cdot 7\cdot 10} + \dfrac{1}{7\cdot 10\cdot 13} + \ldots n$ terms

$+ \ldots \infty$

(211) $\dfrac{4}{1\cdot 2\cdot 3} + \dfrac{5}{2\cdot 3\cdot 4} + \dfrac{6}{3\cdot 4\cdot 5} + \ldots n$ terms

$+ \ldots \infty$

(212) $\dfrac{1}{3\cdot 4\cdot 5} + \dfrac{2}{4\cdot 5\cdot 6} + \dfrac{3}{5\cdot 6\cdot 7} + \ldots n$ terms

$+ \ldots \infty$

(213) $\dfrac{1}{1\cdot 2\cdot 3} + \dfrac{3}{2\cdot 3\cdot 4} + \dfrac{5}{3\cdot 4\cdot 5} + \ldots n$ terms

$+ \ldots \infty$

(214) $\dfrac{3}{1\cdot 2}\cdot\dfrac{1}{2} + \dfrac{4}{2\cdot 3}\cdot\dfrac{1}{2^2} + \dfrac{5}{3\cdot 4}\cdot\dfrac{1}{2^3} + \ldots n$ terms

(215) $\dfrac{1^2}{2\cdot 3}\cdot 4 + \dfrac{2^2}{3\cdot 4}\cdot 4^2 + \dfrac{3^2}{4\cdot 5}\cdot 4^3 + \ldots n$ terms

(216) $\dfrac{1}{1\cdot 3} + \dfrac{2}{1\cdot 3\cdot 5} + \dfrac{3}{1\cdot 3\cdot 5\cdot 7} + \ldots n$ terms

(217) $\dfrac{1\cdot 2}{3!} + \dfrac{2\cdot 2^2}{4!} + \dfrac{3\cdot 2^3}{5!} + \ldots n$ terms

(218) $\dfrac{1\cdot 2}{3} + \dfrac{2\cdot 3}{3^2} + \dfrac{3\cdot 4}{3^3} + \ldots \infty$

(219) $\dfrac{5}{1\cdot 2}\cdot\dfrac{1}{3} + \dfrac{7}{2\cdot 3}\cdot\dfrac{1}{3^2} + \dfrac{9}{3\cdot 4}\cdot\dfrac{1}{3^3} + \ldots n$ terms

$$= \frac{1}{12} - \frac{1}{4(2n + 1)(2n + 3)}$$

$$= \frac{1}{12}$$ F. 322

$$= \frac{1}{24} - \frac{1}{6(3n + 1)(3n + 4)}$$

$$= \frac{1}{24}$$ F. 322

$$= \frac{5}{4} - \frac{2n + 5}{2(n + 1)(n + 2)}$$

$$= \frac{5}{4}$$ F. 322

$$= \frac{1}{6} - \frac{1}{n + 3} + \frac{2}{(n + 3)(n + 4)}$$

$$= \frac{1}{6}$$ F. 322

$$= \frac{3}{4} - \frac{2}{n + 2} + \frac{1}{2(n + 1)(n + 2)}$$

$$= \frac{3}{4}$$ F. 322

$$= 1 - \frac{1}{n + 1} \cdot \frac{1}{2^n}$$ F. 333

$$= \frac{n - 1}{n + 2} \cdot \frac{4^{n+1}}{3} + \frac{2}{3}$$ F. 333

$$= \frac{1}{2} - \frac{1}{2} \frac{1}{1 \cdot 3 \cdot 5 \cdot 7 \ldots (2n + 1)}$$ F. 333

$$= 1 - \frac{2^{n+1}}{(n + 2)!}$$ F. 333

$$= \frac{9}{4}$$ F. 332

$$= 1 - \frac{1}{n + 1} \cdot \frac{1}{3^n}$$ F. 331

Series No.

(220) $\dfrac{1}{3} + \dfrac{3}{3\cdot 7} + \dfrac{5}{3\cdot 7\cdot 11} + \ldots n$ terms

(221) $\dfrac{1}{1\cdot 3} + \dfrac{1}{2\cdot 4} + \dfrac{1}{3\cdot 5} + \ldots \dfrac{1}{n(n+2)}$

(222) $\displaystyle\sum_{1}^{n} \dfrac{1}{(1+nx)(1+\overline{n+1}x)}$

(223) $\dfrac{1}{(x+1)(x+2)} + \dfrac{1!}{(x+1)(x+2)(x+3)}$

$\qquad\qquad + \dfrac{2!}{(x+1)(x+2)(x+3)(x+4)} + \ldots \infty$

(224) $\displaystyle\sum_{1}^{\infty} \dfrac{1}{(x+n)(x+n+1)}$

(225) $\dfrac{1}{a} + \dfrac{x}{a(a+1)} + \dfrac{x^2}{a(a+1)(a+2)} + \ldots \infty$

(226) $\dfrac{a}{b} + \dfrac{a(a+1)}{b(b+1)}x + \dfrac{a(a+1)(a+2)}{b(b+1)(b+2)}x^2 + \ldots \infty$

(227) $\dfrac{1}{2n+2} + \dfrac{1}{2}\cdot\dfrac{1}{2n+4} + \dfrac{1\cdot 3}{2\cdot 4}\cdot\dfrac{1}{2n+6}$

$\qquad\qquad + \dfrac{1\cdot 3\cdot 5}{2\cdot 4\cdot 6}\cdot\dfrac{1}{2n+8} + \ldots \infty$

(228) $1 + \dfrac{a}{b} + \dfrac{a(a+1)}{b(b+1)} + \dfrac{a(a+1)(a+2)}{b(b+1)(b+2)} + \ldots \infty$

$$= \frac{1}{2} - \frac{1}{2} \frac{1}{3 \cdot 7 \cdot 11 \ldots (4n - 1)}$$

F. 331

$$= \frac{3n^2 + 5n}{4(n + 1)(n + 2)}$$

W. 57

$$= \frac{n}{(1 + x)\{1 + \overline{n + 1}x\}}$$

$$= \frac{1}{(1 + x)^2}$$

$$= \frac{1}{x + 1}$$

$$= \frac{(a - 1)!}{x^a} \left\{ \epsilon^x - \sum_{n=0}^{a-1} \frac{x^n}{n!} \right\} \text{ where } a \text{ is positive}$$

T. 118

$$= (b - a) \binom{b - 1}{a - 1} \left\{ \frac{(-1)^{b-a} \log h (1 - x)}{x^b} (1 - x)^{b-a-1} \right.$$

$$\left. + \frac{1}{x^a} \sum_{k=1}^{b-a} (-1)^k \binom{b - a - 1}{k - 1} \sum_{n=1}^{a+k-1} \frac{x^{n-k}}{n} \right\} \text{ where } a \text{ and } b \text{ are }$$

positive and $a < b$; $\binom{b - 1}{a - 1}$, etc., are binomial co-

efficients

T. 118

$$= \frac{2 \cdot 4 \cdot 6 \ldots 2n}{3 \cdot 5 \cdot 7 \ldots (2n + 1)}$$

1Z. 267

$$= \frac{b - 1}{b - a - 1} \text{ where } b - 1 > a > 0$$

A. 48

Series No.

(229) $\dfrac{a}{b} + \dfrac{2a(a + 1)}{b(b + 1)} + \dfrac{3a(a + 1)(a + 2)}{b(b + 1)(b + 2)} + \ldots \infty$

(230) $\dfrac{1}{x(x + 1)} + \dfrac{1}{x(x + 1)(x + 2)}$

$$+ \dfrac{1 \cdot 2}{x(x + 1)(x + 2)(x + 3)} + \ldots \infty$$

(231) $\dfrac{1}{(1 + x)(1 + 2x)} + \dfrac{1}{(1 + 2x)(1 + 3x)} + \ldots n \text{ terms}$

(232) $\dfrac{1}{(1 + x)(1 + ax)} + \dfrac{a}{(1 + ax)(1 + a^2x)} + \ldots n \text{ terms}$

XI. Other Inverse Products

(233) $\dfrac{1}{1 \cdot 3} + \dfrac{1}{3 \cdot 5} + \dfrac{1}{5 \cdot 7} + \ldots \infty$

(234) $\dfrac{1}{1 \cdot 2} + \dfrac{1}{2 \cdot 4} + \dfrac{1}{3 \cdot 6} + \dfrac{1}{4 \cdot 8} + \ldots \infty$

(235) $\dfrac{1}{1 \cdot 2} - \dfrac{1}{2 \cdot 3} + \dfrac{1}{3 \cdot 4} - \dfrac{1}{4 \cdot 5} + \ldots \infty$

(236) $\dfrac{1}{1 \cdot 2 \cdot 3} + \dfrac{1}{3 \cdot 4 \cdot 5} + \dfrac{1}{5 \cdot 6 \cdot 7} + \ldots \infty$

(237) $\dfrac{1}{1 \cdot 2 \cdot 3} - \dfrac{1}{3 \cdot 4 \cdot 5} + \dfrac{1}{5 \cdot 6 \cdot 7} - \ldots \infty$

(238) $\dfrac{1}{1 \cdot 3 \cdot 5} + \dfrac{1}{5 \cdot 7 \cdot 9} + \dfrac{1}{9 \cdot 11 \cdot 13} + \ldots \infty$

(239) $\dfrac{1}{1 \cdot 3 \cdot 5} + \dfrac{1}{3 \cdot 5 \cdot 7} + \dfrac{1}{5 \cdot 7 \cdot 9} + \ldots \infty$

(240) $\dfrac{1}{1 \cdot 3 \cdot 5} - \dfrac{1}{3 \cdot 5 \cdot 7} + \dfrac{1}{5 \cdot 7 \cdot 9} - \ldots \infty$

(241) $\left(\dfrac{1}{1 \cdot 2 \cdot 3}\right)^2 + \left(\dfrac{1}{2 \cdot 3 \cdot 4}\right)^2 + \left(\dfrac{1}{3 \cdot 4 \cdot 5}\right)^2 + \ldots \infty$

$$= \frac{a(b - 1)}{(b - a - 1)(b - a - 2)} \quad \text{where } b - 2 > a > 0 \qquad \text{A. 48}$$

$$= \frac{1}{x^2}$$

$$= \frac{n}{(1 + x)(1 + x.\overline{n + 1})} \qquad \text{F. 313}$$

$$= \frac{1}{1 - a}\left(\frac{1}{1 + x} - \frac{a^n}{1 + a^n x}\right) \qquad \text{F. 313}$$

$$= \frac{1}{2} \qquad \text{T. 143}$$

$$= \frac{\pi^2}{12} \qquad \text{E. 158}$$

$$= \operatorname{logh} \frac{4}{\epsilon} \qquad \text{C. 252}$$

$$= \operatorname{logh} 2 - \frac{1}{2} = 0.193147\ldots \qquad \text{F. 338}$$

$$= 0.153426 = \frac{1}{2}(1 - \operatorname{logh} 2) \qquad \text{H. 476}$$

$$= \frac{\pi}{16} - \frac{1}{8}$$

$$= \frac{1}{12}$$

$$= \frac{\pi}{8} - \frac{1}{3} \qquad \text{C. 372}$$

$$= \frac{\pi^2}{4} - \frac{39}{16} \qquad \text{O. 370}$$

Series No.

(242) $\dfrac{1}{1\cdot2\cdot3\cdot4} + \dfrac{1}{5\cdot6\cdot7\cdot8} + \dfrac{1}{9\cdot10\cdot11\cdot12} + \ldots \infty$

(243) $\dfrac{1}{1\cdot3\cdot5\cdot7} + \dfrac{1}{9\cdot11\cdot13\cdot15} + \dfrac{1}{17\cdot19\cdot21\cdot23} + \ldots \infty$

(244) $\dfrac{1}{2\cdot3\cdot4} - \dfrac{1}{4\cdot5\cdot6} + \dfrac{1}{6\cdot7\cdot8} - \ldots \infty$

(245) $\dfrac{5}{1\cdot2} - \dfrac{3}{2\cdot3} + \dfrac{9}{3\cdot4} - \dfrac{7}{4\cdot5} + \dfrac{13}{5\cdot6} - \dfrac{11}{6\cdot7} + \ldots n$ terms

(246) $\dfrac{2}{1\cdot5} - \dfrac{4}{5\cdot7} + \dfrac{8}{7\cdot17} - \dfrac{16}{17\cdot31} + \dfrac{32}{31\cdot65} - \ldots n$ terms

(247) $\dfrac{1}{(1\cdot3)^2} + \dfrac{1}{(3\cdot5)^2} + \dfrac{1}{(5\cdot7)^2} + \ldots \infty$

(248) $\dfrac{1}{2\cdot4} + \dfrac{1\cdot3}{2\cdot4\cdot6} + \dfrac{1\cdot3\cdot5}{2\cdot4\cdot6\cdot8} + \ldots n$ terms

(249) $\dfrac{1}{2\cdot3\cdot4} + \dfrac{1}{4\cdot5\cdot6} + \dfrac{1}{6\cdot7\cdot8} + \ldots \infty$

(250) $\dfrac{1}{1\cdot2\cdot3} + \dfrac{1}{4\cdot5\cdot6} + \dfrac{1}{7\cdot8\cdot9} + \ldots \infty$

(251) $\dfrac{1}{2\cdot3\cdot4} + \dfrac{1}{6\cdot7\cdot8} + \dfrac{1}{10\cdot11\cdot12} + \ldots \infty$

(252) $\dfrac{1}{1\cdot2\cdot3\cdot4} + \dfrac{1}{4\cdot5\cdot6\cdot7} + \dfrac{1}{7\cdot8\cdot9\cdot10} + \ldots \infty$

(253) $\dfrac{1}{1\cdot2\cdot3} + \dfrac{1}{5\cdot6\cdot7} + \dfrac{1}{9\cdot10\cdot11} + \ldots \infty$

(254) $1 - \dfrac{1}{2} + \dfrac{1\cdot3}{2\cdot4} - \dfrac{1\cdot3\cdot5}{2\cdot4\cdot6} + \ldots \infty$

(255) $1 + \dfrac{1}{2} - \dfrac{1\cdot1}{2\cdot4} + \dfrac{1\cdot1\cdot3}{2\cdot4\cdot6} - \dfrac{1\cdot1\cdot3\cdot5}{2\cdot4\cdot6\cdot8} + \ldots \infty$

$$= \frac{1}{4} \log h \, 2 - \frac{\pi}{24}$$ O. 371

$$= \frac{\pi}{96(2 + \sqrt{2})}$$ O. 371

$$= \frac{1}{4}(\pi - 3)$$ A. 190

$$= 3 - \frac{2 + (-1)^n}{n + 1}$$ F. 339

$$= \frac{1}{3}\left\{ 1 + \frac{(-1)^{n+1}}{2^{n+1} + (-1)^{n+1}} \right\}$$ F. 339

$$= \frac{\pi^2 - 8}{16}$$

$$= \frac{1}{2} - \frac{1 \cdot 3 \cdot 5 \ldots (2n + 1)}{2 \cdot 4 \cdot 6 \ldots (2n + 2)}$$ F. 333

$$= \frac{3}{4} - \log h \, 2$$ T. 144

$$= \frac{1}{4}\left(\frac{\pi}{\sqrt{3}} - \log h \, 3 \right)$$ T. 144

$$= \frac{\pi}{8} - \frac{1}{2} \log h \, 2$$ T. 144

$$= \frac{1}{6}\left(1 + \frac{\pi}{2\sqrt{3}} \right) - \frac{1}{4} \log h \, 3$$ T. 144

$$= \frac{1}{4} \log h \, 2$$ C. 252

$$= \frac{1}{\sqrt{2}}$$

$$= \sqrt{2}$$

Series No.

(256) $\dfrac{1}{3} + \dfrac{2}{3\cdot5} + \dfrac{3}{3\cdot5\cdot7} + \dfrac{4}{3\cdot5\cdot7\cdot9} + \ldots \infty$

(257) $\dfrac{1}{3} + \dfrac{2}{3\cdot5} + \dfrac{3}{3\cdot5\cdot7} + \dfrac{4}{3\cdot5\cdot7\cdot9} + \ldots n$ terms

(258) $1 + \dfrac{1}{3} + \dfrac{1\cdot2}{3\cdot5} + \dfrac{1\cdot2\cdot3}{3\cdot5\cdot7} + \ldots \infty$

(259) $1 + \dfrac{1}{3} + \dfrac{1\cdot2}{3\cdot5} + \dfrac{1\cdot2\cdot3}{3\cdot5\cdot7} + \ldots \infty$

$$= 1 + \dfrac{2}{3}\cdot\dfrac{1}{2} + \dfrac{2\cdot4}{3\cdot5}\cdot\dfrac{1}{2^2} + \dfrac{2\cdot4\cdot6}{3\cdot5\cdot7}\cdot\dfrac{1}{2^3} + \ldots$$

(260) $1 + \dfrac{1}{2\cdot3} + \dfrac{1\cdot3}{2\cdot4\cdot5} + \dfrac{1\cdot3\cdot5}{2\cdot4\cdot6\cdot7} + \ldots \infty$

(261) $1 + \dfrac{1}{3}\cdot\dfrac{1}{2} + \dfrac{1\cdot2}{3\cdot5}\cdot\dfrac{1}{2^2} + \dfrac{1\cdot2\cdot3}{3\cdot5\cdot7}\cdot\dfrac{1}{2^3} + \ldots \infty$

(262) $\dfrac{1}{2} + \dfrac{1\cdot3}{2\cdot4}\cdot\dfrac{1}{2} + \dfrac{1\cdot3\cdot5}{2\cdot4\cdot6}\cdot\dfrac{1}{3} + \ldots \infty$

(263) $\dfrac{1}{2\cdot5} + \dfrac{1}{8\cdot11} + \dfrac{1}{14\cdot17} + \ldots \infty$

(264) $1 - \dfrac{1}{7} + \dfrac{1}{9} - \dfrac{1}{15} + \dfrac{1}{17} - \ldots \infty$

(265) $\dfrac{1}{1\cdot5} + \dfrac{1}{2\cdot7} + \dfrac{1}{3\cdot9} + \ldots \infty$

(266) $\dfrac{1}{1\cdot5} + \dfrac{1}{9\cdot13} + \dfrac{1}{17\cdot21} + \dfrac{1}{25\cdot29} + \ldots \infty$

(267) $1 - \dfrac{2}{3}\cdot\dfrac{1}{2} + \dfrac{2\cdot4}{3\cdot5}\cdot\dfrac{1}{2^2} - \dfrac{2\cdot4\cdot6}{3\cdot5\cdot7}\cdot\dfrac{1}{2^3} + \ldots \infty$

(268) $\displaystyle\sum_{1}^{\infty} \dfrac{2}{(t+n-1)(t+n)(t+n+1)}$

$$= \frac{1}{2}$$
C. 225

$$= \frac{1}{2} \left\{ 1 - \frac{1}{3 \cdot 5 \cdot 7 \ldots (2n + 1)} \right\}$$
A. 431

$$= \frac{\pi}{2}$$
Y. 505

$$= \frac{\pi}{2}$$
A. 197

$$= \frac{\pi}{2}$$
A. 184

$$= \frac{2\pi}{3\sqrt{3}}$$
Y. 505

$$= 2 \log h\, 2$$
1Z. 136

$$= \frac{1}{9} \left(\frac{\pi}{\sqrt{3}} - \log h\, 2 \right)$$
1Z. 164

$$= \frac{\pi}{8} (1 + \sqrt{2})$$
1Z. 165

$$= \frac{8}{9} - \frac{2}{3} \log h\, 2$$
1Z. 165

$$= \frac{\sqrt{2}}{32} \{ \pi + \log h\, (3 + 2\sqrt{2}) \}$$
1Z. 165

$$= \frac{2}{\sqrt{3}} \log h\, \frac{1 + \sqrt{3}}{\sqrt{2}}$$
A. 197

$$= \frac{1}{t(t + 1)}$$
A. 52

Series No.

(269) $\displaystyle\sum_1^\infty \frac{3}{(t + n - 1)(t + n)(t + n + 1)(t + n + 2)}$

(270) $\displaystyle\frac{1}{2} + \frac{1}{2\cdot3\cdot2^3} + \frac{1\cdot3}{2\cdot4\cdot5\cdot2^5} + \ldots \infty$

(271) $\displaystyle\frac{1}{1\cdot2^2\cdot3} + \frac{1}{5\cdot6^2\cdot7} + \frac{1}{9\cdot10^2\cdot11} + \ldots \infty$

(272) $\displaystyle\frac{1}{1^2\cdot2} + \frac{1}{2^2\cdot3} + \frac{1}{3^2\cdot4} + \ldots \infty$

(273) $\displaystyle 1 - \frac{1}{3\cdot3} + \frac{1}{5\cdot3^2} - \frac{1}{7\cdot3^3} + \ldots \infty$

(274) $\displaystyle 1 + \left(\frac{1}{2}\right)^2 + \left(\frac{1}{2\cdot4}\right)^2 + \left(\frac{1\cdot3}{2\cdot4\cdot6}\right)^2 + \left(\frac{1\cdot3\cdot5}{2\cdot4\cdot6\cdot8}\right)^2 + \ldots \infty$

(275) $\displaystyle 1 + \frac{1}{3}\left(\frac{1}{2}\right) + \frac{1\cdot2}{3\cdot5}\left(\frac{1}{2}\right)^2 + \frac{1\cdot2\cdot3}{3\cdot5\cdot7}\left(\frac{1}{2}\right)^3 + \ldots \infty$

(276) $\displaystyle 1 + \frac{1}{2\cdot3} + \frac{1}{3}\cdot\frac{1\cdot2}{3\cdot5} + \frac{1}{4}\cdot\frac{1\cdot2\cdot3}{3\cdot5\cdot7} + \ldots \infty$

(277) $\displaystyle 1 + \frac{1}{2}\cdot\frac{1}{3}\left(\frac{1}{2}\right) + \frac{1}{3}\cdot\frac{1\cdot2}{3\cdot5}\left(\frac{1}{2}\right)^2 + \frac{1}{4}\cdot\frac{1\cdot2\cdot3}{3\cdot5\cdot7}\left(\frac{1}{2}\right)^3 + \ldots \infty$

(278) $\displaystyle 1 + \frac{3}{6} + \frac{3\cdot6}{6\cdot10} + \frac{3\cdot6\cdot9}{6\cdot10\cdot14} + \ldots \infty$

(279) $\displaystyle\frac{1}{1\cdot2\cdot3} + \frac{x}{2\cdot3\cdot4} + \frac{x^2}{3\cdot4\cdot5} + \ldots \infty$

(280) $\displaystyle\frac{1}{1\cdot2\cdot3} + \frac{x}{3\cdot4\cdot5} + \frac{x^2}{5\cdot6\cdot7} + \ldots \infty$

(281) $\displaystyle\frac{1}{1\cdot2\cdot3} - \frac{x}{3\cdot4\cdot5} + \frac{x^2}{5\cdot6\cdot7} - \ldots \infty$

$$= \frac{1}{t(t + 1)(t + 2)}$$ A. 52

$$= \frac{\pi}{6}$$ H. 468

$$= \frac{\pi}{8}\left(1 - \frac{\pi}{4}\right)$$ D. 495

$$= \frac{\pi^2 - 6}{6}$$ C. 372

$$= \frac{\pi}{2\sqrt{3}}$$ H. 476

$$= \frac{\Gamma(2)}{[\Gamma(3/2)]^2} = \frac{4}{\pi}$$ A. 190

$$= \frac{2\pi}{3\sqrt{3}}$$ L. 236

$$= \frac{\pi^2}{8}$$ L. 237

$$= \frac{\pi^2}{9}$$ L. 237

$$= \frac{4\pi}{3\sqrt{3}}$$ L. 237

$$= \frac{3}{4x} - \frac{1}{2x^2} + \frac{(1 - x)^2}{2x^3} \operatorname{logh} \frac{1}{1 - x} \quad \text{where } x^2 < 1 \quad \text{T. 125}$$

$$= \frac{1}{4x}\left\{\frac{1 + x}{\sqrt{x}} \operatorname{logh} \frac{1 + \sqrt{x}}{1 - \sqrt{x}} + 2 \operatorname{logh}(1 - x) - 2\right\} \quad \text{where}$$
$$0 < x < 1 \quad \text{T. 125}$$

$$= \frac{1}{2x}\left\{1 - \operatorname{logh}(1 + x) - \frac{1 - x}{\sqrt{x}} \tan^{-1} x\right\} \quad \text{where } 0 < x \leqslant 1$$
$$\text{T. 125}$$

Series No.

XII. Simple Factorials

(282) $\dfrac{1}{3!} + \dfrac{5}{4!} + \dfrac{11}{5!} + \ldots n$ terms

(283) $\dfrac{2}{1!} + \dfrac{12}{2!} + \dfrac{28}{3!} + \dfrac{50}{4!} + \dfrac{78}{5!} + \ldots \infty$

(284) $\dfrac{1}{n!} + \dfrac{2!}{(n+1)!} + \dfrac{3!}{(n+2)!} + \ldots \infty$

(285) $\dfrac{0!}{n!} + \dfrac{1!}{(n+1)!} + \dfrac{2!}{(n+2)!} + \ldots \infty$

(286) $\displaystyle\sum_{0}^{\infty} \dfrac{(2n)!}{2^{2n}n!n!} \cdot \dfrac{1}{x+n}$

(287) $\displaystyle\sum_{n=0}^{\infty} \dfrac{(-1)^n a(a-1)(a-2)\ldots(a-n)}{n!} \cdot \dfrac{1}{x+n}$

(288) $\displaystyle\sum_{1}^{n} n(n!)$

(289) $\displaystyle\sum_{1}^{\infty} (-1)^{n+1} \dfrac{1}{n(n!)}$

(290) $\dfrac{1}{m} - \dfrac{n}{1!} \dfrac{1}{m+1} + \dfrac{n(n-1)}{2!} \cdot \dfrac{1}{m+2} - \ldots$

(291) $\dfrac{1}{3!} + \dfrac{5}{4!} + \dfrac{11}{5!} + \ldots \dfrac{n^2+n-1}{(n+2)!}$

XIII. Other Power Series (Bernoulli's and Euler's Numbers)

(292) $\displaystyle\operatorname*{Lt}_{n=\infty} \left[\dfrac{1^2}{n^3+1^3} + \dfrac{2^2}{n^3+2^3} + \dfrac{3^2}{n^3+3^3} + \ldots + \dfrac{n^2}{n^3+n^3} \right]$

(293) $\displaystyle\operatorname*{Lt}_{n=\infty} \left[\dfrac{1}{n+1} + \dfrac{1}{n+2} + \dfrac{1}{n+3} + \ldots + \dfrac{1}{n+n} \right]$

$$= \frac{1}{2} - \frac{n + 1}{(n + 2)!}$$ F. 333

$$= 5\epsilon + 2$$ F. 334

$$= \frac{1}{(n - 2)(n - 1)!}$$ F. 338

$$= \frac{1}{(n - 1)(n - 1)!}$$ AC. 63

$$= \frac{\Gamma(x)\Gamma(\frac{1}{2})}{\Gamma(x + \frac{1}{2})}$$ Q. 259

$$= \frac{\Gamma(x)\Gamma(a + 1)}{\Gamma(x + a)}$$ Q. 260

$$= (n + 1)! - 1$$

$$= 0.7965996 = \int_0^1 \frac{1 - \epsilon^{-x}}{x} \, dx$$

$$= \frac{(m - 1)!}{(n + 1)(n + 2)\ldots(n + m)}$$ C. 211

$$= \frac{1}{2} - \frac{1}{(n + 2)(n!)}$$

$$= \frac{1}{3} \log h \, 2$$ 1Z. 324

$$= \log h \, 2$$ 1Z. 326

Series No.

(294) $\displaystyle \operatorname*{Lt}_{n=\infty} \left[\frac{n}{n^2 + 1^2} + \frac{n}{n^2 + 2^2} + \ldots + \frac{n}{n^2 + n^2} \right]$

(295) $\displaystyle \operatorname*{Lt}_{n=\infty} \left[\frac{1}{\sqrt{2n - 1^2}} + \frac{1}{\sqrt{4n - 2^2}} + \frac{1}{\sqrt{6n - 3^2}} + \ldots \right.$

$\displaystyle \left. + \frac{1}{\sqrt{2n^2 - n^2}} \right]$

(296) $\displaystyle \operatorname*{Lt}_{n=\infty} \left[\frac{(n - m)^{1/3}}{n} + \frac{(2^2 n - m)^{1/3}}{2n} + \frac{(3^2 n - m)^{1/3}}{3n} + \ldots \right.$

$\displaystyle \left. + \frac{(n^3 - m)^{1/3}}{n^2} \right]$

(297) $\displaystyle \operatorname*{Lt}_{n=\infty} \left[\frac{\sqrt{n - 1}}{n} + \frac{\sqrt{2n - 1}}{2n} + \frac{\sqrt{3n - 1}}{3n} + \ldots + \frac{\sqrt{n^2 - 1}}{n^2} \right]$

(298) $\displaystyle \operatorname*{Lt}_{n=\infty} \left[\frac{1}{\sqrt{2a^2 n - 1}} + \frac{1}{\sqrt{4a^2 n - 1}} + \ldots + \frac{1}{\sqrt{2a^2 n^2 - 1}} \right]$

(299) $\displaystyle \operatorname*{Lt}_{n=\infty} \left[\frac{n^2}{(n^2 + 1^2)^{3/2}} + \frac{n^2}{(n^2 + 2^2)^{3/2}} + \ldots \right.$

$\displaystyle \left. + \frac{n^2}{\{n^2 + (n - 1)^2\}^{3/2}} \right]$

(300) $\displaystyle \operatorname*{Lt}_{n=\infty} \left[\frac{\sqrt{n - a}}{n - c} + \frac{\sqrt{2n - a}}{2n - c} + \ldots + \frac{\sqrt{n^2 - a}}{n^2 - c} \right]$

(301) $\displaystyle \frac{1}{n + 1} + \frac{2}{n^2 + 1} + \frac{4}{n^4 + 1} + \ldots \infty$

(302) $\displaystyle \sum_1^\infty \frac{n - 1}{n!}$

$= \dfrac{\pi}{4}$ 1Z. 326

$= \dfrac{\pi}{2}$ 1Z. 326

$= \dfrac{3}{2}$ 1Z. 326

$= 2$ 1Z. 326

$= \dfrac{\sqrt{2}}{a}$ 1Z. 326

$= \dfrac{1}{\sqrt{2}}$ 1Z. 326

$= 2$ 1Z. 354

$= \dfrac{1}{n-1}$ where $|n| > 1$ A. 66

$= 1$ A. 52

Series No.

(303) $\left(n + \frac{1}{2}\right) \log h \, n - n + \frac{1}{2} \log h \, (2\pi) + \frac{1}{12n} - \frac{1}{360n^3} - \ldots \infty$

(304) $n^{n+1/2} \sqrt{2\pi} \, \epsilon^{-n} \left\{ 1 + \frac{1}{12n} - \frac{1}{360n^3} + \frac{1}{1260n^5} - \ldots \infty \right\}$

$\qquad\qquad\qquad\qquad\qquad\qquad\qquad\qquad\qquad\qquad$ *n* large

On the series Nos. (305) to (330), see No. (1130) for values of α, β, etc.; see No. (330) for general note covering Nos. (305) through (329).

(305) $1 + \frac{1}{2^n} + \frac{1}{3^n} + \frac{1}{4^n} + \ldots \infty$

(306) $1 - \frac{1}{2^n} + \frac{1}{3^n} - \frac{1}{4^n} + \ldots \infty$

(307) $1 + \frac{1}{3^n} + \frac{1}{5^n} + \frac{1}{7^n} + \frac{1}{9^n} + \ldots \infty$

(308)† $1 - \frac{1}{3^n} + \frac{1}{5^n} - \frac{1}{7^n} + \frac{1}{9^n} - \ldots \infty$

(309) $1 + \frac{1}{2^n} + \frac{1}{4^n} + \frac{1}{5^n} + \frac{1}{7^n} + \frac{1}{8^n} + \ldots \infty$

(310) $1 - \frac{1}{2^n} + \frac{1}{4^n} - \frac{1}{5^n} + \frac{1}{7^n} - \frac{1}{8^n} + \ldots \infty$

(311) $1 + \frac{1}{2^n} - \frac{1}{4^n} - \frac{1}{5^n} + \frac{1}{7^n} + \frac{1}{8^n} - \ldots \infty$

† $u_1 = \frac{\pi}{4}$
$u_2 = 0.91596\,56\ldots$
$u_4 = 0.98894\,455\ldots$
$u_6 = 0.99868\,522.$
A table of n from 1 to 38 to 18 decimal places is given by Glaisher, *Messenger of Mathematics*, **42**; 49, 1913.

$= \log h (n!)$

$$= n! = \sqrt{2\pi n}\left(\frac{n}{\epsilon}\right)^n$$

$= \mathcal{S}_n, \quad \mathcal{S}_{2n} = \dfrac{\frac{1}{2}(2\pi)^{2n}B_n}{(2n)!}$

$= s_n, \quad s_{2n} = \dfrac{\pi^{2n}\beta_n}{2\cdot(2n)!}$

$= U_n, \quad U_{2n} = \dfrac{\pi^{2n}\alpha_n}{4\cdot(2n)!}$

$= u_n, \quad u_{2n+1} = \dfrac{\left(\frac{\pi}{2}\right)^{2n+1}E_n^*}{2(2n)!}$

$= G_n, \quad G_{2n} = \dfrac{\frac{2}{3}(\frac{2}{3}\pi)^{2n}\gamma_n}{(2n)!}$

$= g_n, \quad \sqrt{3}g_{2n+1} = \dfrac{(\frac{2}{3}\pi)^{2n+1}I_n}{(2n)!}$

$= j_n, \quad \sqrt{3}j_{2n+1} = \dfrac{(\frac{1}{3}\pi)^{2n+1}J_n}{(2n)!}$

Series No.

(312) $1 - \dfrac{1}{2^n} - \dfrac{1}{4^n} + \dfrac{1}{5^n} + \dfrac{1}{7^n} - \dfrac{1}{8^n} - \ldots \infty$

(313) $1 + \dfrac{1}{5^n} + \dfrac{1}{7^n} + \dfrac{1}{11^n} + \dfrac{1}{13^n} + \dfrac{1}{17^n} + \ldots \infty$

(314) $1 - \dfrac{1}{5^n} + \dfrac{1}{7^n} - \dfrac{1}{11^n} + \dfrac{1}{13^n} - \dfrac{1}{17^n} + \ldots \infty$

(315) $1 + \dfrac{1}{5^n} - \dfrac{1}{7^n} - \dfrac{1}{11^n} + \dfrac{1}{13^n} + \dfrac{1}{17^n} - \ldots \infty$

(316) $1 - \dfrac{1}{5^n} - \dfrac{1}{7^n} + \dfrac{1}{11^n} + \dfrac{1}{13^n} - \dfrac{1}{17^n} - \ldots \infty$

(317) $1 + \dfrac{1}{3^n} - \dfrac{1}{5^n} - \dfrac{1}{7^n} + \dfrac{1}{9^n} + \dfrac{1}{11^n} - \ldots \infty$

(318) $1 - \dfrac{1}{3^n} - \dfrac{1}{5^n} + \dfrac{1}{7^n} + \dfrac{1}{9^n} - \dfrac{1}{11^n} - \ldots \infty$

(319) $1 + \dfrac{1}{2^{2n}} + \dfrac{1}{3^{2n}} + \ldots \infty$

(320) $1 - \dfrac{1}{2^{2n}} + \dfrac{1}{3^{2n}} - \dfrac{1}{4^{2n}} + \ldots \infty$

(321) $1 - \dfrac{1}{2^{2n+1}} + \dfrac{1}{4^{2n+1}} - \dfrac{1}{5^{2n+1}} + \ldots \infty$

(322) $1 + \dfrac{1}{2^{2n}} - \dfrac{2}{3^{2n}} + \dfrac{1}{4^{2n}} + \dfrac{1}{5^{2n}} - \dfrac{2}{6^{2n}} + \ldots \infty$

(323) $1 + \dfrac{1}{2^{2n+1}} - \dfrac{1}{4^{2n+1}} - \dfrac{1}{5^{2n+1}} + \ldots \infty$

(324) $1 - \dfrac{1}{3^{2n+1}} + \dfrac{1}{5^{2n+1}} - \dfrac{1}{7^{2n+1}} + \ldots \infty$

$$= v_n, \quad v_{2n} = \frac{\frac{4}{3}(\frac{1}{3}\pi)^{2n}\eta_n}{(2n)!}$$
     AC. 42

$$= W_n, \quad W_{2n} = \frac{2(\frac{1}{3}\pi)^{2n}\theta_n}{(2n)!}$$
     AC. 42

$$= h_n, \quad \sqrt{3}h_{2n+1} = \frac{(\frac{1}{3}\pi)^{2n+1}H_n}{(2n)!}$$
     AC. 42

$$= r_n, \quad r_{2n+1} = \frac{2(\frac{1}{6}\pi)^{2n+1}R_n}{(2n)!}$$
     AC. 42

$$= t_n, \quad \sqrt{3}t_{2n} = \frac{6(\frac{1}{6}\pi)^{2n}T_n}{(2n-1)!}$$
     AC. 42

$$= p_n, \quad p_{2n+1} = \frac{\sqrt{2}(\frac{1}{4}\pi)^{2n+1}P_n}{(2n)!}$$
     AC. 42

$$= q_n, \quad q_{2n} = \frac{\sqrt{2}(\frac{1}{4}\pi)^{2n}Q_n}{(2n-1)!}$$
     AC. 42

$$= \frac{(2\pi)^{2n}}{2(2n)!} B_n$$
     AE. 3

$$= \frac{2^{2n-1}\pi^{2n}}{(2n)!} \left(1 - \frac{1}{2^{2n-1}}\right) B_n$$
     AE. 26

$$= \frac{(-1)^{n+1}(2\pi)^{2n+1}}{\sqrt{3}(2n)!} B_{2n+1}\left(\frac{1}{3}\right)$$
     AE. 34

$$= \frac{(-1)^n(2\pi)^{2n}}{(2n-1)!} A_{2n}\left(\frac{1}{3}\right)$$
     AE. 34

$$= \frac{(-1)^{n+1}(2\pi)^{2n+1}}{\sqrt{3}(2n)!} B_{2n+1}\left(\frac{1}{6}\right)$$
     AE. 40

$$= \frac{(-1)^{n+1}2^{2n}\pi^{2n+1}}{(2n)!} B_{2n+1}\left(\frac{1}{4}\right)$$
     AE. 30

$$= \frac{\pi^{2n+1}}{2^{2n+2}(2n)!} E_n{}^*$$
     AE. 30

Series No.

(325) $\dfrac{1}{2^{2n}} - \dfrac{1}{4^{2n}} + \dfrac{1}{6^{2n}} - \dfrac{1}{8^{2r}} + \ldots \infty$

(326) $1 + \dfrac{1}{3^{2n+1}} - \dfrac{1}{5^{2n+1}} - \dfrac{1}{7^{2n+1}} + \dfrac{1}{9^{2n+1}} + \ldots \infty$

(327) $1 - \dfrac{1}{3^{2n}} - \dfrac{1}{5^{2n}} + \dfrac{1}{7^{2n}} + \dfrac{1}{9^{2n}} - \ldots \infty$

(328) $1 + \dfrac{1}{5^{2n+1}} - \dfrac{1}{7^{2n+1}} - \dfrac{1}{11^{2n+1}} + \ldots \infty$

(329) $1 - \dfrac{1}{5^{2n}} - \dfrac{1}{7^{2n}} + \dfrac{1}{11^{2n}} + \ldots \infty$

(330) General note on Nos. (305) through (329):

(a) The values of Bernoulli's and Euler's numbers are given in Nos. (1129) and (1131).

(b) The values of $B_n(x)$ and $A_n(x)$, etc., are given in Nos. (1134) to (1146).

(c) The coefficients $\mathcal{S}$, etc., in Nos. (305) to (312) are given in No. (1130).   See also No. (1101).

(d) The values of p_{2n+1}, q_{2n}, r_{2n+1}, and t_{2n} are given in the table opposite for values of $n = 0$ to 4.

(e) The summation of No. (305) to 16 places of decimals is given in No. (1133).

(f) Some of these series are derived from No. (546), etc., giving θ appropriate values.

(g) Between Nos. (305) to (318) and (319) to (329) there is some duplication, as the series are collected from different sources, but the results are compatible.

$$= \frac{(-1)^n (2\pi)^{2n}}{2(2n+1)!} \left\{ B_{2n}\left(\frac{1}{4}\right) + (-1)^{n-1} \frac{B_n}{2n} \right\} \qquad \text{AE. 30}$$

$$= p_{2n+1} \qquad \text{AE. 59}$$

$$= q_{2n} \qquad \text{AE. 64}$$

$$= r_{2n+1} \qquad \text{AE. 69}$$

$$= t_{2n} \qquad \text{AE. 74}$$

n	p_{2n+1}	q_{2n}	r_{2n+1}	t_{2n}
0	$\dfrac{\pi}{2\sqrt{2}}$	—	$\dfrac{\pi}{3}$	—
1	$\dfrac{3\pi^3}{\sqrt{2}\cdot 2^6}$	$\dfrac{\pi^2}{\sqrt{2}\cdot 2^3}$	$\dfrac{7\pi^3}{6^3}$	$\dfrac{\pi^2}{2\cdot 3\sqrt{3}}$
2	$\dfrac{19\pi^5}{\sqrt{2}\cdot 2^{12}}$	$\dfrac{11\pi^4}{3\sqrt{2}\cdot 2^8}$	$\dfrac{5\cdot 61\pi^5}{2^7\cdot 3^6}$	$\dfrac{23\pi^4}{2^4\cdot 3^4\sqrt{3}}$
3	$\dfrac{307\pi^7}{5\sqrt{2}\cdot 2^{17}}$	$\dfrac{19^2\cdot \pi^6}{3\cdot 5\sqrt{2}\cdot 2^{14}}$	$\dfrac{61\cdot 547\pi^7}{2^{10}\cdot 3^9\cdot 5}$	$\dfrac{41^2\pi^6}{2^8\cdot 3^6\cdot 5\sqrt{3}}$
4	—	$\dfrac{24611\pi^8}{2^{19}\cdot 3^2\cdot 5\cdot 7\sqrt{2}}$	—	$\dfrac{11\cdot 13\cdot 1801\pi^8}{2^{11}\cdot 3^9\cdot 5\cdot 7\sqrt{3}}$
Ref.:	AE. 63	AE. 66	AE. 73	AE. 77

Series No.

(331) $\dfrac{(-1)^{n+1}(2\pi)^{2n+1}}{2 \cdot (2n)!}\left\{B_{2n+1}\left(\dfrac{1}{8}\right) - \dfrac{1}{2^{2n+1}}B_{2n+1}\left(\dfrac{1}{4}\right)\right\}$

(332) $\dfrac{(-1)^{n-1}(2\pi)^{2n}}{2(2n-1)!}\left\{A_{2n}\left(\dfrac{1}{8}\right) - \dfrac{1}{2^{2n}}A_{2n}\left(\dfrac{1}{4}\right)\right\}$

(333) $\dfrac{(-1)^{n+1}(2\pi)^{2n+1}}{2 \cdot (2n)!}\left\{B_{2n+1}\left(\dfrac{5}{12}\right) + \dfrac{1}{2^{2n+1}}B_{2n+1}\left(\dfrac{1}{6}\right)\right.$

$$\left. - \dfrac{1}{3^{2n+1}}B_{2n+1}\left(\dfrac{1}{4}\right)\right\}$$

(334) $\dfrac{(-1)^{n-1}(2\pi)^{2n}}{2(2n-1)!}\left\{A_{2n}\left(\dfrac{1}{12}\right) - \dfrac{1}{2^{2n}}A_{2n}\left(\dfrac{1}{6}\right)\right\}$

In the above four series see also No. (1146) for an amplification of the coefficients A_n, B_n, etc.

(335) If $\displaystyle\sum_1^\infty \dfrac{1}{n^s}$

$$\dfrac{1}{1^s} \quad \dfrac{1}{3^s} \quad \dfrac{1}{5^s} + \ldots \infty$$

$$\dfrac{1}{1^s} \quad \dfrac{1}{5^s} \quad \dfrac{1}{7^s} + \ldots \infty$$

Generally

$$1 + \Sigma' n^{-s}$$

The dash sign indicates that only those values of n (greater than p) which are prime to $2 \cdot 3 \cdot 4 \ldots p$ occur in the summation

(336) $1 + \dfrac{1}{2^2} + \dfrac{1}{3^2} + \dfrac{1}{4^2} + \ldots \infty$

(337) $1 - \dfrac{1}{2^2} + \dfrac{1}{3^2} - \dfrac{1}{4^2} + \ldots \infty$

(338) $1 + \dfrac{1}{5^2} + \dfrac{1}{7^2} + \dfrac{1}{11^2} + \ldots \infty$

$$= \frac{1}{\sqrt{2}} p_{2n+1}$$ AE. 59

$$= \frac{1}{\sqrt{2}} q_{2n}$$ AE. 64

$$= \frac{1}{2} r_{2n+1}$$ AE. 73

$$= \frac{\sqrt{3}}{2} t_{2n}$$ AE. 74

$= \zeta(s)$ 2, 3, 5...p—are prime numbers in order

$= \zeta(s)(1 - 2^{-s})$

$= \zeta(s)(1 - 2^{-s})(1 - 3^{-s})$

$= \zeta(s)(1 - 2^{-s})...(1 - p^{-s})$ Q. 272

$$= \frac{\pi^2}{6}$$ E. 154

$$= \frac{\pi^2}{12}$$ E. 158

$$= \frac{\pi^2}{9}$$ 27 P. 281

Series No.

(339) $1 + \dfrac{1}{3^2} + \dfrac{1}{5^2} + \ldots \infty$

(340) $1 + \dfrac{1}{3^3} - \dfrac{1}{5^3} - \dfrac{1}{7^3} + \dfrac{1}{9^3} + \ldots \infty$

(341) $1 - \dfrac{1}{3^3} + \dfrac{1}{5^3} - \dfrac{1}{7^3} + \ldots \infty$

(342) $1 + \dfrac{1}{3^4} + \dfrac{1}{5^4} + \ldots \infty$

(343) $1 + \dfrac{1}{2^4} + \dfrac{1}{3^4} + \dfrac{1}{4^4} + \ldots \infty$

(344) $1 - \dfrac{1}{3^4} - \dfrac{1}{5^4} + \dfrac{1}{7^4} + \dfrac{1}{9^4} - \ldots \infty$

(345) $1 - \dfrac{1}{3^5} + \dfrac{1}{5^5} - \dfrac{1}{7^5} + \ldots \infty$

(346) $\dfrac{1}{5^2} + \dfrac{1}{7^2} + \dfrac{1}{17^2} + \dfrac{1}{19^2} + \dfrac{1}{29^2} + \dfrac{1}{31^2} + \ldots \infty$

(347) $\dfrac{1}{2^2} - \dfrac{2}{3^2} + \dfrac{3}{4^2} - \dfrac{4}{5^2} + \ldots \infty$

(348) $\dfrac{1}{1^2 \cdot 2} + \dfrac{1}{2^2 \cdot 3} + \dfrac{1}{3^2 \cdot 4} + \ldots \infty$

(349) $\dfrac{1}{3^4} + \dfrac{1+2}{5^4} + \dfrac{1+2+3}{7^4} + \dfrac{1+2+3+4}{9^4} + \ldots \infty$

(350) $1^2 - \dfrac{2^2}{5} + \dfrac{3^2}{5^2} - \dfrac{4^2}{5^3} + \ldots \infty$

(351) $\left(\dfrac{1}{2} - \dfrac{1}{3 \cdot 2^3} + \dfrac{1}{5 \cdot 2^5} + \ldots \infty \right)$

$$+ \left(\dfrac{1}{3} - \dfrac{1}{3 \cdot 3^3} + \dfrac{1}{5 \cdot 3^3} - \ldots \infty \right)$$

$$= \frac{\pi^2}{8}$$ E. 155

$$= \frac{3\pi^3\sqrt{2}}{128}$$ A. 364

$$= \frac{\pi^3}{32}$$ Y. 501

$$= \frac{\pi^4}{96}$$ E. 155

$$= \frac{\pi^4}{90}$$ E. 154

$$= \frac{11\pi^4\sqrt{2}}{1536}$$ A. 364

$$= \frac{5\pi^5}{1536}$$ Y. 501

$$= \frac{\pi^2(2 - \sqrt{3})}{36}$$ A. 528

$$= \frac{\pi^2}{12} - \text{logh } 2$$

$$= \frac{\pi^2 - 6}{6}$$

$$= \frac{\pi^2}{64}\left(1 - \frac{\pi^2}{12}\right)$$ E. 158

$$= \frac{25}{54}$$ F. 332

$$= \frac{\pi}{4}$$ H. 462

Series No.

(352) $1 - \dfrac{1}{2^2} + \dfrac{1}{2^4} - \dfrac{1}{2^6} + \ldots \infty$

(353) $1 - \dfrac{1}{3^2} + \dfrac{1}{3^4} - \dfrac{1}{3^6} + \ldots \infty$

(354) $1 - \dfrac{1}{4^2} + \dfrac{1}{4^4} - \dfrac{1}{4^6} + \ldots \infty$

(355) $1 - \dfrac{1}{5^2} + \dfrac{1}{5^3} - \dfrac{1}{5^6} + \ldots \infty$

(356) $\displaystyle\sum_1^n \dfrac{1}{n^2}$

(357) $\displaystyle\sum_1^n \dfrac{1}{n^3}$

(358) $1 + \dfrac{1}{5^2} + \dfrac{1}{9^2} + \ldots n$ terms

(359) $\displaystyle\sum_1^\infty \dfrac{1}{n \cdot 2^n}$

(360) $\dfrac{x}{1^2} + \dfrac{x^2}{2^2} + \dfrac{x^3}{3^2} + \ldots \infty$ can be summed in five cases only:

(a) $x = 1, \quad \displaystyle\sum_1^\infty \dfrac{x^n}{n^2}$

(b) $x = -1, \quad \displaystyle\sum_1^\infty \dfrac{x^n}{n^2}$

$$= \frac{4}{5}$$

T. 144

$$= \frac{9}{10}$$

T. 144

$$= \frac{16}{17}$$

T. 144

$$= \frac{25}{26}$$

T. 144

$$= \frac{\pi^2}{6} - \frac{b_1}{n+1} - \frac{b_2}{(n+1)(n+2)} - \frac{b_3}{(n+1)(n+2)(n+3)} - \cdots$$

$$\text{where } b_k = \frac{(k-1)!}{k}$$

T. 27

$$= K - \frac{C_2}{(n+1)(n+2)} - \frac{C_3}{(n+1)(n+2)(n+3)} - \cdots$$

$$\text{where } K = 1.2020569 = \sum_1^\infty \frac{1}{k^3}, \text{ see (1133),}$$

$$\text{and } C_k = \frac{(k-1)!}{k}\left(\frac{1}{1} + \frac{1}{2} + \frac{1}{3} + \cdots \frac{1}{k-1}\right)$$

T. 27

$$= 1.0787 - \frac{1}{16}\left[\frac{1}{n+\frac{1}{4}} + \frac{1}{2(n+\frac{1}{4})}\right.$$

$$\left. + \frac{1}{6(n+\frac{1}{4})^3} + \frac{1}{30(n+\frac{1}{4})^5} + \cdots\right]$$

AC. 63
(Glaisher 1876)

$$= \log h\, 2$$

$$= \frac{\pi^2}{6}$$

$$= \frac{\pi^2}{12}$$

Series No.

$$\text{(c)} \quad x = \frac{1}{2}, \quad \sum_{1}^{\infty} \frac{x^n}{n^2}$$

$$\text{(d)} \quad x = 2 \sin \frac{\pi}{10}, \quad \sum_{1}^{\infty} \frac{x^n}{n^2}$$

$$\text{(e)} \quad x = \left(2 \sin \frac{\pi}{10}\right)^2, \quad \sum_{1}^{\infty} \frac{x^n}{n^2}$$

$$(361) \quad \sum_{1}^{\infty} \frac{n^r}{n!}$$

$$(362) \quad \sum_{1}^{\infty} \frac{1}{n^2} \cdot \frac{1}{2^n} = \int_{0}^{1} \text{logh} \left(\frac{1}{x}\right) \frac{dx}{2 - x}$$

$$(363) \quad \sum_{1}^{n} \left(1 + \frac{1}{x^n}\right)^2$$

$$(364) \quad \sum_{1}^{\infty} \frac{n}{(4n^2 - 1)^2}$$

$$(365) \quad \sum_{1}^{\infty} \frac{(-1)^n}{n(n + 1)^2} = \int_{0}^{1} \text{logh} \, x \, \text{logh} \, (1 + x) dx$$

$$(366) \quad \sum_{1}^{\infty} (-1)^{n-1} \frac{1}{4n^2 - 1}$$

$$(367) \quad \sum_{1}^{\infty} \frac{1}{(2n + 1)^2 - 1}$$

$$(368) \quad \sum_{1}^{\infty} (-1)^{n-1} \frac{1}{(2n + 1)^2 - 1}$$

$$(369) \quad \sum_{1}^{\infty} \frac{1}{n^2 - 1}$$

$$= \frac{\pi^2}{12} - \frac{1}{2}\left(\text{logh } \frac{1}{2}\right)^2$$

$$= \frac{\pi^2}{10} - \left(\text{logh } 2 \sin \frac{\pi}{10}\right)^2$$

$$= \frac{\pi^2}{15} - \text{logh}\left(2 \sin \frac{\pi}{10}\right)^2 \qquad \text{2Z. 286}$$

$$= \mathcal{S}_r$$
$$\mathcal{S}_1 = \epsilon \quad \mathcal{S}_2 = 2\epsilon \quad \mathcal{S}_3 = 5\epsilon \quad \mathcal{S}_4 = 15\epsilon$$
$$\mathcal{S}_5 = 52\epsilon \quad \mathcal{S}_6 = 203\epsilon \quad \mathcal{S}_7 = 877\epsilon \quad \mathcal{S}_8 = 4140\epsilon \qquad \text{A. 197}$$

$$= \frac{\pi^2}{12} - \frac{1}{2}(\text{logh } 2)^2 \qquad \text{A. 520}$$

$$= n + \frac{2(1 - x^{-n})}{x - 1} + \frac{1 - x^{-2n}}{x^2 - 1}$$

$$= \frac{1}{8} \qquad \text{A. 52}$$

$$= \sum (-1)^{n-1} \int_0^1 \frac{x^n}{n} \text{logh } x \, dx = 2 - 2 \text{logh } 2 - \frac{\pi^2}{12} \qquad \text{A. 496}$$

$$= \frac{\pi}{4} - \frac{1}{2}$$

$$= \frac{1}{4}$$

$$= \frac{1}{2} \text{logh } 2 - \frac{1}{4}$$

$$= \frac{3}{4}$$

Series No.

(370) $\displaystyle\sum_{1}^{\infty} \frac{x^n}{n + a}$

(371) $\displaystyle\sum_{2}^{n} \frac{1}{n^2 - 1}$

(372) $\displaystyle\sum_{1}^{\infty} \frac{x^{n-1}}{(1 - x^n)(1 - x^{n+1})}$

(373) $\displaystyle\sum_{1}^{\infty} \frac{1}{(4n^2 - 1)^r}$

(374) $\displaystyle\sum_{1}^{\infty} \frac{1}{n(4n^2 - 1)}$

(375) $\displaystyle\sum_{1}^{\infty} \frac{1}{n(9n^2 - 1)}$

(376) $\displaystyle\sum_{1}^{\infty} \frac{1}{n(36n^2 - 1)}$

(377) $1 + x^2 - \dfrac{x^3}{3} + \dfrac{5}{6} x^4 - \dfrac{3}{4} x^5 \ldots \infty$

(378) $\displaystyle\sum_{n=1}^{n=\infty} \left[\frac{1}{(3n - 1)^4} + \frac{1}{(3n + 1)^4} \right]$

(379) $\dfrac{1}{n + 1} + \dfrac{1}{2(n + 1)^2} + \dfrac{1}{3(n + 1)^3} + \ldots \infty$

(380) $1 - \dfrac{n^2}{1} + \dfrac{n^2(n^2 - 1^2)}{1^2 \cdot 2^2} - \dfrac{n^2(n^2 - 1^2)(n^2 - 2^2)}{1^2 \cdot 2^2 \cdot 3^2}$

$\ldots$ to $n + 1$ terms

(381) $\dfrac{x}{3} + \dfrac{1 \cdot 4}{3 \cdot 6} 2^3 \cdot x^2 + \dfrac{1 \cdot 4 \cdot 7}{3 \cdot 6 \cdot 9} \cdot 3^3 \cdot x^3 + \ldots \infty$

$$= -x^{-a}\left\{\frac{x}{1} + \frac{x^2}{2} + \ldots \frac{x^a}{a} + \text{logh}\,(1-x)\right\} \quad \text{where } x < 1$$

C. 246

$$= \frac{3}{4} - \frac{1}{2n} - \frac{1}{2(n+1)}$$

$$= \frac{1}{(1-x)^2} \quad \text{where } |x| < 1 \qquad \qquad \text{Q. 59}$$

$$= \frac{1}{x(1-x)^2} \quad \text{where } |x| > 1$$

$$= S_r$$

$$S_1 = \frac{1}{2} \quad S_2 = \frac{\pi^2 - 8}{16} \quad S_3 = \frac{32 - 3\pi^2}{64}$$

$$S_4 = \frac{\pi^4 + 30\pi^2 - 384}{768} \qquad \text{T. 141}$$

$$= 2\,\text{logh}\,2 - 1 \qquad \qquad \text{T. 142}$$

$$= \frac{3}{2}\,(\text{logh}\,3 - 1) \qquad \qquad \text{T. 142}$$

$$= -3 + \frac{3}{2}\,\text{logh}\,3 + 2\,\text{logh}\,2 \qquad \text{T. 142}$$

$$= (1 + x)^x \qquad \qquad \text{Y. 107}$$

$$= \frac{8\pi^4}{729} - 1 \qquad \qquad \text{E. 190}$$

$$= \frac{1}{n} - \frac{1}{2n^2} + \frac{1}{3n^3} - \ldots \infty \qquad \text{F. 197}$$

$$= 0 \qquad \qquad \text{F. 338}$$

$$= \frac{1}{27} \cdot \frac{x}{(1-x)^{10/3}}\,(x^2 + 18x + 9)$$

Series No.

(382) $\displaystyle\sum_{n=1}^{n=\infty} \frac{1}{\{(2n)^2 - (2m-1)^2\}^2}$

(383) $\displaystyle\sum_{n=1}^{n=\infty} \frac{1}{\{(2n-1)^2 - (2m)^2\}^2}$

(384) $\displaystyle\operatorname*{Lt}_{n=\infty} \frac{\left(\frac{1}{2n}\right)^p + \left(\frac{2}{2n}\right)^p + \left(\frac{3}{2n}\right)^p + \ldots\ 2n\ \text{terms}}{\left(\frac{1}{2} + \frac{1}{2n}\right)^p + \left(\frac{1}{2} + \frac{2}{2n}\right)^p + \ldots\ n\ \text{terms}}$

(385) $\displaystyle\sum_{1}^{\infty} \left\{\frac{1 \cdot 3 \cdot 5 \ldots 2n - 1}{2 \cdot 4 \cdot 6 \ldots 2n}\right\}^2 \frac{1}{2n + r}$

$$S_0 = 2\ \text{logh}\ 2 - \frac{4}{\pi}\ \omega_2$$

$$S_1 = \frac{4}{\pi}\ \omega_2 - 1$$

$$S_2 = \frac{2}{\pi} - \frac{1}{2}$$

$$S_3 = \frac{1}{2\pi}(2\omega_2 + 1) - \frac{1}{3}$$

$$S_4 = \frac{10}{9\pi} - \frac{1}{4}$$

$$S_5 = \frac{1}{32\pi}(18\omega_2 + 13) - \frac{1}{5}$$

$$S_6 = \frac{178}{225\pi} - \frac{1}{6}$$

$$S_7 = \frac{1}{128\pi}(50\omega_2 + 43) - \frac{1}{7}$$

$$\omega_2 = \sum_{0}^{\infty} (-1)^{k-1} \frac{1}{(2k+1)^2}$$

$$= 1 - \frac{1}{3^2} + \frac{1}{5^2} - \frac{1}{7^2} + \ldots \infty$$

$$= 0.9159656$$

When r is a negative integer the value of $n = r/2$ is to be excluded in the summation.

$$= \frac{\pi^2}{16(2m-1)^2} - \frac{1}{2(2m-1)^4} \qquad \text{C. 373}$$

$$= \frac{\pi^2}{64m^2} \qquad \text{C. 373}$$

$$= \frac{1}{1 - \left(\frac{1}{2}\right)^{p+1}} \qquad \text{J. 74}$$

$$= \mathcal{S}_r \qquad \text{T. 142}$$

$$\mathcal{S}_{-1} = 1 - \frac{2}{\pi}$$

$$\mathcal{S}_{-2} = \frac{1}{2}\, \text{logh}\, 2 + \frac{1}{4} - \frac{1}{2\pi}\,(2\omega_2 + 1)$$

$$\mathcal{S}_{-3} = \frac{1}{3} - \frac{10}{9\pi}$$

$$\mathcal{S}_{-4} = \frac{9}{32}\, \text{logh}\, 2 + \frac{11}{128} - \frac{1}{32\pi}\,(18\omega_2 + 13)$$

$$\mathcal{S}_{-5} = \frac{1}{5} - \frac{178}{225\pi}$$

$$\mathcal{S}_{-6} = \frac{25}{128}\, \text{logh}\, 2 + \frac{71}{1536} - \frac{1}{128\pi}\,(50\omega_2 + 43)$$

Series No.

(386) $A_n = \dfrac{1 \cdot 3 \cdot 5 \ldots 2n - 1}{2 \cdot 4 \cdot 6 \ldots 2n}$

(387) $\displaystyle\sum_1^\infty A_n \frac{1}{4n^2 - 1}$

(388) $\displaystyle\sum_1^\infty A_n \frac{1}{2n + 1}$

(389) $\displaystyle\sum_1^\infty (-1)^n A_n \frac{1}{2n + 1}$

(390) $\displaystyle\sum_1^\infty A_n{}^2 \frac{4n + 1}{(2n - 1)(2n + 2)}$

(391) $\displaystyle\sum_1^\infty (-1)^{n+1} A_n{}^3 \frac{4n + 1}{(2n - 1)(2n + 2)}$

(392) $\displaystyle\sum_1^\infty (-1)^n A_n{}^3 (4n + 1)$

(393) $\displaystyle\sum_1^\infty A_n{}^4 \frac{4n + 1}{(2n - 1)(2n + 2)}$

(394) $\displaystyle\sum_{n=1}^\infty \frac{1}{m^2 - n^2}$

(395) $\displaystyle\sum_1^\infty \frac{(-1)^{n-1}}{m^2 - n^2}$

(396) $\displaystyle\sum_2^\infty \frac{n - 1}{n!}$

(397) $\displaystyle\sum_1^\infty \frac{1}{4n^2 - 1}$

(398) $\displaystyle\sum_1^\infty \frac{12n^2 - 1}{n(4n^2 - 1)^2}$

$$= \frac{(2n-1)!}{2^{2n-1}n!(n-1)!}$$ T. 143

$$= 1 - \frac{\pi}{4}$$

$$= \frac{\pi}{2} - 1$$

$$= \text{logh}\,(1 + \sqrt{2}) - 1$$

$$= \frac{1}{2}$$

$$= \frac{2}{\pi} - \frac{1}{2}$$

$$= \frac{2}{\pi} - 1$$

$$= \frac{1}{2} - \frac{4}{\pi^2}$$

$$= -\frac{3}{4m^2} \quad \text{where } m \text{ is an integer and } n = m \text{ omitted}$$ A. 67

$$= \frac{3}{4m^2} \quad \text{where } n \text{ is even and } n = m \text{ omitted}$$ A. 67

$$= 1$$ T. 143

$$= \frac{1}{2}$$ T. 141

$$= 2\,\text{logh}\,2$$ T. 143

Series No.

(399) $1 - \dfrac{1}{2^2} + \dfrac{1}{2^4} - \dfrac{1}{2^6} - \ldots \infty$

(400) $\displaystyle\sum_{2}^{\infty} \dfrac{1}{(n^2-1)^2} = \left[\dfrac{1}{(1\cdot 3)^2} + \dfrac{1}{(2\cdot 4)^2} + \dfrac{1}{(3\cdot 5)^2} + \ldots \infty \right]$

(401) $\displaystyle\sum_{2}^{\infty} \dfrac{(-1)^n}{(n^2-1)^2}$

(402)† $x + aB_2(x) + \dfrac{a^2}{2!} B_3(x) + \dfrac{a^3}{3!} B_4(x) + \ldots \infty$

(403)† $1 + a\left(x - \dfrac{1}{2}\right) + a^2 A_2(x) + \dfrac{a^3}{2!} A_3(x) + \ldots \infty$

(404) $\dfrac{1}{n+1} + \dfrac{1}{2} + \dfrac{n}{2!} B_1{}^* - \dfrac{n(n-1)(n-2)}{4!} B_3{}^* + \ldots \infty$

This series may be used to evaluate $B_n{}^*$ by putting $n = 2, 4, 6$, etc.

(405) $\dfrac{1}{2}\left(\dfrac{2x}{1+x^2}\right) + \dfrac{1}{2\cdot 4}\left(\dfrac{2x}{1+x^2}\right)^3 + \dfrac{1\cdot 3}{2\cdot 4\cdot 6}\left(\dfrac{2x}{1+x^2}\right)^5 + \ldots \infty$

(406) $\displaystyle\sum_{1}^{\infty} \mathcal{S}_n \dfrac{x^n}{n!}$

(407) $\displaystyle\sum_{1}^{\infty} (-1)^{n-1} \mathcal{S}_n \dfrac{2^n}{n!}$

(408) $1 + nx + \dfrac{n^2 x^2}{2!} + \dfrac{n(n^2-1^2)}{3!} x^3 + \dfrac{n^2(n^2-2^2)}{4!} x^4$

$\qquad\qquad + \dfrac{n(n^2-1^2)(n^2-3^2)}{5!} x^5 + \ldots \infty$

(409) $1 + \dfrac{1}{2^2}\left(\dfrac{1}{2}\right)^2 + \dfrac{1}{3^2}\left(\dfrac{1\cdot 3}{2\cdot 4}\right)^2 + \ldots \infty$

(410) $1 + \dfrac{1}{3}\cdot 1^2 + \dfrac{1}{5}\left(\dfrac{2}{3}\right)^2 + \dfrac{1}{7}\left(\dfrac{2\cdot 4}{3\cdot 5}\right)^2 + \ldots \infty$

† For values of $A_n(x)$ and $B_n(x)$, see No. (1146).

$$= \frac{4}{5}$$

$$= \frac{\pi^2}{12} - \frac{11}{16}$$

$$= \frac{\pi^2}{24} - \frac{5}{16}$$

$$= \frac{\epsilon^{ax} - 1}{\epsilon^a - 1} \quad \text{where } x \text{ is a positive integer} \qquad \text{AE. 6}$$

$$= \frac{a\epsilon^{ax}}{\epsilon^a - 1} \qquad\qquad \text{AE. 20}$$

$$= 1 \qquad\qquad \text{Y. 109}$$

$$= x \quad \text{where } 1 > x > -1 \qquad\qquad \text{Y. 459}$$

$$= \frac{1}{x} \quad \text{where } x > 1$$

$$= \frac{1}{4} x\epsilon^x(x^3 + 8x^2 + 14x + 4) \quad \text{where } \mathcal{S}_n = 1^3 + 2^3 + 3^3 + \ldots n^3$$

A. 197

$$= 0 \quad \text{where } \mathcal{S}_n = 1^3 + 2^3 + 3^3 + \ldots n^3 \qquad \text{A. 197}$$

$$= (x + \sqrt{1 + x^2})^n \qquad\qquad \text{Y. 107}$$

$$= \frac{11}{\pi} - 4 \qquad\qquad \text{1Z. 360}$$

$$= \frac{\pi}{2} \qquad\qquad \text{1Z. 360}$$

Series No.

(411) $\dfrac{1}{3^2} \cdot 1^2 + \dfrac{1}{5^2} \left(\dfrac{2}{3}\right)^2 + \dfrac{1}{7^2} \left(\dfrac{2 \cdot 4}{3 \cdot 5}\right)^2 + \ldots \infty$

(412) $\dfrac{x(a + x)}{a} - \dfrac{x^2(a + x)^2}{a^3} + \dfrac{4}{1 \cdot 2} \dfrac{x^3(a + x)^3}{a^5} + \ldots$

$$+ (-1)^{n-1} \dfrac{(2n - 2)!}{n!(n - 1)!} \dfrac{x^n(a + x)^n}{a^{2n-1}} + \ldots \infty$$

(413) $1 - ax(1 - x) + \dfrac{a(a - 3)}{2!} x^2(1 - x)^2$

$$- \dfrac{a(a - 4)(a - 5)}{3!} x^3(1 - x)^3 + \ldots$$

(414) $\displaystyle\operatorname*{Lim}_{x \to 1} \sum_{1}^{\infty} (-1)^{n-1} \dfrac{x^n}{n(1 + x^n)}$

(415) $\displaystyle\operatorname*{Lim}_{x \to 1} \sum_{1}^{\infty} \dfrac{x^n}{1 - x^n}$

(416) $\displaystyle\operatorname*{Lim}_{x \to 1} \left(\dfrac{x}{1 - x} - \dfrac{x^3}{1 - x^3} + \dfrac{x^5}{1 - x^5} + \ldots \infty\right)$

XIV. Trigonometrical Summations

(417) $\sin \theta + \sin 2\theta + \sin 3\theta +$ to n terms

(418) $\cos \theta + \cos 2\theta + \cos 3\theta +$ to n terms

(419) $\sin \theta + \sin 3\theta + \sin 5\theta + \ldots + \sin (2n - 1)\theta$

(420) $\cos \theta + \cos 3\theta + \cos 5\theta + \ldots + \cos (2n - 1)\theta$

(421) $\cos \theta + \sin 3\theta + \cos 5\theta + \ldots + \sin (4n - 1)\theta$

$$= \pi - 3 \qquad\qquad\qquad \text{1Z. 360}$$

$$= x \qquad\qquad\qquad \text{A. 199}$$

$$= (1 - x)^a \quad \text{where} \quad |x(1 - x)| < \frac{1}{4} \qquad\qquad \text{A. 199}$$

$$= \frac{1}{2} \operatorname{logh} 2 \qquad\qquad\qquad \text{A. 201}$$

$$\approx \frac{1}{1 - x} \operatorname{logh} \frac{1}{1 - x} \qquad\qquad\qquad \text{A. 201}$$

$$\approx \frac{\pi}{4} \cdot \frac{1}{1 - x} \qquad\qquad\qquad \text{A. 201}$$

$$= \sin \frac{1}{2} (n + 1)\theta \, \sin \frac{n\theta}{2} \, \operatorname{cosec} \frac{\theta}{2} \qquad\qquad \text{E. 283}$$

$$= \cos \frac{1}{2} (n + 1)\theta \, \sin \frac{n\theta}{2} \, \operatorname{cosec} \frac{\theta}{2} \qquad\qquad \text{E. 283}$$

$$= \sin^2 n\theta \cdot \operatorname{cosec} \theta \qquad\qquad\qquad \text{E. 283}$$

$$= \frac{1}{2} \sin 2n\theta \cdot \operatorname{cosec} \theta \qquad\qquad\qquad \text{E. 287}$$

$$= \sin 2n\theta \, \{\cos 2n\theta + \sin 2n\theta\} \times \{\cos \theta + \sin \theta\} \operatorname{cosec} 2\theta \qquad \text{E. 288}$$

(422) $\operatorname{cosec} \theta + \operatorname{cosec} 2\theta + \operatorname{cosec} 4\theta + \ldots n$ terms

(423) $\cos \dfrac{\theta}{2} + \cos 2\theta + \cos \dfrac{7\theta}{2} + \ldots n$ terms

(424) $\cos \dfrac{\pi}{2n + 1} + \cos \dfrac{3\pi}{2n + 1} + \ldots n$ terms

(425) $1 - 2 \cos \theta + 3 \cos 2\theta - 4 \cos 3\theta + \ldots n$ terms

(426) $3 \sin \theta + 5 \sin 2\theta + 7 \sin 3\theta + \ldots n$ terms

(427) $\displaystyle\sum_{1}^{n-1} k \sin k\theta$

(428) $\displaystyle\sum_{1}^{n-1} k \cos k\theta$

(429) $\displaystyle\sum_{1}^{n} (-1)^k \cos k\theta$

(430) $\displaystyle\sum_{1}^{n} \sin (2k - 1)\theta$

(431) $\displaystyle\sum_{1}^{n+1} (-1)^{k-1} \sin (2k - 1)\theta$

(432) $\tan \theta + \tan \left(\theta + \dfrac{\pi}{n}\right) + \tan \left(\theta + \dfrac{2\pi}{n}\right) + \ldots n$ terms

$$= \cot \frac{\theta}{2} - \cot 2^{n-1}\theta \qquad\qquad \text{E. 125}$$

$$= \cos \frac{1}{4}(3n - 1)\theta \sin \frac{3n\theta}{4} \operatorname{cosec} \frac{3\theta}{4} \qquad\qquad \text{E. 287}$$

$$= \frac{1}{2} \qquad\qquad \text{E. 288}$$

$$= \frac{\cos \theta + (-1)^{n-1}\{(n + 1)\cos (n - 1)\theta + n \cos n\theta\}}{2(1 + \cos \theta)} \qquad\qquad \text{E. 117}$$

$$= \frac{\sin \theta + (2n + 3)\sin n\theta - (2n + 1)\sin (n + 1)\theta}{2(1 - \cos \theta)} \qquad\qquad \text{E. 117}$$

$$= \frac{\sin n\theta}{4 \sin^2 \frac{\theta}{2}} - \frac{n \cos \left(\frac{2n - 1}{2}\right)\theta}{2 \sin \frac{\theta}{2}} \qquad\qquad \text{T. 82}$$

$$= \frac{n \sin \left(\frac{2n - 1}{2}\right)\theta}{2 \sin \frac{\theta}{2}} - \frac{1 - \cos n\theta}{4 \sin^2 \frac{\theta}{2}} \qquad\qquad \text{T. 82}$$

$$= -\frac{1}{2} + (-1)^n \frac{\cos \left(\frac{2n + 1}{2}\right)\theta}{2 \cos \frac{\theta}{2}} \qquad\qquad \text{T. 82}$$

$$= \frac{\sin^2 n\theta}{\sin \theta} \qquad\qquad \text{T. 82}$$

$$= (-1)^n \frac{\sin (2n + 2)\theta}{2 \cos \theta} \qquad\qquad \text{T. 82}$$

$$= -n \cot \left(\frac{n\pi}{2} + n\theta\right) \qquad\qquad \text{E. 73}$$

Series No.

(433) $\cot \theta + \cot \left(\theta + \dfrac{\pi}{n} \right) + \cot \left(\theta + \dfrac{2\pi}{n} \right) + \ldots n$ terms

(434) $\displaystyle\sum_{0}^{n-1} \cos \dfrac{2\pi k^2}{n}$

(435) $\displaystyle\sum_{1}^{n-1} \sin \dfrac{2\pi k^2}{n}$

(436) $\displaystyle\sum_{1}^{n-1} \sin \dfrac{\pi k}{n}$

(437) $\displaystyle\sum_{1}^{n} \sin^2 k\theta$

(438) $\displaystyle\sum_{0}^{n} \cos^2 k\theta$

(439) $\dfrac{1}{\sin^2 \theta} + \dfrac{1}{\sin^2 2\theta} + \ldots + \dfrac{1}{\sin^2 \dfrac{n-1}{2}\theta}$

(440) $\dfrac{1}{\sin^2 \theta} + \dfrac{1}{\sin^2 2\theta} + \ldots + \dfrac{1}{\sin^2 \dfrac{n-2}{2}\theta}$

(441) $\dfrac{1}{\sin^2 \theta} + \dfrac{1}{\sin^2 3\theta} + \ldots + \dfrac{1}{\sin^2 (n-2)\theta}$

(442) $\dfrac{1}{\sin^2 \theta} + \dfrac{1}{\sin^2 3\theta} + \ldots + \dfrac{1}{\sin^2 (n-1)\theta}$

(443) $\displaystyle\sum_{1}^{n-1} \operatorname{cosec}^2 \left(\dfrac{r\pi}{n} \right)$

(444) $\operatorname{cosec}^2 \theta + \operatorname{cosec}^2 \left(\theta + \dfrac{2\pi}{n} \right) + \ldots n$ terms

(445) $\tan^2 \theta + \tan^2 \left(\theta + \dfrac{\pi}{n} \right) + \ldots n$ terms

$$= n \cot n\theta \qquad\qquad \text{E. 73}$$

$$= \frac{\sqrt{n}}{2}\left(1 + \cos\frac{n\pi}{2} + \sin\frac{n\pi}{2}\right) \qquad\qquad \text{T. 83}$$

$$= \frac{\sqrt{n}}{2}\left(1 + \cos\frac{n\pi}{2} - \sin\frac{n\pi}{2}\right) \qquad\qquad \text{T. 83}$$

$$= \cot\frac{\pi}{2n} \qquad\qquad \text{T. 83}$$

$$= \frac{n}{2} - \frac{\cos(n+1)\theta\,\sin n\theta}{2\sin\theta} \qquad\qquad \text{T. 82}$$

$$= \frac{n+2}{2} + \frac{\cos(n+1)\theta\,\sin n\theta}{2\sin\theta} \qquad\qquad \text{T. 82}$$

$$= \frac{n^2 - 1}{6} \quad \text{where } n \text{ is odd} \qquad\qquad \text{A. 210}$$

$$= \frac{n^2 - 4}{6} \quad \text{where } n \text{ is even} \qquad\qquad \text{A. 210}$$

$$= \frac{n^2 - 1}{2} \quad \text{where } n \text{ is odd} \qquad\qquad \text{A. 211}$$

$$= \frac{n^2}{2} \quad \text{where } n \text{ is even} \qquad\qquad \text{A. 211}$$

$$= \frac{1}{3}(n^2 - 1) \quad \text{where } n \text{ is odd} \qquad\qquad \text{A. 223}$$

$$= n^2 \operatorname{cosec}^2 n\theta \quad \text{where } n \text{ is odd}$$
$$= \frac{1}{2}n^2 \operatorname{cosec}^2 \frac{n\theta}{2} \quad \text{where } n \text{ is even} \qquad\qquad \text{E. 73}$$

$$= n^2 \cot^2\left(\frac{n\pi}{2} + n\theta\right) + n(n-1) \qquad\qquad \text{E. 73}$$

(446) $\sin^3 \theta + \sin^3 2\theta + \sin^3 3\theta + \ldots n$ terms

(447) $\cos^3 \theta + \cos^3 2\theta + \cos^3 3\theta + \ldots n$ terms

(448) $\sin^4 \theta + \sin^4 2\theta + \sin^4 3\theta + \ldots n$ terms

(449) $\cos^4 \theta + \cos^4 2\theta + \cos^4 3\theta + \ldots n$ terms

(450) $\displaystyle\sum_{1}^{\frac{n-1}{2}} \tan^4 \left(\frac{r\pi}{n}\right)$

(451) $\cot^2 \dfrac{2\pi}{2n} + \cot^2 \dfrac{4\pi}{2n} + \ldots + \cot^2 \dfrac{(n-1)\pi}{2n}$

(452) $\cot^4 \dfrac{2\pi}{2n} + \cot^4 \dfrac{4\pi}{2n} + \ldots + \cot^4 \dfrac{(n-1)\pi}{2n}$

(453) $1 + a \cos \theta + a^2 \cos 2\theta + \ldots + a^{n-1} \cos (n-1)\theta$

(454) $\displaystyle\sum_{0}^{n-1} a^k \cos k\theta$

Nos. (453) and (454) are equal.

(455) $\displaystyle\sum_{1}^{n-1} a^k \sin k\theta$

$$= \frac{3}{4} \sin \frac{1}{2}(n + 1)\theta \sin \frac{n\theta}{2} \operatorname{cosec} \frac{\theta}{2} - \frac{1}{4} \sin \frac{3}{2}(n + 1)\theta \sin \frac{3n\theta}{2} \operatorname{cosec} \frac{3\theta}{2}$$

E. 288

$$= \frac{3}{4} \cos \frac{1}{2}(n + 1)\theta \sin \frac{n\theta}{2} \operatorname{cosec} \frac{\theta}{2}$$

$$+ \frac{1}{4} \cos \frac{3}{2}(n + 1)\theta \sin \frac{3n\theta}{2} \operatorname{cosec} \frac{3\theta}{2}$$

E. 285

$$= \frac{1}{8} [3n - 4 \cos (n + 1)\theta \sin n\theta \operatorname{cosec} \theta$$

$$+ \cos 2(n + 1)\theta \sin 2n\theta \operatorname{cosec} 2\theta]$$

E. 288

$$= \frac{1}{8} [3n + 4 \cos (n + 1)\theta \sin n\theta \operatorname{cosec} \theta$$

$$+ \cos 2(n + 1)\theta \sin 2n\theta \operatorname{cosec} 2\theta]$$

E. 288

$$= \frac{1}{6} n(n - 1)(n^2 + n - 3) \quad \text{where } n \text{ is odd}$$

A. 223

$$= \frac{1}{6} (n - 1)(n - 2) \quad \text{where } n \text{ is odd}$$

O. 349

$$= \frac{1}{90} (n - 1)(n - 2)(n^2 + 3n - 13) \quad \text{where } n \text{ is odd}$$

O. 349

$$= \frac{1 - a \cos \theta + a^{n+1} \cos (n - 1)\theta - a^n \cos n\theta}{1 - 2a \cos \theta + a^2}$$

$$= \frac{(1 - a \cos \theta)(1 - a^n \cos n\theta) + a^{n+1} \sin \theta \sin n\theta}{1 - 2 a \cos \theta + a^2}$$

T. 82

$$= \frac{a \sin \theta(1 - a^n \cos n\theta) - (1 - a \cos \theta)a^n \sin n\theta}{1 - 2a \cos \theta + a^2}$$

T. 82

Series No.

(456) $a \sin \theta + 2a^2 \sin 2\theta + 3a^3 \sin 3\theta + \dots n$ terms

(457) $\cos^3 \theta - \dfrac{1}{3} \cos^3 3\theta + \dfrac{1}{3^2} \cos^3 3^2\theta + \dfrac{1}{3^3} \cos^3 3^3\theta + \dots$ to

$$n \text{ terms}$$

(458) $\cos \dfrac{\pi}{n} + \cos \dfrac{2\pi}{n} + \dots + \cos \dfrac{(2n-1)\pi}{n}$

(459) $\displaystyle\sum_{0}^{n} \dfrac{1}{2^n} \tan \dfrac{\theta}{2^n}$

(460) $\displaystyle\sum_{1}^{n} \left(\dfrac{1}{2^n} \sec \dfrac{\theta}{2^n} \right)^2$

(461) $\displaystyle\sum_{1}^{n} \left(2^n \sin^2 \dfrac{\theta}{2^n} \right)^2$

(462) $\displaystyle\sum_{0}^{n} \left(\dfrac{1}{2^{2n}} \tan^2 \dfrac{\theta}{2^n} \right)$

(463) $\displaystyle\sum_{1}^{\frac{n-1}{2}} \dfrac{1}{n^2 \sin^2 \left(\dfrac{r\pi}{n} \right)}$

(464) $\displaystyle\sum_{1}^{n-1} \dfrac{1}{n^2 \sin^2 \left(\dfrac{r\pi}{2n} \right)}$

(465) $\sin \theta + \sin (\theta + \beta) + \sin (\theta + 2\beta) + \dots n$ terms

(466) $\cos \theta + \cos (\theta + \beta) + \cos (\theta + 2\beta) + \dots n$ terms

(467) $\sin \theta - \sin (\theta + \beta) + \sin (\theta + 2\beta) - \dots n$ terms

(468) $\cos \theta - \cos (\theta + \beta) + \cos (\theta + 2\beta) - \dots 2n$ terms

$$= [a \sin \theta - a^3 \sin \theta - (n + 1)a^{n+1} \sin (n + 1)\theta$$
$$+ 2(n + 1)a^{n+2} \sin n\theta - (n + 1)a^{n+3} \sin (n - 1)\theta$$
$$+ na^{n+2} \sin (n + 2)\theta - 2na^{n+3} \sin (n + 1)\theta$$
$$+ na^{n+4} \sin n\theta]/(1 - 2a \cos \theta + a^2)^2 \qquad \text{D. 502}$$

$$= \frac{1}{4}\left\{ 3 \cos \theta + \left(-\frac{1}{3} \right)^{n-1} \cos 3^n\theta \right\} \qquad \text{E. 126}$$

$$= -1$$

$$= \frac{1}{2^n} \cot \frac{\theta}{2^n} - 2 \cot 2\theta \qquad \text{T. 83}$$

$$= \operatorname{cosec}^2 \theta - \left(\frac{1}{2^n} \operatorname{cosec} \frac{\theta}{2^n} \right)^2 \qquad \text{T. 82}$$

$$= \left(2^n \sin \frac{\theta}{2^n} \right)^2 - \sin^2 \theta \qquad \text{T. 82}$$

$$= \frac{2^{2n+2} - 1}{3 \cdot 2^{2n-1}} + 4 \cot^2 2\theta - \frac{1}{2^{2n}} \cot \frac{\theta}{2^n} \qquad \text{T. 83}$$

$$= \frac{n^2 - 1}{6n^2} \quad \text{where } n \text{ is odd} \qquad \text{A. 218}$$

$$= \frac{1}{2} \quad \text{where } r \text{ is odd and } n \text{ is even} \qquad \text{A. 218}$$

$$= \sin \left\{ \theta + \frac{1}{2} (n - 1)\beta \right\} \sin \frac{n\beta}{2} \operatorname{cosec} \frac{\beta}{2} \qquad \text{E. 282}$$

$$= \cos \left\{ \theta + \frac{1}{2} (n - 1)\beta \right\} \sin \frac{n\beta}{2} \operatorname{cosec} \frac{\beta}{2} \qquad \text{E. 283}$$

$$= \sin \left\{ \theta + \frac{n - 1}{2} (\beta + \pi) \right\} \sin \frac{n(\beta + \pi)}{2} \sec \frac{\beta}{2} \qquad \text{E. 285}$$

$$= \sin \left\{ \theta + \left(n - \frac{1}{2} \right)\beta \right\} \sin n\beta \sec \frac{\beta}{2} \qquad \text{E. 288}$$

Series No.

(469) $\sin \theta \cdot \sin 2\theta + \sin 2\theta \cdot \sin 3\theta + \ldots n$ terms

(470) $\cos \theta \cdot \sin 2\theta + \sin 2\theta \cdot \cos 3\theta + \ldots 2n$ terms

(471) $\sin \theta \cdot \sin 3\theta + \sin 2\theta \cdot \sin 4\theta + \ldots n$ terms

(472) $\cos \theta \sin \beta + \cos 3\theta \sin 2\beta + \cos 5\theta \sin 3\beta + \ldots n$ terms

(473) $\displaystyle\sum_{1}^{n} r \sin (\phi + r\theta)$

(474) $-6 \sin (a + b) - 5 \sin (2a + b) - \ldots$
$$+ (n - 7) \sin (na + b)$$

(475)† $\sin \theta + a \sin (\theta + \beta) + a^2 \sin (\theta + 2\beta) + \ldots n$ terms

(476) $\tan \theta \tan (\theta + \beta) + \tan (\theta + \beta) \tan (\theta + 2\beta) + \ldots n$ terms

(477) $\operatorname{cosec} \theta \operatorname{cosec} 2\theta + \operatorname{cosec} 2\theta \operatorname{cosec} 3\theta + \ldots n$ terms

(478) $\sec \theta \sec 2\theta + \sec 2\theta \sec 3\theta + \ldots n$ terms

(479) $\displaystyle\sum_{0}^{n} \sin (\theta + k\beta)$

† Sum to infinity $= \dfrac{\sin \theta - a \sin (\theta - \beta)}{1 - 2a \cos \beta + a^2}$ where $a < 1$.

$$= \frac{1}{4} \{(n + 1) \sin 2\theta - \sin 2(n + 1)\theta\} \operatorname{cosec} \theta \qquad \text{E. 288}$$

$$= \frac{1}{2} \sin 2(n + 1)\theta \cdot \sin 2n\theta \operatorname{cosec} \theta \qquad \text{E. 288}$$

$$= \frac{n}{2} \cos 2\theta - \frac{1}{2} \cos (n + 3)\theta \cdot \sin n\theta \cdot \operatorname{cosec} \theta \qquad \text{E. 288}$$

$$= \frac{1}{2} \sin \left\{ n\theta + \frac{1}{2} (n + 1)\beta \right\} \sin \frac{n}{2} (2\theta + \beta) \operatorname{cosec} \frac{1}{2} (2\theta + \beta)$$

$$- \frac{1}{2} \sin \left\{ n\theta - \frac{1}{2} (n + 1)\beta \right\} \sin \frac{n}{2} (2\theta - \beta) \operatorname{cosec} \frac{1}{2} (2\theta - \beta)$$
$$\text{E. 286}$$

$$= \frac{(n + 1) \sin (\phi + n\theta) - \sin \phi - n \sin (\phi + \overline{n + 1}\theta)}{2(1 - \cos \theta)}$$

$$= (n - 7) \sin (na + b) + (n - 8) \frac{\sin \left(na + b - \dfrac{a + \pi}{2} \right)}{2 \sin a/2}$$

$$- \frac{\sin \{na + b - (a + \pi)\}}{2(\sin a/2)^2} - \frac{7 \sin (a + b) - 6 \sin b}{(2 \sin a/2)^2}$$

$$= \frac{\sin \theta - a \sin (\theta - \beta) - a^n \sin (\theta + n\beta) + a^{n+1} \sin \{\theta + (n - 1)\beta\}}{1 - 2a \cos \beta + a^2}$$
$$\text{E. 117}$$

$$= \frac{\tan (\theta + n\beta) - \tan \theta - n \tan \beta}{\tan \beta} \qquad \text{E. 124}$$

$$= \operatorname{cosec} \theta \{\cot \theta - \cot (n + 1)\theta\} \qquad \text{E. 125}$$

$$= \operatorname{cosec} \theta \{\tan (n + 1) \theta - \tan \theta\} \qquad \text{E. 125}$$

$$= \sin \left(\theta + \frac{n\beta}{2} \right) \sin \left(\frac{n + 1}{2} \right) \beta \operatorname{cosec} \frac{\beta}{2} \qquad \text{T. 82}$$

(480) $\displaystyle\sum_0^n \cos(\theta + k\beta)$

(481) $1 - \dfrac{n^2 - 1^2}{2!} \sin^2\theta + \dfrac{(n^2 - 1^2)(n^2 - 3^2)}{4!} \sin^4\theta + \ldots$

$$+ (-1)^{(n-1)/2} 2^{n-1} \sin^{n-1}\theta$$

(482) $n \sin\theta - \dfrac{n(n^2 - 1^2)}{3!} \sin^3\theta + \dfrac{n(n^2 - 1^2)(n^2 - 3^2)}{5!} \sin^5\theta + \ldots$

$$+ (-1)^{(n-1)/2} 2^{n-1} \sin^n\theta$$

(482a) $1 - \dfrac{n^2 - 1^2}{2!} \cos^2\theta + \dfrac{(n^2 - 1^2)(n^2 - 3^2)}{4!} \cos^4\theta$

$$- \dfrac{(n^2 - 1^2)(n^2 - 3^2)(n^2 - 5^2)}{6!} \cos^6\theta + \ldots$$

$$+ (-1)^{(n-1)/2} (2\cos\theta)^{n-1}$$

(482b) $n \cos\theta - \dfrac{n(n^2 - 2^2)}{3!} \cos^3\theta$

$$+ \dfrac{n(n^2 - 2^2)(n^2 - 4^2)}{5!} \cos^5\theta - \ldots$$

$$+ (-1)^{n/2+1} (2\cos\theta)^{n-1}$$

(482c) $n \cos\theta - \dfrac{n(n^2 - 1^2)}{3!} \cos^3\theta$

$$+ \dfrac{n(n^2 - 1^2)(n^2 - 3^2)}{5!} \cos^5\theta - \ldots$$

$$+ (-1)^{(n-1)/2} 2^{n-1} \cos^n\theta$$

(482d) $1 - \dfrac{n^2}{2!} \cos^2\theta + \dfrac{n^2(n^2 - 2^2)}{4!} \cos^4\theta$

$$- \dfrac{n^2(n^2 - 2^2)(n^2 - 4^2)}{6!} \cos^6\theta + \ldots + (-1)^{n/2} 2^{n-1} \cos^n\theta$$

$$= \cos\left(\theta + \frac{n\beta}{2}\right) \sin\left(\frac{n+1}{2}\right) \beta \operatorname{cosec} \frac{\beta}{2}$$

T. 82

$$= \frac{\cos n\theta}{\cos n} \quad \text{where } n \text{ is odd}$$

A. 204

$$= \sin n\theta \quad \text{where } n \text{ is odd}$$

A. 205

$$= (-1)^{(n-1)/2} \frac{\sin n\theta}{\sin \theta} \quad \text{where } n \text{ is odd}$$

$\begin{cases} \text{E. 64} \\ \text{A. 204} \end{cases}$

$$= (-1)^{n/2+1} \frac{\sin n\theta}{\sin \theta} \quad \text{where } n \text{ is even}$$

$\begin{cases} \text{E. 65} \\ \text{A. 204} \end{cases}$

$$= (-1)^{(n-1)/2} \cos n\theta \quad \text{where } n \text{ is odd}$$

$\begin{cases} \text{E. 67} \\ \text{A. 204} \end{cases}$

$$= (-1)^{n/2} \cos n\theta \quad \text{where } n \text{ is even}$$

$\begin{cases} \text{E. 68} \\ \text{A. 204} \end{cases}$

Series No.

(483) $n \sin \theta - \dfrac{n(n^2 - 2^2)}{3!} \sin^3 \theta$

$$+ \dfrac{n(n^2 - 2^2)(n^2 - 4^2)}{5!} \sin^5 \theta + \ldots$$

$$+ (-1)^{n/2+1}(2 \sin \theta)^{n-1}$$

(484)† $1 - \dfrac{n^2}{2!} \sin^2 \theta + \dfrac{n^2(n^2 - 2^2)}{4!} \sin^4 \theta + \ldots$

$$+ (-1)^{n/2}2^{n-1} \sin^n \theta$$

(485) $\displaystyle\sum_{1}^{\frac{n-1}{2}} \{\cot (\theta + ra) + \cot (\theta - ra)\}$

(486) $\displaystyle\sum_{1}^{\frac{n-1}{2}} \{\operatorname{cosec}^2 (\theta + ra) + \operatorname{cosec}^2 (\theta - ra)\}$

(487) $\dfrac{\sin \theta}{2 \cos \theta - 1} + \dfrac{2 \sin 2\theta}{2 \cos 2\theta - 1} + \dfrac{2^2 \sin 2^2\theta}{2 \cos 2^2\theta - 1} + \ldots$

$$n \text{ terms}$$

(488) $\tan^{-1} \dfrac{1}{3} + \tan^{-1} \dfrac{1}{7} + \tan^{-1} \dfrac{1}{13} + \tan^{-1} \dfrac{1}{21} + \ldots$

$$+ \tan^{-1} \dfrac{1}{1 + n(n + 1)}$$

(489) $2 \displaystyle\sum_{1}^{\frac{n-2}{2}} \dfrac{x - a \cos \dfrac{2r\pi}{n}}{x^2 - 2ax \cos \dfrac{2r\pi}{n} + a^2}$

(490) $2 \displaystyle\sum_{1}^{\frac{n-1}{2}} \dfrac{x - a \cos \dfrac{2r\pi}{n}}{x^2 - 2ax \cos \dfrac{2r\pi}{n} + a^2}$

† This summation can be carried to infinity, the sum being $\cos \dfrac{1}{2} n\pi$, where the value of n is unrestricted, and $\theta = \dfrac{\pi}{2}$.

$$= \frac{\sin n\theta}{\cos \theta} \quad \text{where } n \text{ is even}$$

A. 205

$$= \cos n\theta \quad \text{where } n \text{ is even}$$

A. 204

$$= n \cot n\theta - \cot \theta \quad \text{where } na = \pi$$

A. 217

$$= n^2 \operatorname{cosec}^2 n\theta - \operatorname{cosec}^2 \theta \quad \text{where } na = \pi$$

A. 217

$$= \frac{2^n \sin 2^n\theta}{2^n \cos 2^n\theta + 1} - \frac{\sin \theta}{2 \cos \theta + 1}$$

D. 330

$$= \tan^{-1} \frac{n}{n + 2}$$

E. 126

$$= \frac{nx^{n-1}}{x^n - a^n} - \frac{1}{x - a} - \frac{1}{x + a} \quad \text{where } n \text{ is even}$$

Y. 55

$$= \frac{nx^{n-1}}{x^n - a^n} - \frac{1}{x - a} \quad \text{where } n \text{ is odd}$$

Y. 55

A. 207

Series No.

(491) $\displaystyle\lim_{n=\infty}\left[\frac{1}{n}\left\{\sec\frac{\theta}{n}+\sec\frac{2\theta}{n}+\ldots+\sec\frac{(n-1)\theta}{n}\right\}\right]$

(492) $\displaystyle\sum_{1}^{n}\tan^{-1}\left(\sec\frac{2r\pi}{2n+1}\sinh\theta\right)$

(493) $(2\cos\theta)^{n-1}-(n-2)(2\cos\theta)^{n-3}$

$$+\frac{(n-3)(n-4)}{2!}(2\cos\theta)^{n-5}+$$

$$\ldots+(-1)^{(n-1)/2}$$

$$\ldots+(-1)^{n/2-1}(n\cos\theta)$$

(494) $(2\cos\theta)^{n}-n(2\cos\theta)^{n-2}+\dfrac{n(n-3)}{2!}(2\cos\theta)^{n-4}+$

$$\ldots+(-1)^{(n-1)/2}2n\cos\theta\quad(n\text{ is odd})$$

$$\ldots+2(-1)^{n/2}\qquad\qquad(n\text{ is even})$$

(495) $\dfrac{1}{\cos\theta+\cos3\theta}+\dfrac{1}{\cos3\theta+\cos5\theta}+\ldots n$ terms

(496) $\displaystyle\lim_{n=\infty}\left[\frac{1}{n}\left\{\sin^{2k}\frac{\pi}{2n}+\sin^{2k}\frac{2\pi}{2n}+\ldots+\sin^{2k}\frac{\pi}{2}\right\}\right]$

(497) $\displaystyle\lim_{x\to1}[1-x\cos\theta+x^4\cos2\theta-x^9\cos3\theta+\ldots\infty]$

(498) $\displaystyle\lim_{x\to1}[x\sin\theta-x^4\sin2\theta+x^9\sin3\theta-\ldots\infty]$

(499) $\displaystyle\sum_{1}^{\infty}a^n\sin n\theta$

(500) $\displaystyle\sum_{0}^{\infty}a^n\cos n\theta$

(501) $\cos\theta+a\cos3\theta+a^2\cos5\theta+\ldots a^n\cos(2n+1)\theta+$

$$\ldots\infty$$

$$= \frac{1}{\theta} \text{logh} \tan \left(\frac{\theta}{2} + \frac{\pi}{4} \right) \quad \text{where } \pi > \theta > \frac{\pi}{2}$$ 1Z. 355

$$= \tan^{-1} \frac{\sinh n\theta}{\cosh (n + 1)\theta} \quad \text{where } n \text{ is even}$$ A. 528

$$= \sin n\theta \cdot \text{cosec } \theta \quad \text{where } n \text{ is odd}$$
$$= \sin n\theta \cdot \text{cosec } \theta \quad \text{where } n \text{ is even}$$ E. 61

$$= 2 \cos n\theta$$ E. 63

$$= \frac{1}{2} \text{cosec } \theta \{\tan (n + 1)\theta - \tan \theta\}$$ E. 125

$$= \frac{(2k - 1)(2k - 3)\ldots 1}{2k(2k - 2)\ldots 2} \quad \text{where } k \text{ is a positive integer}$$ 1Z. 326

$$= \frac{1}{2}$$ A. 276

$$= \frac{1}{2} \tan \frac{\theta}{2}$$ A. 276

$$= \frac{a \sin \theta}{1 - 2a \cos \theta + a^2} \quad \text{where } a^2 < 1$$ T. 139

$$= \frac{1 - a \cos \theta}{1 - 2a \cos \theta + a^2} \quad \text{where } a^2 < 1$$ T. 139

$$= \frac{(1 - a) \cos \theta}{1 - 2a \cos 2\theta + a^2} \quad \text{where } |a| < 1$$ A. 223

Series No.

(502) $\tan \theta + \tan \left(\theta + \dfrac{2\pi}{5} \right) + \tan \left(\theta + \dfrac{4\pi}{5} \right) + \ldots \tan \left(\theta + \dfrac{8\pi}{5} \right)$

(503) $\cos \theta + \dfrac{1}{2} \cos 2\theta + \dfrac{1}{3} \cos 3\theta + \ldots \infty$

(504) $\cos \theta - \dfrac{1}{2} \cos 2\theta + \dfrac{1}{3} \cos 3\theta + \ldots \infty$

(505) $\cos \theta + \dfrac{1}{3} \cos 3\theta + \dfrac{1}{5} \cos 5\theta + \ldots \;\; \infty$

(506) $\cos \theta - \dfrac{1}{3} \cos 3\theta + \dfrac{1}{5} \cos 5\theta + \ldots \infty$

(507) $\cos 2\theta + \dfrac{1}{2} \cos 4\theta + \dfrac{1}{3} \cos 6\theta + \ldots \infty$

(508) $\sin \theta + \dfrac{1}{2} \sin 2\theta + \dfrac{1}{3} \sin 3\theta + \ldots \infty$

(509) $\sin \theta - \dfrac{1}{2} \sin 2\theta + \dfrac{1}{3} \sin 3\theta + \ldots \infty$

(510) $\sin \theta + \dfrac{1}{3} \sin 3\theta + \dfrac{1}{5} \sin 5\theta + \ldots \infty$

(511) $\sin \theta - \dfrac{1}{3} \sin 3\theta + \dfrac{1}{5} \sin 5\theta - \ldots \infty$

(512) $\sin 2\theta + \dfrac{1}{2} \sin 4\theta + \dfrac{1}{3} \sin 6\theta + \ldots \infty$

$= 5 \tan 5\theta$

$= -\text{logh } 2 \sin \dfrac{\theta}{2}$ where $0 < \theta < 2\pi$ A. 356

$= \text{logh } 2 \cos \dfrac{\theta}{2}$ where $-\pi < \theta < \pi$ A. 356

$= \dfrac{1}{2} \text{logh } \cot \dfrac{\theta}{2}$ where $0 < \theta < \pi$ A. 356

$= \dfrac{1}{2} \text{logh} \left(-\cot \dfrac{\theta}{2} \right)$ where $\pi < \theta < 2\pi$ A. 356

$= \dfrac{\pi}{4}$ where $-\dfrac{\pi}{2} < \theta < \dfrac{\pi}{2}$ A. 359

$= -\text{logh } (2 \sin \theta)$ where $0 < \theta < \pi$ A. 356

$= \dfrac{1}{2}(\pi - \theta)$ where $0 < \theta < 2\pi$ A. 356

$= \dfrac{\theta}{2}$ where $-\pi < \theta < \pi$ A. 356

$= \dfrac{\pi}{4}$ where $0 < \theta < \pi$ A. 356

$= -\dfrac{\pi}{4}$ where $\pi < \theta < 2\pi$ A. 356

$= \dfrac{1}{2} \text{logh } (\sec \theta + \tan \theta)$ where $-\dfrac{\pi}{2} < \theta < \dfrac{\pi}{2}$ A. 359

$= \dfrac{1}{2}(\pi - 2\theta)$ where $0 < \theta < \pi$ A. 356

Series No.

(513) $\cos \dfrac{\pi}{3} + \dfrac{1}{3} \cos \dfrac{2\pi}{3} + \dfrac{1}{5} \cos \dfrac{3\pi}{3} + \dfrac{1}{7} \cos \dfrac{4\pi}{3} + \dots \infty$

(514) $\tan \theta - \dfrac{1}{3} \tan^3 \theta + \dfrac{1}{5} \tan^5 \theta - \dots \infty$

(515) $\dfrac{1}{2} \sin \theta - \dfrac{2}{5} \sin 2\theta + \dfrac{3}{10} \sin 3\theta - \dfrac{4}{17} \sin 4\theta + \dots \infty$

(516) $\cos \theta + \dfrac{1}{2^2} \cos 2\theta + \dfrac{1}{3^2} \cos 3\theta + \dots \infty$

(517) $\cos \theta - \dfrac{1}{2^2} \cos 2\theta + \dfrac{1}{3^2} \cos 3\theta - \dots \infty$

(518) $\cos \theta + \dfrac{1}{3^2} \cos 3\theta + \dfrac{1}{5^2} \cos 5\theta + \dots \infty$

(519) $\sin \theta - \dfrac{1}{3^2} \sin 3\theta + \dfrac{1}{5^2} \sin 5\theta - \dots \infty$

(520) $\displaystyle\sum_{1}^{\infty} \dfrac{\sin^2 n\theta}{n^2}$

(521) $\sin \theta + \dfrac{1}{2} \sin 2\theta + \dfrac{1}{2^2} \sin 3\theta + \dots \infty$

(522) $\sin \dfrac{\theta}{2} - \dfrac{1}{3^2} \sin \dfrac{3}{2} \theta + \dfrac{1}{5^2} \sin \dfrac{5}{2} \theta + \dots \infty$

(523) $\sin^2 \theta - \dfrac{1}{2} \sin^2 2\theta + \dfrac{1}{3} \sin^2 3\theta - \dots \infty$

(524) $\sin 2\theta + \dfrac{1}{2} \sin 3\theta + \dfrac{1}{3} \sin 4\theta + \dots \infty$

$= \dfrac{1}{8} \{2\sqrt{3} \text{ logh } (2 + \sqrt{3}) - \pi\}$ E. 123

$= \theta \quad \text{where } \dfrac{\pi}{4} > \theta > -\dfrac{\pi}{4}$ E. 107

$= \dfrac{\pi \sinh \theta}{2 \sinh \pi}$ U. 42

$= \dfrac{1}{4} (\theta - \pi)^2 - \dfrac{1}{12} \pi^2 \quad \text{where } 0 \leqslant \theta \leqslant 2\pi$ A. 360

$= \dfrac{\pi^2}{12} - \dfrac{\theta^2}{4} \quad \text{where } -\pi \leqslant \theta \leqslant \pi$ A. 360

$= \dfrac{\pi}{8} (\pi - 2\theta) \quad \text{where } 0 \leqslant \theta \leqslant \pi$ A. 360

$= \dfrac{\pi}{8} (\pi + 2\theta) \quad \text{where } -\pi \leqslant \theta \leqslant 0$ A. 360

$= \dfrac{1}{4} \pi\theta \quad \text{where } -\dfrac{\pi}{2} \leqslant \theta \leqslant \dfrac{\pi}{2}$ A. 360

$= \dfrac{\pi}{4} (\pi - \theta) \quad \text{where } \dfrac{\pi}{2} \leqslant \theta \leqslant \dfrac{3\pi}{2}$ A. 360

$= \dfrac{1}{2} \theta(\pi - \theta) \quad \text{where } 0 \leqslant \theta \leqslant \pi$ Q. 163

$= \dfrac{1}{2} \{\pi|\theta| - \theta^2\} \quad \text{where } -\pi \leqslant \theta \leqslant \pi$ Q. 163

$= \dfrac{4 \sin \theta}{5 - 4 \cos \theta}$ E. 117

$= \dfrac{\pi\theta}{8}$ J. 311

$= \dfrac{1}{2} \text{ logh sec } \theta$ C. 334

$= -\sin \theta \text{ logh } \left(4 \sin^2 \dfrac{\theta}{2}\right) + \dfrac{1}{2} (\pi - \theta) \cos \theta$

Series No.

(525) $\sin \theta + \dfrac{1}{2^3} \sin 2\theta + \dfrac{1}{3^3} \sin 3\theta + \ldots \infty$

(526) $\sin \theta - \dfrac{1}{2^3} \sin 2\theta + \dfrac{1}{3^3} \sin 3\theta - \ldots \infty$

(527) $\sin \theta + \dfrac{1}{3^3} \sin 3\theta + \dfrac{1}{5^3} \sin 5\theta + \ldots \infty$

(528) $\cos \theta - \dfrac{1}{3^3} \cos 3\theta + \dfrac{1}{5^3} \cos 5\theta - \ldots \infty$

(529) $\cos \theta + \dfrac{1}{2^4} \cos 2\theta + \dfrac{1}{3^4} \cos 3\theta + \ldots \infty$

(530) $\cos \theta - \dfrac{1}{2^4} \cos 2\theta + \dfrac{1}{3^4} \cos 3\theta - \ldots \infty$

(531) $\cos \theta + \dfrac{1}{3^4} \cos 3\theta + \dfrac{1}{5^4} \cos 5\theta + \ldots \infty$

(532) $\sin \theta - \dfrac{1}{3^4} \sin 3\theta + \dfrac{1}{5^4} \sin 5\theta - \ldots \infty$

(533) $\sin \theta + \dfrac{1}{2^5} \sin 2\theta + \dfrac{1}{3^5} \sin 3\theta + \ldots \infty$

(534) $\displaystyle\sum_{-\infty}^{+\infty} \dfrac{\cos n\theta}{n - a}$

(535) $\displaystyle\sum_{-\infty}^{+\infty} \dfrac{\sin n\theta}{n - a}$

(536) $a \cos \theta + \dfrac{a^2}{2} \cos 2\theta + \dfrac{a^3}{3} \cos 3\theta + \ldots \infty$

(537) $a \cos \theta + \dfrac{a^3}{3} \cos 3\theta + \dfrac{a^5}{5} \cos 5\theta + \ldots \infty$

$$= \frac{1}{12} \{(\theta - \pi)^3 - \pi^2\theta + \pi^3\} \quad \text{where } 0 \leqslant \theta \leqslant 2\pi \qquad \text{A. 362}$$

$$= \frac{1}{12} (\pi^2\theta - \theta^3) \quad \text{where } -\pi \leqslant \theta \leqslant \pi \qquad \text{A. 362}$$

$$= \frac{1}{8} (\pi^2\theta - \pi\theta^2) \quad \text{where } 0 \leqslant \theta \leqslant \pi$$

$$= \frac{1}{8} (\pi^2\theta + \pi\theta^2) \quad \text{where } -\frac{\pi}{2} \leqslant \theta \leqslant \frac{\pi}{2} \qquad \text{A. 362}$$

$$= \frac{1}{8} \pi \left(\frac{1}{4} \pi^2 - \theta^2\right) \quad \text{where } -\frac{\pi}{2} \leqslant \theta \leqslant \frac{\pi}{2} \qquad \text{A. 362}$$

$$= \frac{1}{48} \{2\pi^2(\theta - \pi)^2 - (\theta - \pi)^4\} - \frac{7\pi^4}{720} \quad \text{where } 0 \leqslant \theta \leqslant 2\pi$$

$$\text{A. 363}$$

$$= \frac{1}{48} \left\{\theta^4 - 2\pi^2\theta^2 + \frac{7}{15} \pi^4\right\} \quad \text{where } -\pi \leqslant \theta \leqslant \pi \qquad \text{A. 363}$$

$$= \frac{\pi}{96} \{4\theta^3 - 6\pi\theta^2 + \pi^3\} \quad \text{where } 0 \leqslant \theta \leqslant \pi \qquad \text{A. 363}$$

$$= \frac{\pi\theta}{96} \{3\pi^2 - 4\theta^2\} \quad \text{where } -\frac{\pi}{2} \leqslant \theta \leqslant \frac{\pi}{2} \qquad \text{A. 363}$$

$$= \frac{\pi^4\theta}{90} - \frac{\pi^2\theta^3}{36} + \frac{\pi\theta^4}{48} - \frac{\theta^5}{240} \quad \text{where } 0 < \theta < 2\pi \qquad \text{T. 138}$$

$$= -\frac{\pi \cos a(\pi - \theta)}{\sin a\pi} \quad \text{where } 0 < \theta < 2\pi \qquad \text{A. 370}$$

$$= \frac{\pi \sin a(\pi - \theta)}{\sin a\pi} \quad \text{where } 0 < \theta < 2\pi \qquad \text{A. 370}$$

$$= -\frac{1}{2} \operatorname{logh} (1 - 2a \cos \theta + a^2) \quad \text{where } a^2 < 1 \text{ and } \theta \neq 2n\pi$$

$$\text{2Z. 302}$$

$$= \frac{1}{4} \operatorname{logh} \frac{1 + 2a \cos \theta + a^2}{1 - 2a \cos \theta + a^2} \quad \text{where } |a| < 1 \qquad \text{E. 122}$$

Series No.

(538) $\log a^2 - 2 \left(\dfrac{1}{a} \cos \theta + \dfrac{1}{2a^2} \cos 2\theta + \dfrac{1}{3a^3} \cos 3\theta + \ldots \infty \right)$

(539) $a \cos \theta - \dfrac{a^3}{3} \cos 3\theta + \dfrac{a^5}{5} \cos 5\theta - \ldots \infty$

(540) $a \sin \theta + \dfrac{a^2}{2} \sin 2\theta + \dfrac{a^3}{3} \sin 3\theta + \ldots \infty$

(541) $(\pi - \theta) - \left(\dfrac{1}{a} \sin \theta + \dfrac{1}{2a^2} \sin 2\theta + \dfrac{1}{3a^3} \sin 3\theta + \ldots \infty \right)$

(542) $a \sin \theta - \dfrac{a^2}{2} \sin 2\theta + \dfrac{a^3}{3} \sin 3\theta - \ldots \infty$

(543) $a \sin \theta + \dfrac{a^3}{3} \sin 3\theta + \dfrac{a^5}{5} \sin 5\theta + \ldots \infty$

(544) $a \sin \theta - \dfrac{a^3}{3} \sin 3\theta + \dfrac{a^5}{5} \sin 5\theta - \ldots \infty$

(545) $\dfrac{1}{a} \cos \theta + \dfrac{1}{a^2} \cos 2\theta + \dfrac{1}{a^3} \cos 3\theta + \ldots \infty$

(546) $\displaystyle\sum_1^\infty \dfrac{a^{2n-1}}{2n-1} \sin (2n-1)\theta$

(547) $\displaystyle\sum_1^\infty (-1)^{n-1} \dfrac{a^{2n-1}}{2n-1} \cos (2n-1)\theta$

(548) $2a \sin \theta + 4a^2 \sin 2\theta + 6a^3 \sin 3\theta + \ldots \infty$

(549) $\displaystyle\sum_0^\infty \dfrac{\cos (n + \frac{1}{2})\theta}{n + \frac{1}{2}}$

(550) $\displaystyle\sum_0^\infty \dfrac{\sin (n + \frac{1}{2})\theta}{n + \frac{1}{2}}$

(551) $\displaystyle\sum_{-\infty}^{+\infty} \dfrac{\sin (n - a)\theta}{n - a}$

$= \operatorname{logh} (1 - 2a \cos \theta + a^2)$ where $a^2 > 1$ 2Z. 302

$= \dfrac{1}{2} \tan^{-1} \dfrac{2a \cos \theta}{1 - a^2}$ where $|a| < 1$ E. 122

$= \tan^{-1} \dfrac{a \sin \theta}{1 - a \cos \theta}$ where $a^2 < 1$ 2Z. 302

$= \tan^{-1} \dfrac{a \sin \theta}{1 - a \cos \theta}$ where $a^2 > 1$ 2Z. 302

$= \tan^{-1} \dfrac{a \sin \theta}{1 + a \cos \theta}$ where $|a| < 1$, $\theta \ne (2n + 1)\pi$ E. 122

$= \dfrac{1}{2} \tan^{-1} \dfrac{2a \sin \theta}{1 - a^2}$ where $|a| < 1$, $\theta \ne n\pi$ E. 122

$= \dfrac{1}{4} \operatorname{logh} \dfrac{1 + 2a \sin \theta + a^2}{1 - 2a \sin \theta + a^2}$ where $|a| < 1$ E. 122

$= \dfrac{a \cos \theta - 1}{1 - 2a \cos \theta + a^2}$ where $a^2 > 1$ 2Z. 302

$= \dfrac{1}{2} \tan^{-1} \dfrac{2a \sin \theta}{1 - a^2}$ where $a^2 < 1$ T. 139

$= \dfrac{1}{2} \tan^{-1} \dfrac{2a \cos \theta}{1 - a^2}$ where $a^2 < 1$ T. 140

$= \dfrac{2a(1 - a^2) \sin \theta}{(1 - 2a \cos \theta + a^2)^2}$ where $a^2 < 1$ 2Z. 303

$= \operatorname{logh} \cot \dfrac{\theta}{4}$ where $0 < \theta < \pi$ A. 392

$= \dfrac{\pi}{2}$ where $0 < \theta < \pi$ A. 392

$= \pi$ where $0 < \theta < 2\pi$ A. 371

Series No.

(552) $\displaystyle\sum_{-\infty}^{+\infty} \frac{\cos(n-a)\theta}{n-a}$

(553) $\displaystyle 2m \sum_{1}^{\infty} \frac{\cos n\theta}{n^2 - m^2}$

(554) $\displaystyle 2 \sum_{1}^{\infty} \frac{n \sin n\theta}{n^2 - m^2}$

(555) $\displaystyle \sum_{1}^{\infty} \frac{\cos n\theta}{n^2 - a^2}$

(556) $\displaystyle \sum_{1}^{\infty} \frac{n \sin n\theta}{n^2 - a^2}$

(557) $\displaystyle \sum_{1}^{\infty} (-1)^{n-1} \frac{n \sin n\theta}{n^2 - a^2}$

(558) $\displaystyle a \sum_{1}^{\infty} (-1)^{n-1} \frac{\cos n\theta}{n^2 - a^2}$

(559) $\displaystyle 2a \sum_{1}^{\infty} \frac{\cos n\theta}{n^2 + a^2}$

(560) $\displaystyle 2 \sum_{1}^{\infty} \frac{n \sin n\theta}{n^2 + a^2}$

(561) $\displaystyle \sum_{1}^{\infty} (-1)^{n-1} \frac{n \sin n\theta}{n^2 + a^2}$

(562) $\displaystyle a \sum_{1}^{\infty} (-1)^{n} \frac{\cos n\theta}{n^2 + a^2}$

(563) $\displaystyle \sum_{2}^{\infty} \frac{(-1)^n}{n} \left[\frac{\cos 2(n-1)\theta}{(n-1)^2} - \frac{\cos 2(n+1)\theta}{(n+1)^2} \right]$

$$= -\pi \cot \pi a \quad \text{where } 0 < \theta < 2\pi \qquad\qquad \text{A. 371}$$

$$= \frac{1}{m} + \frac{\cos m\theta}{2m} - (\pi - \theta) \sin m\theta \quad \text{where } 0 < \theta < 2\pi \text{ and } m \text{ is}$$
$$\text{a positive integer (omit } m = n) \qquad \text{A. 371}$$

$$= (\pi - \theta) \cos m\theta - \frac{\sin m\theta}{2m} \quad \text{where } 0 < \theta < 2\pi \text{ and } m \text{ is a}$$
$$\text{positive integer (omit } m = n) \quad \text{A. 371}$$

$$= \frac{\pi \sin a(\frac{1}{2}\pi - \theta)}{4a \cos \frac{1}{2}\pi a} \quad \text{where } 0 < \theta < \pi \text{ and } n \text{ is odd } (a \text{ unrestricted})$$
$$\text{A. 371}$$

$$= \frac{\pi \cos a(\frac{1}{2}\pi - \theta)}{4 \cos \frac{1}{2}\pi a} \quad \text{where } 0 < \theta < \pi \text{ and } n \text{ is odd } (a \text{ unrestricted})$$
$$\text{A. 371}$$

$$= \frac{\pi \sin a\theta}{2 \sin \pi a} \quad \text{where } -\pi < \theta < \pi \qquad\qquad \text{Q. 191}$$

$$= \frac{\pi \cos a\theta}{2 \sin \pi a} - \frac{1}{2a} \quad \text{where } -\pi < \theta < \pi \qquad\qquad \text{Q. 191}$$

$$= \frac{\pi \cosh a(\pi - \theta)}{\sinh \pi a} - \frac{1}{a} \quad \text{where } 0 < \theta < 2\pi \qquad \begin{cases} \text{A. 393} \\ \text{AE. 5} \end{cases}$$

$$= \frac{\pi \sinh a(\pi - \theta)}{\sinh \pi a} \quad \text{where } 0 < \theta < 2\pi \qquad \begin{cases} \text{A. 393} \\ \text{AE. 4} \end{cases}$$

$$= \frac{\pi \sinh a\theta}{2 \sinh \pi a} \quad \text{where } -\pi < \theta < \pi \qquad\qquad \text{2Z. 717}$$

$$= + \frac{\pi \cosh a\theta}{2 \sinh \pi a} - \frac{1}{2a} \quad \text{where } -\pi < \theta < \pi \qquad\qquad \text{2Z. 717}$$

$$= 1 + \frac{\pi^2}{6} - 2\theta^2 - 2\cos 2\theta - 2\theta \sin 2\theta - \frac{1}{4}\cos 4\theta$$

Series No.

(564) $\dfrac{a}{\pi} \displaystyle\sum_{1}^{\infty} \dfrac{\sin \dfrac{2n\pi\theta}{a}}{n}$

See No. (572)

(565) $\dfrac{a^2}{\pi^2} \displaystyle\sum_{1}^{\infty} \dfrac{\cos \dfrac{2n\pi\theta}{a}}{n^2}$

See No. (573)

(566) $\dfrac{3}{4} \sin \theta + 3 \sin^3 \dfrac{\theta}{3} + 3^2 \sin^3 \dfrac{\theta}{3^2} + \ldots \infty$

(567) $\sin^2 \theta + 2^2 \sin^4 \dfrac{\theta}{2} + 2^4 \sin^4 \dfrac{\theta}{2^2} + 2^6 \sin^4 \dfrac{\theta}{2^3} + \ldots \infty$

(568) $\cos 2\theta - \dfrac{1}{2} \cos 4\theta + \dfrac{1}{3} \cos 6\theta - \dfrac{1}{4} \cos 8\theta$
$$+ \dfrac{1}{5} \cos 10\theta + \ldots \infty$$

(569) $1 - \dfrac{1}{4} \tan^2 2\theta + \dfrac{1}{8} \tan^4 2\theta - \dfrac{5}{64} \tan^6 2\theta + \ldots \infty$

(570) $1 - \dfrac{3}{8} \tan^2 2\theta + \dfrac{31}{128} \tan^4 2\theta - \dfrac{187}{1024} \tan^6 2\theta + \ldots \infty$

(571) $1 - \dfrac{11}{32} \tan^2 2\theta + \dfrac{431}{2048} \tan^4 2\theta - \ldots \infty$

(572)† $2 \displaystyle\sum_{1}^{\infty} \dfrac{\sin 2n\pi\theta}{2n\pi}$

(573)† $2 \displaystyle\sum_{1}^{\infty} \dfrac{\cos 2n\pi\theta}{(2n\pi)^2}$

(574)† $2 \displaystyle\sum_{1}^{\infty} \dfrac{\sin 2n\pi\theta}{(2n\pi)^{2k-1}}$

(575)† $2 \displaystyle\sum_{1}^{\infty} \dfrac{\cos 2n\pi\theta}{(2n\pi)^{2k}}$

† For $\phi_k(\theta)$ see No. (1128). B_k are Bernoulli numbers.

$$= \frac{1}{2} a - \theta \quad \text{where } 0 < \theta < a$$

$$= \left(\frac{1}{2} a - \theta\right)^2 - \frac{a^2}{12} \quad \text{where } 0 \leqslant \theta \leqslant a$$

$$= \frac{3}{4} \theta \qquad\qquad\qquad\qquad\qquad\qquad \text{C. 336}$$

$$= \theta^2 \qquad\qquad\qquad\qquad\qquad\qquad\qquad \text{C. 336}$$

$$= \text{logh } 2 + \text{logh } \cos \theta \quad \text{where } -\pi < \theta < \pi \qquad \text{2Z. 302}$$

$$= \frac{2 \tan \theta}{\tan 2\theta} \qquad\qquad\qquad\qquad\qquad\qquad \text{O. 383}$$

$$= \frac{2 \sin \theta}{\tan 2\theta} \qquad\qquad\qquad\qquad\qquad\qquad \text{O. 383}$$

$$= \frac{4 \sin \dfrac{\theta}{2}}{\tan 2\theta} \qquad\qquad\qquad\qquad\qquad\qquad \text{O. 383}$$

$$= \frac{1}{2} - \phi_1(\theta) = \frac{1}{2} - \theta \quad \text{where } 0 < \theta < 1 \qquad \begin{cases} \text{A. 370} \\ \text{AE. 2} \end{cases}$$

$$= \frac{1}{2!} \{\phi_2(\theta) + B_1\} = \frac{1}{2} \left(\theta^2 - \theta + \frac{1}{6}\right) \quad \text{where } 0 < \theta < 1 \begin{cases} \text{A. 370} \\ \text{AE. 2} \end{cases}$$

$$= \frac{(-1)^k}{(2k - 1)!} \phi_{2k-1}(\theta) \quad \text{where } k > 1 \text{ and } 0 < \theta < 1 \qquad \text{A. 370}$$

$$= \frac{(-1)^{k-1}}{(2k)!} \{\phi_{2k}(\theta) + (-1)^{k-1} B_k\} \quad \text{where } 0 < \theta < 1 \qquad \text{A. 370}$$

Series No.

(576)† $\sin 2\pi\theta + \dfrac{\sin 4\pi\theta}{2^{2n+1}} + \dfrac{\sin 6\pi\theta}{3^{2n+1}} + \ldots \infty$

(577)† $\cos 2\pi\theta + \dfrac{\cos 4\pi\theta}{2^{2n}} + \dfrac{\cos 6\pi\theta}{3^{2n}} + \ldots \infty$

(578) $\displaystyle\sum_1^\infty \tan^{-1} \dfrac{2\theta^2}{n^2}$

(579) $\displaystyle\sum_1^\infty (-1)^{n-1} \tan^{-1} \dfrac{2\theta^2}{n^2}$

(580) $\tan^{-1} \dfrac{\theta}{1-\theta^2} - \tan^{-1}\dfrac{3\theta}{3^2-\theta^2} + \tan^{-1}\dfrac{5\theta}{5^2-\theta^2} - \ldots \infty$

(581) $\dfrac{1}{2}\tan\dfrac{\theta}{2} + \dfrac{1}{2^2}\tan\dfrac{\theta}{2^2} + \dfrac{1}{2^3}\tan\dfrac{\theta}{2^3} + \ldots \infty$

(582) $\dfrac{1}{2^2}\sec^2\dfrac{\theta}{2} + \dfrac{1}{2^4}\sec^2\dfrac{\theta}{2^2} + \dfrac{1}{2^6}\sec^2\dfrac{\theta}{2^3} + \ldots \infty$

(583) $\left\{\dfrac{\pi^2}{1} - \dfrac{4}{1^3}\right\}\sin\theta - \dfrac{\pi^2}{2}\sin 2\theta + \left\{\dfrac{\pi^2}{3} - \dfrac{4}{3^3}\right\}\sin 2\theta$

$\qquad\qquad\qquad\qquad - \dfrac{\pi^2}{4}\sin 4\theta + \ldots \infty$

(584) $\left\{\dfrac{\pi^3}{1} - \dfrac{6\pi}{1^3}\right\}\sin\theta - \left\{\dfrac{\pi^3}{2} - \dfrac{6\pi}{2^3}\right\}\sin 2\theta$

$\qquad\qquad\qquad\qquad + \left\{\dfrac{\pi^3}{3} - \dfrac{6\pi}{3^3}\right\}\sin 3\theta - \ldots \infty$

(585) $\dfrac{1}{2}(1+\epsilon^\pi)\sin\theta + \dfrac{2}{5}(1-\epsilon^\pi)\sin 2\theta + \dfrac{3}{10}(1+\epsilon^\pi)\sin 3\theta$

$\qquad\qquad\qquad\qquad + \dfrac{4}{17}(1-\epsilon^\pi)\sin 4\theta - \ldots \infty$

(586) $\left\{\dfrac{\pi^2}{1^2} - \dfrac{4}{1^4}\right\}\cos\theta - \dfrac{\pi^2}{2^2}\cos 2\theta + \left\{\dfrac{\pi^2}{3^2} - \dfrac{4}{3^4}\right\}\cos 3\theta$

$\qquad\qquad - \dfrac{\pi^2}{4^2}\cos 4\theta + \left\{\dfrac{\pi^2}{5^2} - \dfrac{4}{5^4}\right\}\cos 5\theta - \ldots \infty$

† For values of $B_n(\theta)$, see No. (1142).

$$= (-1)^{n+1} \frac{2^{2n}\pi^{2n+1}}{(2n)!} B_{2n+1}(\theta) \quad \text{where } 0 < \theta < 1 \qquad \text{AE. 3}$$

$$= (-1)^{n-1} \frac{2^{2n-1}\pi^{2n}}{(2n-1)!} \left\{ B_{2n}(\theta) + (-1)^{n-1} \frac{B_n}{2n} \right\} \quad \text{where } 0 < \theta < 1$$
$$\text{AE. 3}$$

$$= \frac{\pi}{4} - \tan^{-1} \frac{\tanh \pi\theta}{\tan \pi\theta} \qquad \text{A. 314}$$

$$= -\frac{\pi}{4} + \tan^{-1} \frac{\sinh \pi\theta}{\sin \pi\theta} \qquad \text{A. 314}$$

$$= \tan^{-1} \frac{\sinh \dfrac{\pi\theta}{4}}{\cos \dfrac{\sqrt{3}\pi\theta}{4}} \qquad \text{A. 314}$$

$$= \frac{1}{\theta} - \cot \theta \qquad \text{Y. 54}$$

$$= \operatorname{cosec}^2 \theta - \frac{1}{\theta^2} \qquad \text{Y. 54}$$

$$= \frac{\pi\theta^2}{2} \qquad \text{U. 41}$$

$$= \frac{\pi\theta^3}{2} \qquad \text{U. 41}$$

$$= \frac{\pi\epsilon^\theta}{2} \qquad \text{U. 42}$$

$$= \left\{ \frac{\pi^3}{4} - \theta^3 \right\} \frac{\pi}{6} \qquad \text{U. 45}$$

Series No.

(587) $\quad \epsilon^a \cos \theta - \dfrac{1}{3} \epsilon^{3a} \cos 3\theta + \dfrac{1}{5} \epsilon^{5a} \cos 5\theta - \dots \infty$

(588) $\quad \dfrac{8a}{\pi^2} \sum_0^\infty \left\{ \dfrac{\cos (2n + 1) \dfrac{\pi\theta}{2a}}{2n + 1} \right\}^2$

(589) $\quad \displaystyle\sum_1^\infty \dfrac{n}{n^2 + a^2} \{1 + (-1)^{n-1} \epsilon^{a\pi}\} \sin n\theta$

(590) $\quad 1 + a^2 + 4a \cos \theta + 2a^2(3 - a^2) \cos 2\theta$
$\quad\quad + 2a^3(4 - 2a^2) \cos 3\theta + \dots$
$\quad\quad + 2a^n\{n(1 - a^2) + (1 + a^2)\} \cos n\theta + \dots \infty$

(591) $\quad a^2 + 1 + 4a \cos \theta + \dfrac{2(3a^2 - 1)}{a^2} \cos 2\theta + \dots$
$\quad\quad\quad + \dfrac{2\{n(a^2 - 1) + (a^2 + 1)\}}{a^n} \cos n\theta + \dots \infty$

(592) $\quad \displaystyle\sum_1^\infty \dfrac{na^{n-1}}{2(1 - a^2)^3} [n(1 - a^2) + (1 + a^2)] \sin \theta$

(593) $\quad \displaystyle\sum_1^\infty \dfrac{n}{2(a^2 - 1)^3} \dfrac{1}{a^{n+1}} [n(a^2 - 1) + (a^2 + 1)] \sin n\theta$

Memorandum: Consult Edwards *Integral Calculus*, Vol. II, for extension to these series.

(594) $\quad \dfrac{\epsilon^{-q\theta} \sin \theta}{1} + \dfrac{\epsilon^{-2q\theta} \sin 2\theta}{2} + \dfrac{\epsilon^{-3q\theta} \sin 3\theta}{3} + \dots \infty$

(595) $\quad \dfrac{\epsilon^{-q\theta} \cos \theta}{1} + \dfrac{\epsilon^{-2q\theta} \cos 2\theta}{2} + \dfrac{\epsilon^{-3q\theta} \cos 3\theta}{3} + \dots \infty$

(596) $\quad \dfrac{4}{3} \sin 2\theta + \dfrac{8}{15} \sin 4\theta + \dots + \dfrac{1 + (-1)^n}{n^2 - 1} n \sin n\theta + \dots \infty$

$$= -\frac{1}{2} \tan^{-1}(\cos\theta \operatorname{cosech} a)$$ E. 123

$$= a - \theta \quad \text{where } \theta \text{ is positive, } |\theta| < a$$

$$= a + \theta \quad \text{where } \theta \text{ is negative, } |\theta| < a$$ J. 309

$$= \frac{\pi}{2} \epsilon^{a\theta} \quad \text{where } 0 < \theta < \pi$$ U. 42

$$= \frac{(1 - a^2)^3}{(1 - 2a\cos\theta + a^2)^2} \quad \text{where } a^2 < 1$$ 2Z. 303

$$= \frac{(a^2 - 1)^3}{(1 - 2a\cos\theta + a^2)^2} \quad \text{where } a^2 > 1$$ 2Z. 304

$$= \frac{\sin\theta}{(1 - 2a\cos\theta + a^2)^3} \quad \text{where } a^2 < 1$$ 2Z. 305

$$= \frac{\sin\theta}{(1 - 2a\cos\theta + a^2)^3} \quad \text{where } a^2 > 1$$ 2Z. 305

$$= \tan^{-1}\frac{\sin\theta}{\epsilon^{q\theta} - \cos\theta} \quad \text{where } q \text{ is positive}$$ 2Z. 194

$$= -\operatorname{logh}\sqrt{1 - 2\epsilon^{-q\theta}\cos\theta + \epsilon^{-2q\theta}} \quad \text{where } q \text{ is positive}$$
2Z. 194

$$= \frac{\pi\cos\theta}{2} \quad \text{where } 0 < \theta < \pi$$

Series No.

(597) $\dfrac{1}{2} (1 + \cosh \pi) \sin \theta + \dfrac{2}{5} (1 - \cosh \pi) \sin 2\theta$

$$+ \dfrac{3}{10} (1 + \cosh \pi) \sin 3\theta + \ldots \infty$$

(598) $\dfrac{1 + \epsilon^a}{a^2 + \pi^2} \sin \dfrac{\pi\theta}{a} + \dfrac{2(1 - \epsilon^a)}{a^2 + 4\pi^2} \sin \dfrac{2\pi a}{a}$

$$+ \dfrac{3(1 + \epsilon^a)}{a^2 + 9\pi^2} \sin \dfrac{3\pi\theta}{a} + \ldots \infty$$

(599) $\displaystyle\sum_{1}^{\infty} \dfrac{(-1)^{n-1}}{n^2} \cos \dfrac{n\pi\theta}{a}$

(600) $\displaystyle\sum_{1}^{\infty} \dfrac{\cos 2n\theta}{(2n - 1)(2n + 1)}$

(601) $\dfrac{6}{\pi} \displaystyle\sum_{1}^{\infty} \dfrac{\sin \frac{1}{3}(2n - 1)\pi \cdot \sin (2n - 1)\theta}{(2n - 1)^2}$

(602) $\displaystyle\sum_{1}^{\infty} \dfrac{\cos (2n + 2)\theta}{n(n + 1)}$

(603) $\displaystyle\sum_{1}^{\infty} \dfrac{\sin (2n + 2)\theta}{n(n + 1)}$

(604) $\dfrac{\sin 2\theta}{1 \cdot 3} + \dfrac{\sin 3\theta}{2 \cdot 4} + \ldots \infty = \displaystyle\sum_{2}^{\infty} \dfrac{\sin n\theta}{n^2 - 1}$

(605) $\dfrac{\cos 2\theta}{1 \cdot 3} + \dfrac{\cos 3\theta}{2 \cdot 4} + \ldots \infty = \displaystyle\sum_{2}^{\infty} \dfrac{\cos n\theta}{n^2 - 1}$

(606) $\dfrac{\cos 2\theta}{1 \cdot 3} - \dfrac{\cos 4\theta}{3 \cdot 5} + \ldots \infty = -\displaystyle\sum_{2}^{\infty} \dfrac{\cos \frac{n\pi}{2} \cos n\theta}{n^2 - 1}$

$$= \frac{\pi \cosh \theta}{2}$$

U. 42

$$= \frac{\epsilon^\theta}{2\pi} \quad \text{where } 0 < \theta < a$$

U. 51

$$= \frac{\pi^2}{4a^2} \left(\frac{a^2}{3} - \theta^2 \right) \quad \text{where } -a \leqslant \theta \leqslant a$$

T. 139

$$= \frac{1}{2} - \frac{\pi}{4} \sin \theta \quad \text{where } 0 \leqslant \theta \leqslant \frac{\pi}{2}$$

T. 139

$$= \frac{3}{2} \theta \quad \text{where } 0 \leqslant \theta \leqslant \frac{1}{3}\pi$$

$$= \frac{\pi}{2} \quad \text{where } \frac{1}{3}\pi \leqslant \theta \leqslant \frac{2}{3}\pi$$

AB. 243

$$= \frac{3}{2}(\pi - \theta) \quad \text{where } \frac{2}{3}\pi \leqslant \theta \leqslant \pi$$

$$= \cos 2\theta - \left(\frac{\pi}{2} - \theta \right) \sin 2\theta + \sin^2 \theta \, \text{logh} \, (4 \sin^2 \theta)$$
$$\text{where } 0 \leqslant \theta \leqslant \pi \qquad$$

T. 139

$$= \sin 2\theta - (\pi - 2\theta) \sin^2 \theta - \sin \theta \cos \theta \, \text{logh} \, (4 \sin^2 \theta)$$
$$\text{where } 0 \leqslant \theta \leqslant \pi$$

T. 139

$$= \frac{1}{4} \sin \theta - \sin \theta \, \text{logh} \left(2 \sin \frac{\theta}{2} \right) \quad \text{where } 0 < \theta < 2\pi$$

A. 368

$$= \frac{1}{2} + \frac{1}{4} \cos \theta - \frac{1}{2}(\pi - \theta) \sin \theta \quad \text{where } 0 < \theta < 2\pi$$

A. 368

$$= \frac{\pi}{4} \cos \theta - \frac{1}{2}$$

Series No.

(607) $\dfrac{2 \sin 2\theta}{1 \cdot 3} - \dfrac{4 \sin 4\theta}{3 \cdot 5} + \ldots \infty = -\sum_{2}^{\infty} \dfrac{\cos \dfrac{n\pi}{2} \, n \sin n\theta}{n^2 - 1}$

(608) $\dfrac{\cos 2\theta}{1 \cdot 3} - \dfrac{\cos 3\theta}{2 \cdot 4} + \ldots \infty = +\sum_{2}^{\infty} \dfrac{(-1)^n \cos n\theta}{n^2 - 1}$

(609) $\dfrac{1}{2} - \dfrac{\cos 2\theta}{1 \cdot 3} - \dfrac{\cos 4\theta}{3 \cdot 5} - \dfrac{\cos 6\theta}{5 \cdot 7} - \ldots \infty$

(610) $\dfrac{1}{2} + \dfrac{1}{4} \cos \theta - \dfrac{1}{1 \cdot 3} \cos 2\theta - \dfrac{1}{2 \cdot 4} \cos 3\theta - \dfrac{1}{3 \cdot 5} \cos 4\theta - \ldots \infty$

(611) $\dfrac{\cos 3\theta}{2 \cdot 4} + \dfrac{\cos 5\theta}{4 \cdot 6} + \ldots \infty = \sum_{2}^{\infty} \dfrac{\sin^2 \dfrac{n\pi}{2} \cos n\theta}{n^2 - 1}$

(612) $\dfrac{\sin 3\theta}{2 \cdot 4} - \dfrac{\sin 5\theta}{4 \cdot 6} + \ldots \infty = -\sum_{2}^{\infty} \dfrac{\sin \dfrac{n\pi}{2} \sin n\theta}{n^2 - 1}$

(613) $\dfrac{\sin 3\theta}{2 \cdot 4} + \dfrac{\sin 5\theta}{4 \cdot 6} + \ldots \infty = \sum_{2}^{\infty} \dfrac{\sin^2 \dfrac{n\pi}{2} \sin n\theta}{n^2 - 1}$

(614) $\dfrac{3 \cos 3\theta}{2 \cdot 4} - \dfrac{5 \cos 5\theta}{4 \cdot 6} + \ldots \infty = -\sum_{2}^{\infty} \dfrac{\sin \dfrac{n\pi}{2} \, n \cos n\theta}{n^2 - 1}$

(615) $\dfrac{2 \cos 2\theta}{1 \cdot 3} + \dfrac{3 \cos 3\theta}{2 \cdot 4} + \ldots \infty = \sum_{2}^{\infty} \dfrac{n \cos n\theta}{n^2 - 1}$

(616) $\sum_{0}^{\infty} \dfrac{(-1)^n \cos n\theta}{(n + 1)(n + 2)}$

(617) $\dfrac{1}{2} \sin \theta + \dfrac{1 \cdot 3}{2 \cdot 4} \sin 2\theta + \dfrac{1 \cdot 3 \cdot 5}{2 \cdot 4 \cdot 6} \sin 3\theta + \ldots \infty$

$$= \frac{\pi}{4} \sin \theta$$

$$= \frac{1}{2} - \frac{1}{4} \cos \theta - \frac{1}{2} \theta \sin \theta$$

$$= \frac{\pi}{4} \sin \theta \qquad\qquad \text{T. 139}$$

$$= \frac{1}{2} (\pi - \theta) \sin \theta \quad \text{where } 0 \leqslant \theta \leqslant \pi \qquad\qquad \text{Q. 166}$$

$$= \frac{1}{2} (\pi - \theta) \sin \theta \quad \text{where } \pi \leqslant \theta \leqslant 2\pi$$

$$= - \frac{1}{2} (\pi + \theta) \sin \theta \quad \text{where } -\pi \leqslant \theta \leqslant 0$$

$$= \frac{1}{4} \cos \theta - \frac{\pi}{4} \sin \theta + \frac{1}{2} \theta \sin \theta$$

$$= \frac{1}{2} \theta \cos \theta - \frac{1}{4} \sin \theta$$

$$= \frac{1}{4} \sin \theta - \frac{1}{2} \sin \theta \operatorname{logh} (2 \sin \theta)$$

$$= - \frac{1}{2} \theta \sin \theta + \frac{1}{4} \cos \theta$$

$$= - \frac{1}{2} - \frac{1}{4} \cos \theta - \cos \theta \operatorname{logh} \left(2 \sin \frac{\theta}{2} \right)$$

$$= (\cos \theta + \cos 2\theta) \operatorname{logh} \left(2 \cos \frac{\theta}{2} \right) + \frac{1}{2} \theta (\sin 2\theta + \sin \theta) - \cos \theta$$

Q. 190

$$= \left(2 \sin \frac{\theta}{2} \right)^{-1/2} \sin \frac{\pi - \theta}{4} \qquad\qquad \text{E. 116}$$

Series No.

(618) $1 + \dfrac{1}{2} \cos \theta + \dfrac{1 \cdot 3}{2 \cdot 4} \cos 2\theta + \ldots \infty$

(619) $\dfrac{\sin 2\theta}{1 \cdot 2 \cdot 3} + \dfrac{\sin 3\theta}{2 \cdot 3 \cdot 4} + \ldots \infty = \sum_{2}^{\infty} \dfrac{\sin n\theta}{(n-1)n(n+1)}$

(620) $\cos \theta + \dfrac{1}{2} \cdot \dfrac{\cos 3\theta}{3} + \dfrac{1 \cdot 3}{2 \cdot 4} \cdot \dfrac{\cos 5\theta}{5} + \ldots \infty$

(621) $\sin \theta + \dfrac{1}{2} \sin 3\theta + \dfrac{1 \cdot 3}{2 \cdot 4} \cdot \sin 5\theta + \ldots \infty$

(622) $1 + \dfrac{1}{2} \cos 2\theta - \dfrac{1}{2 \cdot 4} \cos 4\theta + \dfrac{1 \cdot 3}{2 \cdot 4 \cdot 6} \cos 6\theta - \ldots \infty$

(623) $\dfrac{\sin \theta}{3} - \dfrac{\sin 3\theta}{1 \cdot 3 \cdot 5} - \dfrac{\sin 5\theta}{3 \cdot 5 \cdot 7} - \ldots \infty = -\sum_{1}^{\infty} \dfrac{\sin n\theta}{n(n^2 - 4)}$

(624) $1 - \dfrac{\sin^2 \theta}{3} - \dfrac{2}{3} \cdot \dfrac{\sin^4 \theta}{5} - \dfrac{2 \cdot 4}{3 \cdot 5} \dfrac{\sin^6 \theta}{7} - \ldots \infty$

(625) $\sin \theta + \dfrac{2}{3} \sin^3 \theta + \dfrac{2 \cdot 4}{3 \cdot 5} \sin^5 \theta + \dfrac{2 \cdot 4 \cdot 6}{3 \cdot 5 \cdot 7} \sin^7 \theta + \ldots \infty$

(626) $\dfrac{\cos \theta}{1 \cdot 2 \cdot 3} + \dfrac{\cos 2\theta}{2 \cdot 3 \cdot 4} + \dfrac{\cos 3\theta}{3 \cdot 4 \cdot 5} + \ldots \infty$

(627) $\dfrac{\cos 3\theta}{1 \cdot 3 \cdot 5} - \dfrac{\cos 5\theta}{3 \cdot 5 \cdot 7} + \dfrac{\cos 7\theta}{5 \cdot 7 \cdot 9} - \ldots \infty$

(628) $\dfrac{1}{2} \cdot \dfrac{\sin^2 \theta}{2} + \dfrac{1 \cdot 3}{2 \cdot 4} \dfrac{\sin^4 \theta}{4} + \dfrac{1 \cdot 3 \cdot 5}{2 \cdot 4 \cdot 6} \dfrac{\sin^6 \theta}{6} + \ldots \infty$

(629) $1 + \dfrac{2}{3} \sin^2 \theta + \dfrac{2 \cdot 4}{3 \cdot 5} \sin^4 \theta + \dfrac{2 \cdot 4 \cdot 6}{3 \cdot 5 \cdot 7} \sin^6 \theta + \ldots \infty$

$= 1 + \dfrac{2^2}{3!} \sin^2 \theta + \dfrac{2^2 \cdot 4^2}{5!} \sin^4 \theta + \dfrac{2^2 \cdot 4^2 \cdot 6^2}{7!} \sin^6 \theta + \ldots \infty$

(630) $\sin \theta + a \cos \theta - \dfrac{a^2}{2!} \sin \theta - \dfrac{a^3}{3!} \cos \theta + \ldots \infty$

(631) $1 + a \cos \theta + \dfrac{a^2}{2!} \cos 2\theta + \dfrac{a^3}{3!} \cos 3\theta + \ldots \infty$

$$= \left(2 \sin \frac{\theta}{2}\right)^{-1/2} \cos \frac{\pi - \theta}{4}$$ E. 116

$$= \frac{3}{4} \sin \theta - \frac{1}{2}(\pi - \theta) + \frac{1}{2}(\pi - \theta) \cos \theta$$

$$= \frac{1}{2} \cos^{-1}(1 - 2 \sin \theta)$$ C. 334

$$= \frac{1}{\sqrt{2 \sin \theta}} \sin\left(\frac{\pi}{4} + \frac{\theta}{2}\right)$$ E. 117

$$= \sqrt{\cos \theta(1 + \cos \theta)} \quad \text{where } -\frac{\pi}{2} < \theta < \frac{\pi}{2}$$ E. 118

$$= \frac{\pi}{8} \sin^2 \theta \quad \text{where } n \text{ is odd}$$ X. 54

$$= \theta \cot \theta$$ Y. 86

$$= \theta \sec \theta$$ Y. 505

$$= \frac{1}{2} \cos \theta - \frac{1}{4} \cos 2\theta$$ C. 421

$$= \frac{\pi}{8} \cos^2 \theta - \frac{1}{3} \cos \theta \quad \text{where } -\frac{\pi}{2} \leqslant \theta \leqslant \frac{\pi}{2}$$ A. 369

$$= \text{logh} \sec^2 \frac{\theta}{2}$$ H. 498

$$= \frac{2\theta}{\sin 2\theta}$$ L. 78

$$= \sin(\theta + a)$$ Y. 84

$$= \epsilon^{a \cos \theta} \cos(a \sin \theta)$$ X. 72

Series No.

(632) $a \sin \theta + \dfrac{a^2}{2!} \sin 2\theta + \dfrac{a^3}{3!} \sin 3\theta + \ldots \infty$

(633) $1 + \dfrac{a^2 \cos 2\theta}{2!} + \dfrac{a^4 \cos 4\theta}{4!} + \ldots \infty$

(634) $\dfrac{a^2 \sin 2\theta}{2!} + \dfrac{a^4 \sin 4\theta}{4!} + \ldots \infty$

(635) $\displaystyle\sum_0^\infty \dfrac{a^{2n} \cos 2n\theta}{(2n)!}$

(636) $\displaystyle\sum_0^\infty \dfrac{a^{2n+1} \cos (2n + 1)\theta}{(2n + 1)!}$

(637) $\displaystyle\sum_0^\infty \dfrac{a^{2n+1} \sin (2n + 1)\theta}{(2n + 1)!}$

(638) $\displaystyle\sum_1^\infty \dfrac{a^{2n} \sin 2n\theta}{(2n)!}$

(639) $1 - \theta \sin \theta + \dfrac{\theta^2 \cos 2\theta}{2!} + \dfrac{2^2\theta^3 \sin 3\theta}{3!} - \dfrac{3^3\theta^4 \cos 4\theta}{4!} - \ldots \infty$

(640) $\theta \cos \theta + \dfrac{\theta^2 \sin 2\theta}{2!} - \dfrac{2^2\theta^3 \cos 3\theta}{3!} - \dfrac{3^3\theta^4 \sin 4\theta}{4!} + \ldots \infty$

(641) $r\theta \sin \phi + \dfrac{r^2\theta^2}{2!} \sin 2\phi + \dfrac{r^3\theta^3}{3!} \sin 3\phi + \ldots \infty$

$\left(r = \sqrt{a^2 + b^2}, \right.$

(642) $1 + \sin \theta + \dfrac{(1 + 1^2) \sin^2 \theta}{2!} + \dfrac{(1 + 2^2) \sin^3 \theta}{3!} + \ldots \infty$

(643) $1 + 2^{1/2} \cos \dfrac{\pi}{4} \theta + 2^{2/2} \cos \dfrac{2\pi}{4} \dfrac{\theta^2}{2!} + 2^{3/2} \cos \dfrac{3\pi}{4} \dfrac{\theta^3}{3!} + \ldots \infty$

$= \displaystyle\sum_0^\infty 2^{n/2} \cos \dfrac{n\pi}{4} \cdot \dfrac{\theta^n}{n!}$

(644) $\cos \theta + n \cos 3\theta + \dfrac{n(n - 1)}{2!} \cos 5\theta + \ldots \infty$

$$= \epsilon^{a \cos \theta} \sin (a \sin \theta) \qquad\qquad\qquad \text{X. 72}$$

$$= \frac{1}{2} \cos (a \sin \theta)\{\epsilon^{a \cos \theta} + \epsilon^{-a \cos \theta}\} \qquad \text{E. 118}$$

$$= \frac{1}{2} \sin (a \sin \theta)\{\epsilon^{a \cos \theta} - \epsilon^{-a \cos \theta}\} \qquad \text{E. 118}$$

$$= \cosh (a \cos \theta) \cos (a \sin \theta) \quad \text{where } a^2 < 1 \qquad \text{T. 127}$$

$$= \sinh (a \cos \theta) \cos (a \sin \theta) \quad \text{where } a^2 < 1 \qquad \text{T. 127}$$

$$= \cosh (a \cos \theta) \sin (a \sin \theta) \quad \text{where } a^2 < 1 \qquad \text{T. 127}$$

$$= \sinh (a \cos \theta) \sin (a \sin \theta) \quad \text{where } a^2 < 1 \qquad \text{T. 127}$$

$$\left.\begin{array}{l} = \cos \theta \\ \\ = \sin \theta \end{array}\right\} \text{ where } |\theta| < \frac{1}{\epsilon} \qquad \text{A. 312}$$

$$\phi = \tan^{-1}\frac{b}{a}\Big) = \epsilon^{a\theta} \sin b\theta \qquad\qquad \text{E. 131}$$

$$= \frac{\epsilon^{\theta}}{\cos \theta} \qquad\qquad\qquad\qquad\qquad \text{L. 79}$$

$$= \epsilon^{\theta} \cos \theta \qquad\qquad\qquad\qquad\qquad \text{Y. 84}$$

$$= 2^n \cos^n \theta \cos (n + 1)\theta \qquad\qquad\qquad \text{X. 72}$$

Series No.

(645) $\sin \theta + n \sin 3\theta + \dfrac{n(n-1)}{2!} \sin 5\theta + \ldots \infty$

(646) $\dfrac{1}{2} + \dfrac{a}{a+2} \cos 2\theta + \dfrac{a(a-2)}{(a+2)(a+4)} \cos 4\theta + \ldots \infty$

(647) $\cos^n \theta - \dfrac{n(n-1)}{2!} \cos^{n-2} \theta \sin^2 \theta$

$\qquad + \dfrac{n(n-1)(n-2)(n-3)}{4!} \cos^{n-4} \theta \sin^4 \theta - \ldots$ zero

(648) $n \cos^{n-1} \theta \sin \theta - \dfrac{n(n-1)(n-2)}{3!} \cos^{n-3} \theta \sin^3 \theta + \ldots$ zero

(649) $\cos n\theta + n \cos (n-2)\theta + \dfrac{n(n-1)}{2!} \cos (n-4)\theta + \ldots$

If n is odd there is an even number of terms so that the last term contains $\cos \theta$.

(650) $\cos n\theta - n \cos (n-2)\theta + \dfrac{n(n-1)}{2!} \cos (n-4)\theta + \ldots$

$\qquad + \dfrac{1}{2}(-1)^{n/2} \dfrac{n!}{\left\{ \left(\dfrac{n}{2} \right)! \right\}^2}$

(651) $\sin n\theta - n \sin (n-2)\theta + \dfrac{n(n-1)}{2!} \sin (n-4)\theta + \ldots$

$\qquad + (-1)^{(n-1)/2} \dfrac{n!}{\left(\dfrac{n-1}{2} \right)! \left(\dfrac{n+1}{2} \right)!} \sin \theta$

In the series Nos. (652) through (659) $_nC_r$ are the binomial coefficients.

$$_nC_r = \dfrac{n(n-1)(n-2)\ldots(n-r+1)}{r!}$$

(652) $\cos 2n\theta + {}_{2n}C_1 \cos (2n-2)\theta + {}_{2n}C_2 \cos (2n-4)\theta + \ldots$

$\qquad + \dfrac{1}{2} \, {}_{2n}C_n$

(653) $\cos (2n+1)\theta + {}_{2n+1}C_1 \cos (2n-1)\theta + \ldots + {}_{2n+1}C_n \cos \theta$

$= 2^n \cos^n \theta \sin (n + 1)\theta$ X. 72

$= \dfrac{2^{a-1} \left\{ \Gamma\left(\dfrac{a}{2} + 1\right) \right\}^2}{\Gamma(a + 1)} \cos{^a\theta}$ where a is positive but not

necessarily an integer and $-\dfrac{\pi}{2} \leqslant \theta \leqslant \dfrac{\pi}{2}$ Q. 263

$= \cos n\theta$ E. 33

$= \sin n\theta$ E. 33

$- 2^{n-1} \cos^n \theta$ E. 55

$= 2^{n-1}(-1)^{n/2} \sin^n \theta$ where n is even   E. 57

$= 2^{n-1}(-1)^{(n-1)/2} \sin^n \theta$ where n is odd   E. 58

$= 2^{2n-1} \cos^{2n} \theta$ where n is even   C. 278

$= 2^{2n} \cos^{2n+1} \theta$ C. 278

Series No.

(654) $\cos 2n\theta - {}_{2n}C_1 \cos (2n - 2)\theta + {}_{2n}C_2 \cos (2n - 4)\theta + \ldots$
$$+ (-1)^n \frac{1}{2} \cdot {}_{2n}C_n$$

(655) $\sin (2n + 1)\theta - {}_{2n+1}C_1 \sin (2n - 1)\theta$
$$+ {}_{2n+1}C_2 \sin (2n - 3)\theta + \ldots + (-1)^n {}_{2n+1}C_n \sin \theta$$

(656) $1 + {}_nC_1 \cos 2\theta + {}_nC_2 \cos 4\theta + {}_nC_3 \cos 6\theta + \ldots + \cos 2n\theta$

(657) ${}_nC_1 \sin 2\theta + {}_nC_2 \sin 4\theta + {}_nC_3 \sin 6\theta + \ldots + \sin 2n\theta$

(658) $1 - {}_nC_1 \cos 2\theta + {}_nC_2 \cos 4\theta - {}_nC_3 \cos 6\theta + \ldots - \cos 2n\theta$
$\quad {}_nC_1 \sin 2\theta - {}_nC_2 \sin 4\theta + {}_nC_3 \sin 6\theta - \ldots - \sin 2n\theta$

(659) ${}_nC_1 \sin 2\theta - {}_nC_2 \sin 4\theta + {}_nC_3 \sin 6\theta - \ldots + \sin 2n\theta$
$\quad 1 - {}_nC_1 \cos 2\theta + {}_nC_2 \cos 4\theta - {}_nC_3 \cos 6\theta + \ldots + \cos 2n\theta$

(660) $1 - a\theta \sin b\theta - \dfrac{a(a - 2b)}{2!} \theta^2 \cos 2b\theta$
$$+ \frac{a(a - 3b)^2}{3!} \theta^3 \sin 3b\theta + \ldots \infty$$

(661) $\dfrac{1}{2} + \dfrac{2n - 1}{2n + 1} \cos 2\theta + \dfrac{(2n - 1)(2n - 3)}{(2n + 1)(2n + 3)} \cos 4\theta + \ldots \infty$

(662) $\sin^2 \theta + \dfrac{2}{3} \cdot \dfrac{1}{2} \sin^4 \theta + \dfrac{2 \cdot 4}{3 \cdot 5} \cdot \dfrac{1}{3} \sin^6 \theta + \ldots \infty$

(663) $\cos \theta - \dfrac{1}{7} \cos 3\theta + \dfrac{1}{7} \cdot \dfrac{5}{11} \cos 5\theta - \dfrac{1}{7} \cdot \dfrac{5}{11} \cdot \dfrac{9}{15} \cos 7\theta + \ldots \infty$

$$\text{where } h = \frac{4}{\pi} \int_0^{\pi/2} \cos^{3/2} \theta \, d\theta$$

(664) General case of (663)
$$\cos \theta - \frac{1 - n}{3 + n} \cos 3\theta + \frac{1 - n}{3 + n} \cdot \frac{3 - n}{5 + n} \cos 5\theta$$
$$- \frac{1 - n}{3 + n} \cdot \frac{3 - n}{5 + n} \cdot \frac{5 - n}{7 + n} \cos 7\theta + \ldots \infty$$

When *n* is odd, this series terminates.

$= 2^{2n-1}(-1)^n \sin^{2n} \theta$ C. 278

$= 2^{2n}(-1)^n \sin^{2n+1} \theta$ C. 278

$= 2^n \cos n\theta \cos^n \theta$ where n can be odd or even

$= 2^n \cos^n \theta \sin n\theta$ where n can be odd or even

$= (-1)^{(n-1)/2} 2^n \sin^n \theta \sin n\theta$ where n is odd

$= (-1)^{(n+2)/2} 2^n \sin^n \theta \sin n\theta$ where n is even

$= (-1)^{(n-1)/2} 2^n \sin^n \theta \cos n\theta$ where n is odd

$= (-1)^{n/2} 2^n \sin^n \theta \cos n\theta$ where n is even

$= \cos a\theta$ Y. 511

$= \dfrac{\pi}{4} \cdot \dfrac{1 \cdot 3 \cdot 5 \ldots (2n-1)}{2 \cdot 4 \cdot 6 \ldots (2n-2)} |\cos^{2n-1}\theta|$ where n is an integer Q. 191

$= \theta^2$ Q. 130

$= \dfrac{1}{h} \cos^{1/2} \theta$

$= \dfrac{4}{\pi} \cdot \dfrac{\sqrt{\pi}}{2} \dfrac{\Gamma\left(\dfrac{5}{4}\right)}{\Gamma\left(\dfrac{7}{4}\right)} = 1.113$ X. 56

$= \dfrac{1}{C} \cos^n \theta$ where $C = \dfrac{4}{\pi} \displaystyle\int_0^{\pi/2} \cos^{n+1}\theta \, d\theta = \dfrac{4}{\pi} \cdot \dfrac{2}{\sqrt{\pi}} \cdot \dfrac{\Gamma\left(\dfrac{n}{2}+1\right)}{\Gamma\left(\dfrac{n}{2}+\dfrac{3}{2}\right)}$

where n is any value X. 63

Series No.

(665) $\sin^4 \theta + \dfrac{4}{3} \cdot \dfrac{2}{5} \left(1 + \dfrac{1}{2^2}\right) \sin^6 \theta + \ldots$

$\qquad + \dfrac{4 \cdot 6 \ldots (2n-2)}{5 \cdot 7 \ldots (2n-1)} \cdot \dfrac{2}{n} \left\{ 1 + \dfrac{1}{2^2} + \ldots + \dfrac{1}{(n-1)^2} \right\} \sin^{2n}\theta + \ldots \infty$

(666) $1 + \dfrac{2^2}{3 \cdot 4} \sin^2 \theta + \dfrac{2^2 \cdot 4^2}{3 \cdot 4 \cdot 5 \cdot 6} \sin^4 \theta$

$\qquad\qquad\qquad + \dfrac{2^2 \cdot 4^2 \cdot 6^2}{3 \cdot 4 \cdot 5 \cdot 6 \cdot 7 \cdot 8} \sin^6 \theta + \ldots \infty$

(667) $\dfrac{1}{2} \cos^2 \theta - \dfrac{1}{3} \left(1 + \dfrac{1}{2}\right) \cos^3 \theta$

$\qquad\qquad\qquad + \dfrac{1}{4} \left(1 + \dfrac{1}{2} + \dfrac{1}{3}\right) \cos^4 \theta - \ldots \infty$

(667a) $\dfrac{1}{2} \cos 2\theta - \dfrac{1}{3} \left(1 + \dfrac{1}{2}\right) \cos 3\theta + \dfrac{1}{4} \left(1 + \dfrac{1}{2} + \dfrac{1}{3}\right) \cos 4\theta - \ldots \infty$

(668) $\dfrac{\sin \theta}{2!} + 1^2 \cdot 3^2 \left(\dfrac{1}{1^2} + \dfrac{1}{3^2}\right) \dfrac{\sin^3 \theta}{4!}$

$\qquad\qquad + 1^2 \cdot 3^2 \cdot 5^2 \left(\dfrac{1}{1^2} + \dfrac{1}{3^2} + \dfrac{1}{5^2}\right) \dfrac{\sin^5 \theta}{6!} + \ldots \infty$

(669) $\dfrac{2}{\pi} \displaystyle\sum_{1}^{\infty} \dfrac{n}{k^2 + n^2} (1 - \epsilon^{k\pi} \cos n\pi) \sin n\theta$

(670) $\dfrac{\epsilon^{k\pi} - 1}{k\pi} + \dfrac{2k}{\pi} \displaystyle\sum_{1}^{\infty} \dfrac{\epsilon^{k\pi} \cos n\pi - 1}{k^2 + n^2} \cos n\theta$

(671) $\displaystyle\sum_{r=0}^{r=n-1} \dfrac{x - a \cos \dfrac{2r\pi + \theta}{n}}{x^2 - 2ax \cos \dfrac{2r\pi + \theta}{n} + a^2}$

(672) $\tan^{-1} x + (h \sin \theta) \sin \theta - \dfrac{(h \sin \theta)^2}{2!} \sin 2\theta + \ldots \infty$

(673) $1 + \dfrac{\tan^2 \theta}{3} - \dfrac{2}{3} \dfrac{\tan^4 \theta}{5} + \dfrac{2 \cdot 4}{3 \cdot 5} \dfrac{\tan^6 \theta}{7} + \ldots \infty$

$$= \theta^4$$

$$= \left(\frac{\theta}{\sin \theta} \right)^2$$

$$= \frac{1}{2} \left[\text{logh } 2 \cos^2 \frac{\theta}{2} \right]^2 \quad \text{where } -\pi < \theta < \pi$$

$$= \frac{1}{8} \left[\text{logh } 4 \cos^2 \frac{\theta}{2} \right]^2 - \frac{\theta^2}{8} \quad \text{where } -\pi < \theta < \pi$$

$$= \frac{\theta^2}{\sin 2\theta}$$

$$= \epsilon^{k\theta} \quad \text{where } 0 < \theta < \pi$$

$$= \epsilon^{k\theta} \quad \text{where } 0 < \theta < \pi$$

$$= \frac{nx^{n-1}(x^n - a^n \cos \theta)}{x^{2n} - 2x^n a^n \cos \theta + a^{2n}}$$

$$= \tan^{-1}(x + h) \quad \text{where } x = \cot \theta$$

$$= \frac{gd^{-1}\theta}{\sin \theta}$$

Series No.

(674) $1 - \dfrac{n(n-1)}{2!} \tan^2 \theta$

$$+ \dfrac{n(n-1)(n-2)(n-3)}{4!} \tan^4 \theta + \ldots \infty$$

(675) $\displaystyle\sum_{-\infty}^{+\infty} \left\{ \tan^{-1} \dfrac{y}{n+x} - \dfrac{y}{n} \right\}$

(676) $\displaystyle\sum_{-\infty}^{+\infty} (-1)^n \left\{ \tan^{-1} \dfrac{y}{n+x} - \dfrac{y}{n} \right\}$

(677) $\cos \theta \cos a + \dfrac{1}{2} \cos 2\theta \cos 2a + \dfrac{1}{3} \cos 3\theta \cos 3a + \ldots \infty$

(678) $\cos \theta \cos a - \dfrac{1}{2} \cos 2\theta \cos 2a + \dfrac{1}{3} \cos 3\theta \cos 3a - \ldots \infty$

(679) $\sin \theta \sin a + \dfrac{1}{2} \sin 2\theta \sin 2a + \dfrac{1}{3} \sin 3\theta \sin 2a + \ldots \infty$

(680) $\sin \theta \sin a - \dfrac{1}{2} \sin 2\theta \sin 2a + \dfrac{1}{3} \sin 3\theta \sin 3a - \ldots \infty$

(681) $\cos \theta \cos a + \dfrac{1}{2^2} \cos 2\theta \cos 2a + \dfrac{1}{3^2} \cos 3\theta \cos 3a + \ldots \infty$

(682) $\cos \theta \cos a - \dfrac{1}{2^2} \cos 2\theta \cos 2a + \dfrac{1}{3^2} \cos 3\theta \cos 3a - \ldots \infty$

(683) $\sin \theta \sin a + \dfrac{1}{2^2} \sin 2\theta \sin 2a + \dfrac{1}{3^2} \sin 3\theta \sin 3a + \ldots \infty$

$$= \frac{\cos n\theta}{\cos^n \theta} \quad \text{where } n \text{ is a positive integer} \qquad \text{D. 330}$$

$$= -\tan^{-1}\frac{y}{x} + \tan^{-1}\frac{\tanh \pi y}{\tan \pi x} \quad \text{omit } y = x \qquad \text{A. 314}$$

$$= -\tan^{-1}\frac{y}{x} + \tan^{-1}\frac{\sinh \pi y}{\sin \pi x} \quad \text{omit } y = x \qquad \text{A. 314}$$

$$= -\frac{1}{4}\operatorname{logh}\left[4(\cos\theta - \cos a)^2\right] \quad \text{where } \theta \neq 2n\pi + a \qquad \text{A. 358}$$

$$= \frac{1}{4}\operatorname{logh}\left[4(\cos\theta + \cos a)^2\right] \quad \text{where } \theta \neq (2n+1)\pi \pm a \quad \text{A. 358}$$

$$= \frac{1}{4}\operatorname{logh}\frac{\sin^2\frac{1}{2}(\theta+a)}{\sin^2\frac{1}{2}(\theta-a)} \quad \text{where } \theta \neq 2n\pi \pm a \qquad \text{A. 358}$$

$$= \frac{1}{4}\operatorname{logh}\frac{\cos^2\frac{1}{2}(\theta-a)}{\cos^2\frac{1}{2}(\theta+a)} \quad \text{where } \theta \neq (2n+1)\pi \pm a \qquad \text{A. 358}$$

$$= \frac{1}{4}\theta^2 + \frac{1}{4}(a-\pi)^2 - \frac{1}{12}\pi^2 \quad \text{where } 0 \leqslant \theta \leqslant a \qquad \text{A. 361}$$

$$= \frac{1}{4}a^2 + \frac{1}{4}(\theta-\pi)^2 - \frac{1}{12}\pi^2 \quad \text{where } a \leqslant \theta \leqslant \pi \qquad \text{A. 361}$$

$$= \frac{1}{12}\pi^2 - \frac{1}{4}(a^2+\theta^2) \quad \text{where } -(\pi-a) \leqslant \theta \leqslant (\pi-a) \quad \text{A. 361}$$

$$= \frac{1}{12}\pi^2 - \frac{1}{4}\{(a-\pi)^2 + (\theta-\pi)^2\} \quad \text{where } (\pi-a) \leqslant \theta \leqslant (\pi+a)$$
$$\text{A. 361}$$

$$= \frac{1}{2}\theta(\pi-a) \quad \text{where } -a \leqslant \theta \leqslant a \qquad \text{A. 362}$$

$$= \frac{1}{2}a(\pi-\theta) \quad \text{where } a \leqslant \theta \leqslant (2\pi-a) \qquad \text{A. 362}$$

Series No.

(684) $\sin \theta \cos a + \dfrac{1}{2} \sin 2\theta \cos 2a + \dfrac{1}{3} \sin 3\theta \cos 3a + \ldots \infty$

$\cos \theta \sin a + \dfrac{1}{2} \cos 2\theta \sin 2a + \dfrac{1}{3} \cos 3\theta \sin 3a + \ldots \infty$

(685) $\cos \theta + a \cos (\theta + \beta) + a^2 \cos (\theta + 2\beta) + \ldots \infty$

(686) $\sin \theta + a \sin (\theta + \beta) + a^2 \sin (\theta + 2\beta) + \ldots \infty$

(687) $\cos (\theta + a) + \dfrac{1}{2} \cos 2(\theta + a) + \dfrac{1}{3} \cos 3(\theta + a) + \ldots \infty$

$$\theta \neq 2n\pi \pm a$$

(688) $\cos (\theta - a) + \dfrac{1}{2} \cos 2(\theta - a) + \dfrac{1}{3} \cos 3(\theta - a) + \ldots \infty$

$$\theta \neq 2n\pi \pm a$$

(689) $\sin (\theta + a) + \dfrac{1}{2} \sin 2(\theta + a) + \dfrac{1}{3} \sin 3(\theta + a) + \ldots \infty$

(690) $\sin (\theta - a) + \dfrac{1}{2} \sin 2(\theta - a) + \dfrac{1}{3} \sin 3(\theta - a) - \ldots \infty$

(691) $\sin \theta + a \sin (\theta + \beta) + \dfrac{a^2}{2!} \sin (\theta + 2\beta) + \ldots \infty$

$$= f(\theta) \quad \text{where } f(\theta) = -\frac{1}{2}\theta$$

$$g(\theta) = \frac{1}{2}(\pi - a) \quad \left.\right\} \quad \text{if } 0 < \theta < a$$

$$= g(\theta) \quad \text{where } f(\theta) = \frac{1}{2}(\pi - \theta)$$

$$g(\theta) = -\frac{1}{2}a \quad \left.\right\} \quad \text{if } a < \theta < \pi$$

$$f(a) = \frac{1}{4}(\pi - 2a) = g(a) \qquad \text{A. 358}$$

$$= \frac{\cos\theta - a\cos(\theta - \beta)}{1 - 2a\cos\beta + a^2} \qquad \text{E. 131}$$

$$= \frac{\sin\theta - a\sin(\theta - \beta)}{1 - 2a\cos\beta + a^2} \qquad \text{E. 117}$$

$$= -\frac{1}{2}\operatorname{logh}\left[4\sin^2\frac{1}{2}(\theta + a)\right] \qquad \text{A. 358}$$

$$= -\frac{1}{2}\operatorname{logh}\left[4\sin^2\frac{1}{2}(\theta - a)\right] \qquad \text{A. 358}$$

$$= \frac{1}{2}\{\pi - (\theta + a)\} \quad \text{where} \quad 0 < a < \pi \quad \text{and} \quad 0 < (\theta + a) < 2\pi$$

$$\text{A. 358}$$

$$= \frac{1}{2}\{\pi - (\theta - a)\} \quad \text{where } 0 < a < \pi \quad \text{and} \quad 0 < (\theta - a) < 2\pi;$$

when $\theta < a$ the sum is diminished by π \qquad A. 358

$$= \epsilon^{a\cos\beta}\sin(\theta + a\sin\beta) \qquad \text{E. 121}$$

Series No.

(692) $\cos \theta + a \cos (\theta + \beta) + \dfrac{a^2}{2!} \cos (\theta + 2\beta) + \ldots \infty$

(693) $1 - \cos \theta \cos \beta + \dfrac{\cos^2 \theta}{2!} \cos 2\beta - \dfrac{\cos^3 \theta}{3!} \cos 3\beta + \ldots \infty$

(694) $\sin \theta - \dfrac{1}{2!} \sin (\theta + 2\beta) + \dfrac{1}{4!} \sin (\theta + 4\beta) - \ldots \infty$

(695) $\cos \theta - \dfrac{1}{3!} \cos (\theta + 2\beta) + \dfrac{1}{5!} \cos (\theta + 4\beta) - \ldots \infty$

(696) $a \cos \theta - \dfrac{a^3}{3} \cos (\theta + 2\beta) + \dfrac{a^5}{5} \cos (\theta + 4\beta) + \ldots \infty$

(697) $\displaystyle\sum_{1}^{\infty} \dfrac{1}{n^2} \sin n\theta \sin na \cos n\beta$

(698) $\sin \theta \cos \theta + \sin^2 \theta \cos 2\theta + \ldots \infty$

(699) $\displaystyle\sum_{1}^{\infty} \dfrac{1}{n} \sin 2n\theta \sin^2 n\phi$

(700) $\displaystyle\sum_{1}^{\infty} \dfrac{1}{n^2} \sin^2 n\theta \sin^2 n\phi$

$$= \epsilon^{a \cos \beta} \cos (\theta + a \sin \beta) \qquad\qquad \text{E. 121}$$

$$= \epsilon^{-\cos \theta \cos \beta} \cos (\cos \theta \sin \beta) \qquad\qquad \text{E. 121}$$

$$\doteqdot \sin \theta \cos (\cos \beta) \cosh (\sin \beta) - \cos \theta \sin (\cos \beta) \sinh (\sin \beta)$$
$$\text{E. 121}$$

$$= \sin (\cos \beta) \cosh (\sin \beta) \cos (\theta - \beta)$$
$$- \cos (\cos \beta) \sinh (\sin \beta) \sin (\theta - \beta) \qquad \text{E. 122}$$

$$= \frac{1}{2} \cos (\theta - \beta) \tan^{-1} \frac{2a \cos \beta}{1 - a^2} - \frac{1}{2} \sin (\theta - \beta) \tanh^{-1} \frac{2a \sin \beta}{1 + a^2}$$
$$\text{E. 122}$$

where $0 < \beta < a < \dfrac{\pi}{2}$

$$= \frac{1}{2} \theta(\pi - a) \quad \text{where } 0 < \theta < (a - \beta)$$

$$= \frac{1}{4} \pi(\theta + a - \beta) - \frac{1}{2} a\theta \quad \text{where } (a - \beta) < \theta < (a + \beta)$$

$$= \frac{1}{2} a(\pi - \theta) \quad \text{where } (a + \beta) < \theta < \pi \qquad\qquad \text{A. 390}$$

$$= \frac{\sin \theta (\cos \theta - \sin \theta)}{1 - \sin 2\theta + \sin^2 \theta} \quad \text{where } \theta \neq \pm \frac{\pi}{2} \qquad\qquad \text{E. 117}$$

$$= \frac{1}{4} \pi \quad \text{where } \begin{array}{l} 0 < 2\theta < \pi \\ \theta < \phi < (\pi - \theta) \end{array} \qquad\qquad \text{A. 391}$$

$$= \frac{1}{4} \pi\theta \qquad\qquad \text{A. 391}$$

Series No.

(701) $\displaystyle\sum_{1}^{\infty} \frac{1}{n^2} \sin^4 n\theta \sin^2 n\phi$

(702) $\displaystyle\sum_{1}^{\infty} \frac{1}{n^4} \sin^4 n\theta \sin^2 n\phi$

(703) $\cos \theta \sin \theta + \dfrac{1}{2} \cos^2 \theta \sin 2\theta + \dfrac{1}{3} \cos^3 \theta \sin 3\theta + \ldots \infty$

(704) $\sec^2 \theta - \dfrac{1}{3} \tan^2 \theta \sec^2 \theta + \dfrac{1}{5} \tan^4 \theta \sec^2 \theta + \ldots \infty$

(705) $\cot \theta \operatorname{cosec}^2 \theta - \cot 3\theta \operatorname{cosec}^2 3\theta$
$\qquad\qquad\qquad\qquad + \cot 5\theta \operatorname{cosec}^2 5\theta + \ldots n$ terms

(706) $\theta + \cos \theta \sin \theta + \dfrac{\cos^2 \theta}{2} \sin 2\theta + \dfrac{\cos^3 \theta}{3} \sin 3\theta + \ldots \infty$

(707) $\dfrac{\sin \theta}{\cos \theta} + \dfrac{1}{2} \dfrac{\sin 2\theta}{\cos^2 \theta} + \dfrac{1}{3} \dfrac{\sin 3\theta}{\cos^3 \theta} + \ldots \infty$

(708) $\operatorname{logh} \sin \theta + a \cot \theta - \dfrac{a^2}{2} \operatorname{cosec}^2 \theta + \dfrac{a^3}{3} \dfrac{\cos \theta}{\sin^3 \theta} - \ldots \infty$

(709) $\dfrac{1}{n} + \dfrac{2}{\pi} \displaystyle\sum_{m=1}^{\infty} \dfrac{1}{m} \tan \dfrac{m\pi}{n} \cos 2 m\pi\theta$

(710) $\dfrac{1}{3} + 4\pi^{-1} \displaystyle\sum_{m=1}^{\infty} m^{-1} \sin \dfrac{2}{3} m\pi \cos 2m\pi\theta$

$$= \frac{1}{8} \pi \theta$$

A. 391

$$= \frac{1}{6} \pi \theta^3$$

A. 391

$$= \frac{\pi}{2} - \theta \quad \text{where } 0 < \theta < \frac{\pi}{2}$$

E. 121

$$= \frac{\theta}{\sin \theta \cos \theta}$$

2Z. 246

$$= 2n^3$$

A. 223

$$= \frac{\pi}{2}$$

Y. 108

$$= \frac{\pi}{2}$$

L. 81

$$= \text{logh} \sin (\theta + a)$$

L. 71

$$= (-1)^s \quad \text{if } \theta \text{ is not a multiple of } \frac{1}{n}$$

$$= 0 \quad \text{if } \theta \text{ is a multiple integer of } \frac{1}{n}$$

Q. 191

$$\begin{cases} \theta \text{ is a real variable between 0 and 1} \\ n \text{ is an odd integer} \geqslant 3 \\ s \text{ is the greatest integer in } n\theta \end{cases}$$

$$= 1 \quad \text{when } 0 < \theta < \frac{1}{3} \text{ and } \frac{2}{3} < \theta < 1$$

$$= -1 \quad \text{when } \frac{1}{3} < \theta < \frac{2}{3}$$

Q. 191

Series No.

XV. Hyperbolic Summations

(711) $1 + \cosh\theta + \dfrac{\cosh 2\theta}{2!} + \dfrac{\cosh 3\theta}{3!} + \ldots \infty$

(712) $\sinh\theta + \dfrac{\sinh 2\theta}{2!} + \dfrac{\sinh 3\theta}{3!} + \ldots \infty$

(713) $1 - \dfrac{2}{3}\sinh^2\theta + \dfrac{2\cdot 4}{3\cdot 5}\sinh^4\theta - \ldots \infty$

(714) $1 + a\cosh\theta + a^2\cosh 2\theta + \ldots a^{n-1}\cosh(n-1)\theta$

(715) $a\sinh\theta + a^2\sinh 2\theta + \ldots \infty$

(716) $\sinh\theta - \dfrac{1}{2}\sinh 2\theta + \dfrac{1}{3}\sinh 3\theta - \ldots \infty$

(717) $\sinh^2\theta - 2^2\sinh^4\dfrac{\theta}{2} - 2^4\sinh^4\dfrac{\theta}{2^2} - 2^6\sinh^4\dfrac{\theta}{2^3} - \ldots \infty$

(718) $\tanh\theta + \dfrac{1}{3}\tanh^3\theta + \dfrac{1}{5}\tanh^5\theta + \ldots \infty$

(719) $\coth^2\theta - \displaystyle\sum_{1}^{n}\dfrac{1}{2^{2n}}\tanh^2\dfrac{\theta}{2^n}$

(720)† $\dfrac{1}{n}\displaystyle\sum_{r=0}^{r=\frac{n}{2}-1}\dfrac{\tanh\theta\,\dfrac{2}{n\sin^2\dfrac{2r+1}{2n}\pi}}{1 + \dfrac{\tanh^2\theta}{\tan^2\dfrac{2r+1}{2n}\pi}}$

† $\dfrac{\dfrac{2\tanh\theta}{n\sin^2 R\pi}}{1 + \dfrac{\tanh 2\theta}{\tan^2 R\pi}} = \dfrac{2\sinh 2\theta}{n\{\cosh 2\theta - \cos 2R\pi\}}$

$$= \epsilon^{\cosh \theta} \cosh (\sinh \theta)$$ E. 122

$$= \epsilon^{\cosh \theta} \sinh (\sinh \theta)$$ E. 122

$$= \frac{\theta}{\sinh \theta \cosh \theta}$$ A. 198

$$= \frac{1 - a \cosh \theta - a^n \cosh n\theta + a^{n+1} \cosh (n - 1)\theta}{1 - 2a \cosh \theta + a^2}$$ E. 117

$$= \frac{a \sinh \theta}{1 - 2a \cosh \theta + a^2}$$ E. 117

$$= \frac{\theta}{2}$$ E. 122

$$= \theta^2$$ C. 336

$$= \tan \theta - \frac{1}{3} \tan^3 \theta + \frac{1}{5} \tan^5 \theta - \dots \infty \quad \text{where } \theta \text{ is between } \pm \frac{\pi}{4}$$

E. 123

$$= \frac{1}{2^{2n}} \coth^2 \frac{\theta}{2^{2n}}$$ C. 315

$$= \tanh n\theta \quad \text{where } n \text{ is even}$$

Series No.

$(721)\dagger \quad \dfrac{1}{n}(\tanh\theta + \coth\theta) + \displaystyle\sum_{r=1}^{r=\frac{n}{2}-1} \dfrac{\tanh\theta \ \dfrac{2}{n\sin^2\dfrac{r\pi}{n}}}{1 + \dfrac{\tanh^2\theta}{\tan^2\dfrac{r\pi}{n}}}$

$(722)\dagger \quad \dfrac{\tanh\theta}{n} + \displaystyle\sum_{r=0}^{r=\frac{n-3}{2}} \dfrac{\tanh\theta \ \dfrac{2}{n\sin^2\dfrac{2r+1}{2n}\pi}}{1 + \dfrac{\tanh^2\theta}{\tan^2\dfrac{2r+1}{2n}\pi}}$

$(723)\dagger \quad \dfrac{\coth\theta}{n} + \displaystyle\sum_{r=1}^{r=\frac{n-1}{2}} \dfrac{\tanh\theta \ \dfrac{2}{n\sin^2\dfrac{r\pi}{n}}}{1 + \dfrac{\tanh^2\theta}{\tan^2\dfrac{r\pi}{n}}}$

$(724)\ddagger \quad \dfrac{1}{n} \displaystyle\sum_{r=0}^{r=\frac{n}{2}-1} \dfrac{1}{\dfrac{\sin^2\dfrac{2r+1}{2n}\pi}{\sinh\theta} + \dfrac{1}{2}\tanh\dfrac{\theta}{2}}$

$\dagger \quad \dfrac{\dfrac{2\tanh\theta}{n\sin^2 R\pi}}{1 + \dfrac{\tanh^2\theta}{\tan^2 R\pi}} = \dfrac{2\sinh 2\theta}{n\{\cosh 2\theta - \cos 2R\pi\}}$

$\ddagger \quad \dfrac{1}{\dfrac{\sin^2 R\pi}{\sinh\theta} + \dfrac{1}{2}\tanh\dfrac{\theta}{2}} = \dfrac{2\sinh\theta}{\cosh\theta - \cos 2R\pi}$

$= \coth n\theta$ where n is even

$= \tanh n\theta$ where n is odd

$= \coth n\theta$ where n is odd

$= \tanh \dfrac{n\theta}{2}$ where n is even

Series No.

(725)‡ $\dfrac{1}{n}\left\{2\coth\theta + \displaystyle\sum_{r=1}^{r=\frac{n}{2}-1}\dfrac{1}{\dfrac{\sin^2\dfrac{r\pi}{n}}{\sinh\theta}+\dfrac{1}{2}\tanh\dfrac{\theta}{2}}\right\}$

(726)‡ $\dfrac{1}{n}\left\{\tanh\dfrac{\theta}{2} + \displaystyle\sum_{r=0}^{r=\frac{n-3}{2}}\dfrac{1}{\dfrac{\sin^2\dfrac{2r+1}{2n}\pi}{\sinh\theta}+\dfrac{1}{2}\tanh\dfrac{\theta}{2}}\right\}$

(727)‡ $\dfrac{1}{n}\left\{\coth\dfrac{\theta}{2} + \displaystyle\sum_{r=1}^{r=\frac{n-1}{2}}\dfrac{1}{\dfrac{\sin^2\dfrac{r\pi}{n}}{\sinh\theta}+\dfrac{1}{2}\tanh\dfrac{\theta}{2}}\right\}$

(728) $\dfrac{1}{a} + 2a\displaystyle\sum_{1}^{\infty}\dfrac{\cos n\theta}{a^2+n^2}$

(729) $2\displaystyle\sum_{1}^{\infty}\dfrac{n\sin n\theta}{n^2+a^2}$

(730) $\dfrac{1}{a} + 2a\displaystyle\sum_{1}^{\infty}\dfrac{(-1)^n\cos n\theta}{a^2+n^2}$

(731) $2\displaystyle\sum_{1}^{\infty}\dfrac{(-1)^{n-1}n\sin n\theta}{n^2+a^2}$

XVI. Trigonometrical Expansions

(732) $1 - \dfrac{\theta^2}{2!} + \dfrac{\theta^4}{4!} - \ldots \infty = \displaystyle\sum_{1}^{\infty}(-1)^n\dfrac{\theta^{2n}}{(2n)!}$

(733) $\theta - \dfrac{\theta^3}{3!} + \dfrac{\theta^5}{5!} - \ldots \infty = \displaystyle\sum_{0}^{\infty}(-1)^n\dfrac{\theta^{2n+1}}{(2n+1)!}$

‡ $\dfrac{1}{\dfrac{\sin^2 R\pi}{\sinh\theta}+\dfrac{1}{2}\tanh\dfrac{\theta}{2}} = \dfrac{2\sinh\theta}{\cosh\theta-\cos 2R\pi}$

$$= \coth \frac{n\theta}{2} \quad \text{where } n \text{ is even}$$

$$= \tanh \frac{n\theta}{2} \quad \text{where } n \text{ is odd}$$

$$= \coth \frac{n\theta}{2} \quad \text{where } n \text{ is odd}$$

$$= \pi \frac{\cosh a(\pi - \theta)}{\sinh a\pi} \quad \text{where } 0 \leqslant \theta \leqslant 2\pi \qquad \text{A. 393}$$

$$= \pi \frac{\sinh (\pi - \theta)a}{\sinh a\pi} \quad \text{where } 0 < \theta < 2\pi \qquad \text{A. 393}$$

$$= \pi \frac{\cosh a\theta}{\sinh a\pi} \quad \text{where } -\pi \leqslant \theta \leqslant \pi \qquad \text{A. 368}$$

$$= \pi \frac{\sinh a\theta}{\sinh a\theta} \quad \text{where } -\pi < \theta < \pi \qquad \text{A. 368}$$

$$= \cos \theta \quad \text{where } \theta < \infty$$

$$= \sin \theta \quad \text{where } \theta < \infty$$

Series No.

(734) $\theta - \dfrac{\theta^3}{3} + \dfrac{\theta^5}{5} - \ldots \infty = \displaystyle\sum_0^\infty (-1)^n \dfrac{\theta^{2n+1}}{2n+1}$

In the following series Nos. (735) through (763), see No. (1130) for values of the coefficients.

(735) $1 - B_1 \dfrac{\theta^2}{2!} - B_2 \dfrac{\theta^4}{4!} - \ldots \infty = 1 - \displaystyle\sum_1^\infty B_n \dfrac{\theta^{2n}}{(2n)!}$

(736) $\alpha_1 \dfrac{\theta}{2!} + \alpha_2 \dfrac{\theta^3}{4!} + \ldots \infty = \displaystyle\sum_1^\infty \alpha^n \dfrac{\theta^{2n-1}}{(2n)!}$

(737) $1 + \beta_1 \dfrac{\theta^2}{2!} + \beta_2 \dfrac{\theta^4}{4!} + \ldots \infty = 1 + \displaystyle\sum_1^\infty \beta_n \dfrac{\theta^{2n}}{(2n)!}$

(738) $1 + E_2 \dfrac{\theta^2}{2!} + E_4 \dfrac{\theta^4}{4!} + \ldots \infty = 1 + \displaystyle\sum_1^\infty E_{2n} \dfrac{\theta^{2n}}{(2n)!}$

(739) $2 + \delta_1 \dfrac{\theta^2}{2!} + \delta_2 \dfrac{\theta^4}{4!} + \ldots \infty = 2 + \displaystyle\sum_1^\infty \delta_n \dfrac{\theta^{2n}}{(2n)!}$

(740) $\zeta_1 \dfrac{\theta}{2!} + \zeta_2 \dfrac{\theta^3}{4!} + \zeta_3 \dfrac{\theta^5}{6!} + \ldots \infty = \displaystyle\sum_1^\infty \zeta_n \dfrac{\theta^{2n-1}}{(2n)!}$

(741) $I_0 + I_1 \dfrac{\theta^2}{2!} + I_2 \dfrac{\theta^4}{4!} + \ldots \infty = I_0 + \displaystyle\sum_1^\infty I_n \dfrac{\theta^{2n}}{(2n)!}$

(742) $H_0 + H_1 \dfrac{\theta^2}{2!} + H_2 \dfrac{\theta^4}{4!} + \ldots \infty = H_0 + \displaystyle\sum_1^\infty H_n \dfrac{\theta^{2n}}{(2n)!}$

(743) $\gamma_1 \dfrac{\theta}{2!} + \gamma_2 \dfrac{\theta^3}{4!} + \gamma_3 \dfrac{\theta^5}{6!} + \ldots \infty = \displaystyle\sum_1^\infty \gamma_n \dfrac{\theta^{2n-1}}{(2n)!}$

$= \tan^{-1} \theta$ where $\theta^2 \leqslant 1$ E. 107

$= \dfrac{\theta}{2} \cot \dfrac{\theta}{2}$ AC. 41

$= \tan \dfrac{\theta}{2}$ AC. 41

$= \theta \operatorname{cosec} \theta$ AC. 41

$= \sec \theta$ AC. 41

$= \dfrac{3\theta \cos \dfrac{\theta}{2}}{\sin \dfrac{3}{2} \theta}$ AC. 41

$= \dfrac{\sin \dfrac{\theta}{2}}{\cos \dfrac{3\theta}{2}}$ AC. 41

$= \dfrac{3 \sin \dfrac{\theta}{2}}{2 \sin \dfrac{3\theta}{2}}$ AC. 41

$= \dfrac{3 \cos \dfrac{\theta}{2}}{2 \cos \dfrac{3\theta}{2}}$ AC. 41

$= \dfrac{3 \sin \dfrac{\theta}{2} \sin \theta}{2 \sin \dfrac{3\theta}{2}}$ AC. 41

Series No.

(744) $\theta_1 \dfrac{\theta}{2!} + \theta_2 \dfrac{\theta^3}{4!} + \theta_3 \dfrac{\theta^5}{6!} + \dots \infty = \displaystyle\sum_1^\infty \theta_n \dfrac{\theta^{2n-1}}{(2n)!}$

(745) $1 - \epsilon_1 \dfrac{\theta^2}{2!} - \epsilon_2 \dfrac{\theta^4}{4!} - \dots \infty = 1 - \displaystyle\sum_1^\infty \epsilon_n \dfrac{\theta^{2n}}{(2n)!}$

(746) $T_1\theta + T_2 \dfrac{\theta^3}{3!} + T_3 \dfrac{\theta^5}{5!} + \dots \infty = \displaystyle\sum_1^\infty T_n \dfrac{\theta^{2n-1}}{(2n-1)!}$

(747) $J_0 + J_1 \dfrac{\theta^2}{2!} + J_2 \dfrac{\theta^4}{4!} + \dots \infty = J_0 + \displaystyle\sum_1^\infty J_n \dfrac{\theta^{2n}}{(2n)!}$

(748) $S_0 + S_1 \dfrac{\theta^2}{2!} + S_2 \dfrac{\theta^4}{4!} + \dots \infty = S_0 + \displaystyle\sum_1^\infty S_n \dfrac{\theta^{2n}}{(2n)!}$

(749) $\eta_1 \dfrac{\theta}{2!} + \eta_2 \dfrac{\theta^3}{4!} + \eta_3 \dfrac{\theta^5}{6!} + \dots \infty = \displaystyle\sum_1^\infty \eta_n \dfrac{\theta^{2n-1}}{(2n)!}$

(750) $R_0 + R_1 \dfrac{\theta^2}{2!} + R_2 \dfrac{\theta^4}{4!} + \dots \infty = R_0 + \displaystyle\sum_1^\infty R_n \dfrac{\theta^{2n}}{(2n)!}$

(751) $P_0 + P_1 \dfrac{\theta^2}{2!} + P_2 \dfrac{\theta^4}{4!} + \dots \infty = P_0 + \displaystyle\sum_1^\infty P_n \dfrac{\theta^{2n}}{(2n)!}$

(752) $Q_1\theta + Q_2 \dfrac{\theta^3}{2!} + Q_3 \dfrac{\theta^5}{4!} + \dots \infty = \displaystyle\sum_1^\infty Q_n \dfrac{\theta^{2n-1}}{(2n-2)!}$

(753) $1 + E_1\theta + E_2 \dfrac{\theta^2}{2!} + E_3 \dfrac{\theta^3}{3!} + \dots \infty$

(754) $\theta + E_2 \dfrac{\theta^3}{3!} + E_4 \dfrac{\theta^5}{5!} + \dots \infty$

(755) $\text{logh } \theta + \displaystyle\sum_1^\infty \dfrac{(2^{2n-1} - 1)2^{2n}}{n \cdot (2n)!} B_n \theta^{2n}$

(756) $B_1\theta^2 + B_2 \dfrac{2^3}{2 \cdot 4!} \theta^4 + B_3 \dfrac{2^5}{3 \cdot 6!} \theta^6 + \dots \infty$

$$= \frac{\sin \theta \cos \dfrac{\theta}{2}}{2 \cos \dfrac{3\theta}{2}}$$

AC. 41

$$= \frac{3\theta \cos 2\theta}{\sin 3\theta}$$

AC. 41

$$= \frac{\sin 2\theta}{2 \cos 3\theta}$$

AC. 41

$$= \frac{3 \sin 2\theta}{\sin 3\theta}$$

AC. 41

$$= \frac{\cos 2\theta}{\cos 3\theta}$$

AC. 41

$$= \frac{3 \sin^2 \theta}{2 \sin 3\theta}$$

AC. 41

$$= \frac{\cos^2 \theta}{\cos 3\theta}$$

AC. 41

$$= \frac{\cos \theta}{\cos 2\theta}$$

AC. 41

$$= \frac{\sin \theta}{\cos 2\theta}$$

AC. 41

$$= \sec \theta + \tan \theta$$

Y. 500

$$= \text{logh} (\sec \theta + \tan \theta) = gd^{-1}\theta$$

Y. 500

$$= \text{logh} \tan \theta \quad \text{where } \theta^2 < \frac{\pi^2}{4}$$

T. 123

$$= - \text{logh} \frac{\sin \theta}{\theta}$$

B. 245

(757) $\displaystyle\sum_1^\infty \log h\left\{1 - \frac{4\theta^2}{(2n-1)^2\pi^2}\right\} = -\sum_1^\infty \frac{2^{2n-1}(2^n-1)}{n(2n)!}\,B_n\theta^{2n}$

(758) $\displaystyle\log h\,\theta + \sum_1^\infty \log h\left\{1 - \frac{\theta^2}{n^2\pi^2}\right\} = \log h\,\theta - \sum_1^\infty \frac{2^{2n-1}}{n(2n)!}\,B_n\theta^{2n}$

(759) $\displaystyle\frac{B_1}{2}\cdot\frac{\theta^2}{2!} + \frac{B_2}{4}\cdot\frac{\theta^4}{4!} + \frac{B_3}{6}\cdot\frac{\theta^6}{6!} + \dots \infty$

(760) $\displaystyle -\sum_1^\infty 2^{n+1}\cos\frac{n\pi}{2}\,\frac{B_n}{2!}\,\frac{\theta^{2n}}{(2n)!}$

(761) $\displaystyle\frac{1}{\theta} + \frac{\theta}{3!} + \frac{7}{3\cdot 5!}\,\theta^3 + \dots \infty$

$$= \frac{1}{\theta} + \sum_0^\infty \frac{2(2^{2n+1}-1)}{(2n+2)!}\,B_{n+1}\theta^{2n+1}$$

(762) $\displaystyle\frac{1}{\theta} - \frac{\theta}{3} - \frac{\theta^3}{45} - \dots \infty = \frac{1}{\theta} - \sum_1^\infty \frac{2^{2n}}{(2n)!}\,B_n\theta^{2n-1}$

(763) $\displaystyle\theta + \frac{\theta^3}{3} + \frac{2\theta^5}{15} + \dots \infty = \sum_1^\infty \frac{2^{2n}(2^{2n}-1)}{(2n)!}\,B_n\theta^{2n-1}$

(764) $\displaystyle\sum_0^\infty \frac{8\theta}{(2n+1)^2\pi^2 - 4\theta^2}\,\theta$

(765) $\displaystyle\frac{2}{\pi - 2\theta} - \frac{2}{\pi + 2\theta} + \frac{2}{3\pi - 2\theta} - \frac{2}{3\pi + 2\theta} + \dots \infty$

(766) $\displaystyle 2\sum_1^\infty \frac{\theta}{\left(\dfrac{2n-1}{2}\right)^2\pi^2 - \theta^2}$

(767) $\displaystyle\frac{1}{\theta} + \frac{1}{\theta - \pi} + \frac{1}{\theta + \pi} + \frac{1}{\theta - 2\pi} + \frac{1}{\theta + 2\pi} + \dots \infty$

$$= \frac{1}{\theta} - \sum_1^\infty \frac{2\theta}{n^2\pi^2 - \theta^2}$$

(768) $\displaystyle\frac{4}{\pi - 2\theta} - \frac{4}{3\pi + 2\theta} + \frac{4}{5\pi - 2\theta} - \frac{4}{7\pi + 2\theta} + \dots \infty$

$= \text{logh} \cos \theta \quad$ where $\theta^2 < \dfrac{\pi^2}{4}$ 　　　　　　　B. 237

$= \text{logh} \sin \theta \quad$ where $\theta^2 < \pi^2$ 　　　　　　　B. 237

$= \text{logh} \dfrac{\theta}{2 \sin \dfrac{\theta}{2}}$ 　　　　　　　A. 315

$= \text{logh} \dfrac{\cosh \theta - \cos \theta}{\theta^2}$ 　　　　　　　A. 315

$= \text{cosec } \theta \quad$ where $\theta^2 < \pi^2$ 　　　　　　　T. 121

$= \cot \theta \quad$ where $\theta^2 < \pi^2$ 　　　　　　　T. 121

$= \tan \theta \quad$ where $\theta^2 < \dfrac{\pi^2}{4}$ 　　　　　　　T. 121

$= \tan \theta \quad$ where $\theta \neq n\pi$ 　　　　　　　A. 296

$= \tan \theta \quad$ where $\theta \neq \dfrac{(2n + 1)\pi}{2}$ 　　　　　　　C. 360

$= \tan \theta$ 　　　　　　　B. 237

$= \cot \theta \quad$ where $\theta \neq n\pi$ 　　　　　　　C. 360

$= \sec \theta + \tan \theta \quad$ where $\dfrac{\pi}{2} > \theta > -\dfrac{\pi}{2}$ 　　　　　　　Y. 501

Series No.

(769) $\dfrac{1}{\theta} + \dfrac{1}{\pi - \theta} - \dfrac{1}{\pi + \theta} - \dfrac{1}{2\pi - \theta} + \dfrac{1}{2\pi + \theta} + \ldots \infty$

$$= \dfrac{1}{\theta} + 2\theta \sum_{1}^{\infty} \dfrac{(-1)^{n-1}}{n^2\pi^2 - \theta^2}$$

(770) $\dfrac{2}{\pi - 2\theta} + \dfrac{2}{\pi + 2\theta} - \dfrac{2}{3\pi - 2\theta} - \dfrac{2}{3\pi + 2\theta} - \ldots \infty$

$$= \sum_{1}^{\infty} (-1)^{n-1} \dfrac{(2n - 1)\pi}{\left(\dfrac{2n - 1}{2}\right)^2 \pi^2 - \theta^2}$$

(771) $\dfrac{1}{\pi - 4\theta^2} - \dfrac{3}{3^2\pi^2 - 4\theta^2} + \dfrac{5}{5^2\pi^2 - 4\theta^2} - \ldots \infty$

(772) $\dfrac{1}{\theta^2} - \dfrac{1}{\theta^2 - \pi^2} + \dfrac{1}{\theta^2 - 2^2\pi^2} - \ldots \infty$

(773) $\dfrac{1}{(\pi - 2\theta)^2} + \dfrac{1}{(\pi + 2\theta)^2} + \dfrac{1}{(3\pi - 2\theta)^2} + \dfrac{1}{(3\pi + 2\theta)^2} + \ldots \infty$

(774) $1 + 2\theta + 2\theta^2 + \dfrac{8\theta^3}{3} + \dfrac{10\theta^4}{3} + \ldots \infty$

(775) $\theta + \dfrac{1}{2} \cdot \dfrac{\theta^3}{3} + \dfrac{1 \cdot 3}{2 \cdot 4} \cdot \dfrac{\theta^5}{5} + \ldots \infty = \sum_{0}^{\infty} \dfrac{(2n)!}{2^{2n}(n!)^2(2n + 1)} \theta^{2n+1}$

(776) $1 + \dfrac{\theta^2}{3!} + \dfrac{14\theta^4}{6!} + \ldots \infty$

(777) $1 - \theta^2 + \dfrac{2^3\theta^4}{4!} - \dfrac{2^5\theta^6}{6!} + \ldots \infty$

(778) $\theta^2 + \dfrac{2}{3} \cdot \dfrac{\theta^4}{2} + \dfrac{2 \cdot 4}{3 \cdot 5} \cdot \dfrac{\theta^6}{3} + \ldots \infty = \sum_{0}^{\infty} \dfrac{2^{2n}(n!)^2}{(2n + 1)!(n + 1)} \theta^{2n+2}$

(779) $1 + \dfrac{1}{3 \cdot 4} \theta + \dfrac{1 \cdot 3}{5 \cdot 4^2} \dfrac{\theta^2}{2!} + \ldots \infty$

$$= 1 + \sum_{1}^{\infty} \dfrac{1 \cdot 3 \ldots (2n - 1)}{(2n + 1)4^n} \cdot \dfrac{\theta^n}{n!}$$

(780) $\theta + \dfrac{1}{3} \cdot \dfrac{\theta^2}{2} + \dfrac{1 \cdot 2}{3 \cdot 5} \dfrac{\theta^3}{3} + \ldots \infty = \theta + \sum_{2}^{\infty} \dfrac{(n - 1)!}{3 \cdot 5 \ldots 2n - 1} \dfrac{\theta^n}{n}$

$= \operatorname{cosec} \theta$ where $\theta \neq n\pi$ C. 361

$= \sec \theta$ where $\theta \neq \dfrac{2n \pm 1}{2} \pi$ C. 361

$= \dfrac{\sec \theta}{4\pi}$ E. 158

$= \dfrac{1 + \theta \operatorname{cosec} \theta}{2\theta^2}$ E. 158

$= \dfrac{\sec^2 \theta}{4}$ E. 159

$= \tan\left\{\dfrac{\pi}{4} + \theta\right\}$ H. 498

$= \sin^{-1} \theta = \dfrac{\pi}{2} - \cos^{-1} \theta$ where $\theta^2 \leqslant 1$ T. 121

$= \dfrac{\theta}{\sin \theta}$ H. 498

$= \cos^2 \theta$ H. 498

$= (\sin^{-1} \theta)^2$ where $|\theta^2| < |$ T. 122

$= \dfrac{\operatorname{vers}^{-1} \theta}{\sqrt{2\theta}}$ Y. 505

$= \dfrac{(\operatorname{vers}^{-1} \theta)^2}{2}$ Y. 505

Series No.

(781) $\dfrac{\theta^5}{1\cdot3\cdot5} - \dfrac{\theta^7}{3\cdot5\cdot7} + \dfrac{\theta^9}{5\cdot7\cdot9} - \ldots \infty$

(782) $\theta^2 - \dfrac{\theta^4}{3} + \dfrac{2\theta^6}{45} - \ldots \infty$

(783) $\theta + \dfrac{2^2}{3!}\theta^3 + \dfrac{2^2\cdot4^2}{5!}\theta^5 + \dfrac{2^2\cdot4^2\cdot6^2}{7!}\theta^7 + \ldots \infty$

(784) $\theta - \dfrac{\theta^3}{3} - \dfrac{2}{3}\cdot\dfrac{\theta^5}{5} - \dfrac{2\cdot4}{3\cdot5}\dfrac{\theta^7}{7} - \ldots \infty$

(785) $\dfrac{\theta^3}{1\cdot3} - \dfrac{\theta^5}{3\cdot5} + \dfrac{\theta^7}{5\cdot7} - \ldots \infty$

(786) $1 + \theta - \dfrac{2\theta^3}{3!} - \dfrac{2^2\theta^4}{4!} - \dfrac{2^2\theta^5}{5!} + \dfrac{2^3\theta^7}{7!} - \ldots \infty$

(787) $\theta + \theta^2 + \dfrac{2\theta^3}{3!} - \dfrac{2^2\theta^5}{5!} - \dfrac{2^3\theta^6}{6!} - \dfrac{2^3\theta^7}{7!} - \ldots \infty$

(788) $\dfrac{\theta^2}{3} + \dfrac{7\theta^4}{90} + \dfrac{17\,\theta^6}{30} + \ldots \infty$

(789) $2\theta + \dfrac{4}{3}\theta^3 + \dfrac{4}{3}\theta^5 + \ldots \infty$

(790) $\theta - \dfrac{\theta^2}{2} + \dfrac{\theta^3}{6} - \dfrac{\theta^4}{12} + \dfrac{\theta^5}{24} - \ldots \infty$

(791) $-\dfrac{\theta^2}{3} + \dfrac{13}{90}\theta^4 - \dfrac{251}{5\cdot7\cdot9^2}\theta^6 + \ldots \infty$

(793) † $\theta^2 - \dfrac{2}{3}\theta^4 + \dfrac{61}{120}\theta^6 - \ldots \infty$

(794) $-\dfrac{\theta^2}{3} - \dfrac{7}{90}\theta^4 - \dfrac{62}{2835}\theta^6 - \ldots \infty$

(795) $\theta - \dfrac{\theta^2}{2} + \dfrac{2\theta^3}{3} - \ldots \infty$

(796) $\dfrac{\theta^2}{2} + \dfrac{\theta^4}{12} + \dfrac{\theta^6}{45} + \ldots \infty$

† No. (792) has been omitted because it duplicates a previous series.—Ed.

$$= \frac{(\theta^2 + 1)^2}{8} \tan^{-1} \theta - \frac{5\theta^3 + 3\theta}{24}$$ 1Z. 135

$$= \sin^2 \theta$$ D. 336

$$= \frac{\sin^{-1} \theta}{\sqrt{1 - \theta^2}} \text{ where } |\theta| < 1$$ L. 78

$$= \sqrt{1 - \theta^2} \sin^{-1} \theta$$ A. 191

$$= \frac{1}{2} (1 + \theta^2) \tan^{-1} \theta - \frac{1}{2} \theta$$ H. 475

$$= \epsilon^\theta \cos \theta$$ H. 497

$$= \epsilon^\theta \sin \theta$$ H. 497

$$= \text{logh} \frac{\tan \theta}{\theta}$$ L. 80

$$= \text{logh} \tan \left\{ \frac{\pi}{4} + \theta \right\}$$ H. 498

$$= \text{logh} (1 + \sin \theta)$$ H. 498

$$= \text{logh} \frac{\tan^{-1} \theta}{\theta}$$ Y. 80

$$= \text{logh} (1 + \theta \sin \theta)$$ Y. 106

$$= \text{logh} \theta \cot \theta$$ Y. 80

$$= \text{logh} (1 + \tan \theta)$$ L. 79

$$= \text{logh} \sec \theta$$ H. 497

Series No.

(797) $1 + \theta + \dfrac{\theta^2}{2} - \dfrac{\theta^4}{8} - \dfrac{\theta^5}{15} + \dfrac{\theta^6}{240} - \dots \ \infty$

(798) $\epsilon \left\{ 1 - \dfrac{\theta^2}{2!} + \dfrac{4\theta^4}{4!} - \dfrac{31\theta^6}{6!} + \dots \ \infty \right\}$

(799) $1 + \theta^2 + \dfrac{1}{3}\theta^4 + \dfrac{1}{120}\theta^6 + \dots \ \infty$

(800) $-\dfrac{\theta^2}{2!} - \dfrac{2\theta^4}{4!} - \dfrac{16\theta^6}{6!} - \dfrac{2720\theta^8}{8!} - \dots \ \infty$

(801) $1 + \theta + \dfrac{\theta^2}{2!} + \dfrac{2\theta^3}{3!} + \dfrac{5\theta^4}{4!} + \dots \ \infty$

(802) $1 + \theta + \dfrac{\theta^2}{2} - \dfrac{\theta^3}{3} - \dfrac{11\theta^4}{24} - \dfrac{\theta^5}{5} - \dots \ \infty$

(803) $1 + \dfrac{\theta^3}{3!} + \dfrac{\theta^6}{6!} + \dfrac{\theta^9}{9!} + \dots \ \infty$

(804) $\theta + \dfrac{\theta^4}{4!} + \dfrac{\theta^7}{7!} + \dfrac{\theta^{10}}{10!} + \dots \ \infty$

(805) $\dfrac{\pi}{2} - \dfrac{1}{\theta} + \dfrac{1}{3\theta^3} - \dfrac{1}{5\theta^5} + \dfrac{1}{7\theta^7} - \dots \ \infty$

$$= \dfrac{\pi}{2} - \sum_0^\infty (-1)^n \dfrac{1}{(2n+1)\theta^{2n+1}}$$

(806) $\dfrac{\pi}{2} - \dfrac{1}{\theta} - \dfrac{1}{2\cdot3}\dfrac{1}{\theta^3} - \dots \ \infty = \dfrac{\pi}{2} - \sum_0^\infty \dfrac{(2n)!}{2^{2n}(n!)^2(2n+1)}\theta^{-2n-1}$

(807) $1 + \theta + \dfrac{\theta^2}{2!} + \dfrac{3\theta^3}{3!} + \dfrac{9\theta^4}{4!} + \dfrac{37\theta^5}{5!} + \dots \ \infty$

(808) $1 + \theta + \dfrac{\theta^2}{2} - \dfrac{\theta^3}{6} + \dfrac{7\theta^4}{24} - \dots \ \infty$

(809) $1 + \theta + \dfrac{\theta^2}{2} + \dfrac{2\theta^3}{3} + \dots \ \infty$

(810) $\dfrac{2\theta}{1^2 - \theta^2} + \dfrac{2\theta}{3^2 - \theta^2} + \dfrac{2\theta}{5^2 - \theta^2} + \dots \ \infty$

$= \epsilon^{\sin \theta}$ L. 73

$= \epsilon^{\cos \theta}$ T. 126

$= \epsilon^{\theta} \sin \theta$ Y. 80

$= \text{logh} \cos \theta$ Y. 107

$= \epsilon^{\sin^{-1} \theta}$ T. 126

$= \epsilon^{\theta} \cos \theta$ L. 79

$= \dfrac{1}{3} \left\{ \epsilon^{\theta} + 2\epsilon^{-\theta/2} \cos \dfrac{\theta\sqrt{3}}{2} \right\}$ E. 190

$= \dfrac{1}{3} \epsilon^{\theta} - \dfrac{1}{3} \epsilon^{-\theta/2} \left\{ \cos \dfrac{\theta\sqrt{3}}{2} - \sqrt{3} \sin \dfrac{\theta\sqrt{3}}{2} \right\}$ E. 190

$= \tan^{-1} \theta \quad \text{where } \theta^2 \geqslant 1$ T. 122

$= \sec^{-1} \theta = \dfrac{\pi}{2} - \text{cosec}^{-1} \theta \quad \text{where } \theta > 1$ T. 122

$= \epsilon^{\tan \theta}$ T. 126

$= \epsilon^{\tan^{-1} \theta}$ T. 126

$= \epsilon^{\theta} \sec \theta$ Y. 107

$= \dfrac{\pi}{2} \tan \left\{ \dfrac{\pi\theta}{2} \right\}$ A. 225

Series No.

(811) $\tan^{-1}\theta + \dfrac{h}{1 + \theta^2} - \dfrac{\theta h^2}{(1 + \theta^2)^2} - \dfrac{(1 - 3\theta^2)h^3}{3(1 + \theta^2)^3} + \ldots \infty$

(812) $\sin^{-1}\theta + \dfrac{h}{\sqrt{1 - \theta^2}} + \dfrac{\theta}{(1 - \theta^2)^{3/2}}\dfrac{h^2}{2!}$

$$+ \dfrac{1 + 2\theta^2}{(1 - \theta^2)^{5/2}}\cdot\dfrac{h^3}{3!} + \ldots \infty$$

(813) $\sec^{-1}\theta + \dfrac{h}{\theta\sqrt{\theta^2 - 1}} - \dfrac{2\theta^2 - 1}{\theta^2(\theta^2 - 1)^{3/2}}\cdot\dfrac{h^2}{2!} + \ldots \infty$

(814) $\dfrac{\theta}{1 + \theta^2}\displaystyle\sum_0^\infty \dfrac{2^{2n}(n!)^2}{(2n + 1)!}\left(\dfrac{\theta^2}{1 + \theta^2}\right)^n$

(815) $\dfrac{1}{\theta} + \displaystyle\sum_{-\infty}^{+\infty}\dfrac{\theta}{n(\theta - n)} = \dfrac{1}{\theta} + \sum_1^\infty\dfrac{2\theta}{\theta^2 - n^2}$

(816) $\dfrac{1}{n^2 - 1} - \dfrac{1}{3^3 n^2 - 3} + \dfrac{1}{5^3 n^2 - 5} - \dfrac{1}{7^3 n^2 - 7} + \ldots \infty$

(817) $1 - \dfrac{n^2}{1^2} + \dfrac{n^2(n^2 - 1)}{1^2\cdot 2^2} - \dfrac{n^2(n^2 - 1^2)(n^2 - 2^2)}{1^2\cdot 2^2\cdot 3^2} + \ldots \infty$

(818) $\left(1 + \dfrac{1}{1}\right) - \dfrac{\theta^2}{2!}\left(1 - \dfrac{1}{3}\right) + \dfrac{\theta^4}{4!}\left(1 + \dfrac{1}{5}\right) - \dfrac{\theta^6}{6!}\left(1 - \dfrac{1}{7}\right) + \ldots \infty$

(819) $\dfrac{1}{4}\left[(1 + 3) - (3^2 + 3)\dfrac{\theta^2}{2} + \ldots\right.$

$$\left. + (-1)^n\{3^{2n} + 3\}\dfrac{\theta^{2n}}{(2n)!} + \ldots \infty\right]$$

(820) $\dfrac{\theta^2}{2} - \left(1 + \dfrac{1}{3}\right)\dfrac{\theta^4}{4} + \left(1 + \dfrac{1}{3} + \dfrac{1}{5}\right)\dfrac{\theta^6}{6} - \ldots \infty$

(821) $\dfrac{1}{2}\cdot\dfrac{\theta^3}{3} - \left\{\dfrac{1}{2} + \dfrac{1}{4}\left(1 + \dfrac{1}{3}\right)\right\}\dfrac{\theta^5}{5}$

$$+ \left\{\dfrac{1}{2} + \dfrac{1}{4}\left(1 + \dfrac{1}{3}\right) + \dfrac{1}{6}\left(1 + \dfrac{1}{3} + \dfrac{1}{5}\right)\right\}\dfrac{\theta^7}{7} - \ldots \infty$$

(822) $\displaystyle\sum_{-\infty}^{+\infty}\dfrac{1}{(\theta - n)^2} = \dfrac{1}{\theta^2} + 2\sum_1^\infty\dfrac{\theta^2 + n^2}{(\theta^2 - n^2)^2}$

Reference

$= \tan^{-1}(\theta + h)$ L. 71

$= \sin^{-1}(\theta + h)$ L. 71

$= \sec^{-1}(\theta + h)$ L. 71

$= \tan^{-1}\theta$ where $\theta^2 < \infty$ T. 122

$= \pi \cot \pi\theta$ $(n = 0$ excluded$)$ A. 217

$= \dfrac{\pi}{4}\left(\sec \dfrac{\pi}{2n} - 1\right)$ A. 225

$= \dfrac{\sin n\pi}{n\pi}$ C. 421

$= \cos\theta + \dfrac{\sinh\theta}{\theta}$ A. 389

$= \cos^3\theta$ Y. 79

$= \dfrac{1}{2}(\tan^{-1}\theta)^2$ where $|x| < 1$ A. 191

$= \dfrac{(\tan^{-1}\theta)^3}{3!}$ Y. 89

$= \pi^2 \operatorname{cosec}^2 \pi\theta$ A. 218

Series No.

(823) $\displaystyle\sum_{-\infty}^{+\infty} \frac{1}{(\theta - n)^3} = \frac{1}{\theta^3} + 2\sum_{1}^{\infty} \frac{\theta(\theta^2 + 3n^2)}{(\theta^2 - n^2)^3}$

(824) $\displaystyle\sum_{-\infty}^{+\infty} \frac{1}{(\theta - n)^4} = \frac{1}{\theta^4} + 2\sum_{1}^{\infty} \frac{\theta^4 + 6\theta^2 n^2 + n^4}{(\theta^2 - n^2)^4}$

(825) $\displaystyle\frac{1^4 - (1^2 - \theta^2)^2}{(1^2 - \theta^2)^2} + \frac{3^4 - (3^2 - \theta^2)^2}{(1^2 - \theta^2)^2(3^2 - \theta^2)^2} + \ldots \infty$

(826) $\displaystyle\frac{1}{\theta^2} + \frac{1}{3} + \frac{1}{15}\theta^2 + \frac{2}{189}\theta^4 + \ldots \infty$

(827) $\displaystyle\sum_{-\infty}^{+\infty} \frac{a - \theta}{(\theta - n)(a - n)}$

(828) $\displaystyle 1 - \frac{n\theta^2}{3!} + \frac{n(5n - 2)}{3\cdot 5!}\theta^4 + \ldots \infty$

(829) $\displaystyle\frac{1}{4}\left\{(3^3 - 3)\frac{\theta^3}{3!} + \ldots (-1)^n \frac{3^{2n-1} - 3}{(2n - 1)!}\theta^{2n-1} - \ldots \infty\right\}$

(830) $\displaystyle\frac{1}{\theta} + \frac{1}{\theta - 2} + \frac{1}{\theta + 2} + \frac{1}{\theta - 4} + \frac{1}{\theta + 4} + \ldots \infty$

(831) $\displaystyle -\left(\frac{1}{\theta - 1} + \frac{1}{\theta + 1}\right) - \left(\frac{1}{\theta - 3} + \frac{1}{\theta + 3}\right) - \ldots \infty$

(832) $\displaystyle\frac{1}{2}\frac{\theta^3}{3} + \left(\frac{1}{1^2} + \frac{1}{3^2}\right)\frac{1\cdot 3}{2\cdot 4}\frac{\theta^5}{5} + \frac{1\cdot 3\cdot 5}{2\cdot 4\cdot 6}\left(\frac{1}{1^2} + \frac{1}{3^2} + \frac{1}{5^2}\right)\frac{\theta^7}{7} + \ldots \infty$

(833) $\displaystyle 1 + a\theta + \frac{(a^2 + 1^2)\theta^2}{2!} + \frac{a(a^2 + 2^2)\theta^3}{3!} + \ldots \infty$

(834) $\displaystyle\theta + \frac{2}{3}\theta^3 + \frac{2\cdot 4}{3\cdot 5}\theta^5 + \ldots \infty$

(835) $\displaystyle\frac{mn}{m^2 + n^2}\left\{1 + \frac{2}{3}\cdot\frac{m^2}{m^2 + n^2} + \frac{2\cdot 4}{3\cdot 5}\left(\frac{m^2}{m^2 + n^2}\right)^2 + \ldots \infty\right\}$

$= \pi^3 \cot \pi\theta \, \text{cosec}^2 \, \pi\theta$ A. 225

$= \pi^4 \left\{ \text{cosec}^4 \, \pi\theta - \dfrac{2}{3} \, \text{cosec}^2 \, \pi\theta \right\}$ A. 225

$= \tan^2 \dfrac{\pi\theta}{2}$ C. 421

$= \text{cosec}^2 \, \theta$ A. 222

$= \pi \left(\cot \pi\theta - \cot \pi a \right)$ A. 225

$= \left(\dfrac{\sin \theta}{\theta} \right)^n$ H. 498

$= \sin^3 \theta$ Y. 79

$= \dfrac{\pi}{2} \cot \dfrac{\pi\theta}{2}$ A. 225

$= \dfrac{\pi}{2} \tan \dfrac{\pi\theta}{2}$ A. 225

$= \dfrac{1}{6} (\sin^{-1} \theta)^3 \quad \text{where} - \dfrac{\pi}{2} < \theta < \dfrac{\pi}{2}$ A. 223

$= \dfrac{\epsilon^{a \sin^{-1} \theta}}{\sqrt{1 - \theta^2}}$ L. 79

$= \dfrac{1}{\sqrt{1 - \theta^2}} \sin^{-1} \theta \quad \text{where} \, |\theta| < 1$ A. 197

$= \tan^{-1} \dfrac{m}{n}$ A. 196

Series No.

(836) $\theta(1 + \theta^2) - \dfrac{4}{1} \cdot \dfrac{\theta^3(1 + \theta^2)^3}{3} + \dfrac{6 \cdot 7}{1 \cdot 2} \dfrac{\theta^5(1 + \theta^2)^5}{5}$

$$- \dfrac{8 \cdot 9 \cdot 10}{1 \cdot 2 \cdot 3} \cdot \dfrac{\theta^7(1 + \theta^2)^7}{7} + \ldots \infty$$

(837) $1 - \dfrac{n(n - 1)}{2!} + \dfrac{n(n - 1)(n - 2)(n - 3)}{4!} - \ldots \infty$

(838) $(2^2 - 1) \dfrac{2}{2!} B_1 \theta^2 + \dfrac{1}{2} (2^4 - 1) \dfrac{2^3}{4!} B_2 \theta^4$

$$+ \dfrac{1}{3} (2^6 - 1) \dfrac{2^5}{6!} B_3 \theta^6 + \ldots \infty$$

(839) $1 + a\theta + \dfrac{a^2\theta^2}{2!} + \dfrac{a(a^2 + 1)}{3!} \theta^3$

$$+ \dfrac{a^2(a^2 + 2^2)}{4!} \theta^4 + \dfrac{a(a^2 + 1)(a^2 + 3^2)}{5!} \theta^5 + \ldots \infty$$

(840) $\displaystyle\sum_{n=1}^{\infty} \dfrac{1}{(1 - n^2 m^2)^2}$

(841) $m\theta - \dfrac{m(m - 1)(m - 2)}{3!} \theta^3$

$$+ \dfrac{m(m - 1)(m - 2)(m - 3)(m - 4)}{5!} \theta^5 + \ldots \infty$$

(842) $1 - \dfrac{m(m - 1)}{2!} \theta^2 + \dfrac{m(m - 1)(m - 2)(m - 3)}{4!} \theta^4 + \ldots \infty$

(843) $1 + a\theta + \dfrac{a^2 - b^2}{2!} \theta^2 + \dfrac{a(a^2 - 3b^2)}{3!} \theta^3$

$$+ \dfrac{a^4 - 6a^2b^2 + b^4}{4!} \theta^4 + \ldots$$

$$+ \dfrac{(a^2 + b^2)^{n/2}}{n!} \theta^n \cos \left(n \tan^{-1} \dfrac{b}{a} \right) + \ldots \infty$$

(844) $m\theta - \dfrac{m(m^2 - 1^2)}{3!} \theta^3 + \dfrac{m(m^2 - 1^2)(m^2 - 3^2)}{5!} \theta^5 - \ldots \infty$

$= \tan^{-1} \theta$ where $|\theta(1 + \theta^2)|^2 < \dfrac{4}{27}$

A. 199

$= 2^{n/2} \cos \dfrac{n\pi}{4}$ where n is positive

A. 311

$= - \operatorname{logh} \cos \theta$ where $\theta^2 < \dfrac{\pi^2}{4}$

B. 245

$= \epsilon^{a \sin^{-1} \theta}$

L. 77

$= \dfrac{\pi^2}{4m^2} \operatorname{cosec}^2 \dfrac{\pi}{m} + \dfrac{\pi}{4m} \cot \dfrac{\pi}{m} - \dfrac{1}{2}$

$\begin{cases} \text{A. 217} \\ \text{A. 218} \end{cases}$

$= \sin (m \tan^{-1} \theta)(1 + \theta^2)^{m/2}$

L. 81

$= \cos (m \tan^{-1} \theta)(1 + \theta^2)^{m/2}$

L. 81

$= \epsilon^{a\theta} \cos b\theta$

L. 73

$= \sin (m \sin^{-1} \theta)$

L. 76

Series No.

(845) $1 - \dfrac{m^2\theta^2}{2!} + \dfrac{m^2(m^2 - 2^2)}{4!}\,\theta^4$
$$- \dfrac{m^2(m^2 - 2^2)(m^2 - 4^2)}{6!}\,\theta^6 + \ldots \infty$$

(846) $\displaystyle\sum_{-\infty}^{+\infty}\left\{\log h\left(1 + \dfrac{\theta}{n}\right) - \dfrac{\theta}{n}\right\}$

(847) $\displaystyle\sum_{-\infty}^{+\infty}(-1)^n\left\{\log h\left(1 + \dfrac{\theta}{n}\right) - \dfrac{\theta}{n}\right\}$

(848) $\theta^2 + \left(1 - \dfrac{1}{3} + \dfrac{1}{5}\right)\dfrac{\theta^6}{3} + \left(1 - \dfrac{1}{3} + \dfrac{1}{5} - \dfrac{1}{7} + \dfrac{1}{9}\right)\dfrac{\theta^{10}}{5} + \ldots \infty$

(849) $S_2\dfrac{\theta^3}{3} - S_4\dfrac{\theta^5}{5} + S_6\dfrac{\theta^7}{7} - \ldots \infty$

$$S_{2n} = 1 + \dfrac{1}{2} + \dfrac{1}{3} + \ldots \dfrac{1}{2n}$$

(850) $\displaystyle\sum_{-\infty}^{+\infty}(-1)^n\left(\dfrac{1}{\theta - n} + \dfrac{1}{n}\right)$

(851) $\displaystyle\sum_{-\infty}^{+\infty}\left\{\dfrac{1}{n + x + (-1)^{n-1}y} - \dfrac{1}{n}\right\}$

In Series Nos. (852) to (854), see No. (1134) for values of $A_n(x)$ and $B_n(x)$.

(852) $2a\left(x - \dfrac{1}{2}\right) - \dfrac{(2a)^3}{2!}\,B_3(x) + \dfrac{(2a)^5}{4!}\,B_5(x) - \ldots \infty$

(853) $-(2a)^2 B_2(x) + \dfrac{(2a)^4}{3!}\,B_4(x) - \dfrac{(2a)^6}{5!}\,B_6(x) + \ldots \infty$

(854) $1 - (2a)^2 A_2(x) + \dfrac{(2a)^4}{3!}\,A_4(x) - \dfrac{(2a)^6}{5!}\,A_6(x) + \ldots \infty$

(855) $\displaystyle\sum_{1}^{\infty}(-1)^{n-1}\dfrac{r!\,\theta^{2n-1}}{(2n - 1)!\,[r - (2n - 1)]!}$

See No. (841).

$= \cos (m \sin^{-1} \theta)$ L. 76

$= \text{logh} \sin \pi\theta - \text{logh} \pi\theta$ where $n \neq 0$ A. 314

$= \text{logh} \tan \dfrac{\pi\theta}{2} - \text{logh} \dfrac{\pi\theta}{2}$ where $n \neq 0$ A. 314

$= \dfrac{1}{2} \tan^{-1} \theta \, \text{logh} \dfrac{1 + \theta}{1 - \theta}$ A. 191

$= \dfrac{1}{2} \tan^{-1} \theta \, \text{logh} (1 + \theta^2)$ A. 191

$= \pi \cosec (\pi\theta) - \dfrac{1}{\theta}$ omit $n = 0$

$= \dfrac{\pi \cos \pi x}{\sin \pi x - \sin \pi y} - \dfrac{1}{x - y}$ omit $n = 0$ A. 225

$= \dfrac{a \sin a(2x - 1)}{\sin a}$ AE. 25

$= \dfrac{a \cos a(2x - 1) - a \cos a}{\sin a}$ AE. 25

$= \dfrac{a \cos a(2x - 1)}{\sin a}$ AE. 25

$= (1 + \theta^2)^{r/2} \sin (r \tan^{-1} \theta)$ L. 81

Series No.

(856) $\displaystyle\sum_1^\infty (-1)^n \frac{r!\theta^{2n}}{(2n)!(r-2n)!}$

See No. (842).

(857) $\displaystyle\sum_{-\infty}^{+\infty} \frac{1}{n^4 + \theta^4}$

(858) $\displaystyle\sum_{-\infty}^{+\infty} \frac{1}{(n+x)^2 + y^2}$

(859) $\displaystyle\sum_1^\infty \frac{(-1)^n n}{(\epsilon^{n\pi} - \epsilon^{-n\pi})\{(n\pi)^4 + \frac{1}{4}\theta^4\}}$

In Series Nos. (860) to (862), see No. (1134) for values of $A_n x$.

(860) $2aA_1(x) - \dfrac{(2a)^3}{2!} A_3(x) + \dfrac{(2a)^5}{4!} A_5(x) + \dots$

(861) $2a\left\{A_1(x) - 2A_1\left(\dfrac{x}{2}\right)\right\} - \dfrac{(2a)^3}{2!}\left\{A_3(x) - 2^3 A_3\left(\dfrac{x}{2}\right)\right\}$

$\qquad\qquad + \dfrac{(2a)^5}{4!}\left\{A_5(x) - 2^5 A_5\left(\dfrac{x}{2}\right)\right\} - \dots$

(862) $(2a)^2\left\{A_2(x) - 2^2 A_2\left(\dfrac{x}{2}\right)\right\} - \dfrac{(2a)^4}{3!}\left\{A_4(x) - 2^4 A_4\left(\dfrac{x}{2}\right)\right\}$

$\qquad\qquad + \dfrac{(2a)^6}{5!}\left\{A_6(x) - 2^6 A_6\left(\dfrac{x}{2}\right)\right\} - \dots$

In series Nos. (863) to (873), see No. (330), etc. for values of p, q, r, and t.

(863) $p_1 + q_2 a + p_3 a^2 + q_4 a^3 + \dots$

(864) $r_1 + t_2 a + r_3 a^2 + t_4 a^4 + \dots$

$$= (1 + \theta^2)^{r/2} \cos (r \tan^{-1} \theta) - 1 \qquad \text{L. 81}$$

$$= \frac{\pi}{\theta^3 \sqrt{2}} \frac{\sinh \pi\theta\sqrt{2} + \sin \pi\theta\sqrt{2}}{\cosh \pi\theta\sqrt{2} - \cos \pi\theta\sqrt{2}} \qquad \text{A. 313}$$

$$= \frac{\pi}{y} \frac{\sinh 2\pi y}{\cosh 2\pi y - \cos 2\pi x} \qquad \text{A. 314}$$

$$= \frac{1}{2\pi\theta^2 (\cosh \theta - \cos \theta)} - \frac{1}{2\pi\theta^4} \qquad \text{Q. 135}$$

$$= \frac{a \sin (2x - 1)a}{\sin a} \qquad \text{AE. 93}$$

$$= \frac{a \cos (2x - 1)a}{\cos a} \qquad \text{AE. 93}$$

$$= \frac{a \sin (2x - 1)a}{\cos a} \qquad \text{AE. 93}$$

$$= \frac{\pi}{4} \frac{1}{\sin \left(\dfrac{\pi}{4} - \dfrac{\pi a}{4} \right)} \qquad \text{AE. 80}$$

$$= \frac{\pi}{6} \frac{1}{\sin \left(\dfrac{\pi}{6} - \dfrac{\pi a}{4} \right)} \qquad \text{AE. 80}$$

Series No.

(865) $p_1a + q_2a^2 + p_3a^3 + q_4a^4 + \ldots$

(866) $r_1a + t_2a^2 + r_3a^3 + t_4a^4 + \ldots$

(867) $p_1a + p_3a^3 + p_5a^5 + \ldots$

(868) $r_1a + r_3a^3 + r_5a^5 + \ldots$

(869) $t_2a^2 + t_4a^4 + t_6a^6 + \ldots$

(870) $q_2a^2 + q_4a^4 + q_6a^6 + \ldots$

XVII. Hyperbolic Expansions

(871) $1 + \dfrac{\theta^2}{2!} + \dfrac{\theta^4}{4!} + \ldots \infty = \displaystyle\sum_{0}^{\infty} \dfrac{\theta^{2n}}{(2n)!}$

(872) $\theta + \dfrac{\theta^3}{3!} + \dfrac{\theta^5}{5!} + \ldots \infty = \displaystyle\sum_{0}^{\infty} \dfrac{\theta^{2n+1}}{(2n+1)!}$

$$= \frac{\pi a}{2} \frac{\sin\left(\frac{\pi}{4} + \frac{\pi a}{4}\right)}{\cos\frac{\pi a}{2}}$$ AE. 80

$$= \frac{2\pi a}{3} \frac{\sin\left(\frac{\pi}{6} + \frac{\pi a}{6}\right)}{2\cos\frac{\pi a}{3} - 1}$$ AE. 80

$$= \frac{\pi a}{2\sqrt{2}} \frac{\cos\frac{\pi a}{4}}{\cos\frac{\pi a}{2}}$$ AE. 81

$$= \frac{\pi a}{3} \frac{\cos\frac{\pi a}{6}}{2\cos\frac{\pi a}{3} - 1}$$ AE. 81

$$= \frac{\pi a}{\sqrt{3}} \frac{\sin\frac{\pi a}{6}}{2\cos\frac{\pi a}{3} - 1}$$ AE. 81

$$= \frac{\pi a}{2\sqrt{2}} \frac{\sin\frac{\pi a}{4}}{\cos\frac{\pi a}{2}}$$ AE. 81

$$= \cosh\theta \quad \text{where } \theta^2 < \infty$$ E. 84

$$= \sinh\theta \quad \text{where } \theta^2 < \infty$$ E. 84

Series No.

(873)† $\theta - \dfrac{\theta^3}{3} + \dfrac{2\theta^5}{15} - \dfrac{17\theta^7}{315} \cdots \infty$

$$= \sum_{1}^{\infty} (-1)^{n-1} \frac{2^{2n}(2^{2n} - 1)}{(2n)!} B_n \theta^{2n-1}$$

(874) $1 + \dfrac{m^2}{1^2} + \dfrac{m^2(m^2 + 1^2)}{1^2 \cdot 3^2} + \dfrac{m^2(m^2 + 1^2)(m^2 + 3^2)}{1^2 \cdot 3^2 \cdot 5^2} + \ldots \infty$

(875) $\theta + \dfrac{\theta^3}{3} + \dfrac{\theta^5}{5} + \ldots \infty$

(876) $\displaystyle\sum_{-\infty}^{+\infty} (-1)^{n-1} \frac{4n^2 - 1}{16n^4 + 4n^2 + 1}$

(878)‡ $1 + \displaystyle\sum_{1}^{\infty} (-1)^{n-1} \frac{2^{2n} B_n \theta^{2n}}{(2n)!} = 1 + \dfrac{\theta^2}{3} - \dfrac{\theta^4}{45} + \dfrac{2}{945} \theta^6 - \ldots \infty$

(879)† $1 + 2 \displaystyle\sum_{1}^{\infty} (-1)^n \frac{(2^{2n-1} - 1)B_n \theta^{2n}}{(2n)!}$

$$= 1 - \frac{\theta^2}{6} + \frac{7\theta^4}{360} - \frac{31\theta^6}{15120} + \ldots \infty$$

(880) $\dfrac{1}{\theta} - 2\theta \left(\dfrac{1}{\pi^2 + \theta^2} - \dfrac{1}{4\pi^2 + \theta^2} + \dfrac{1}{9\pi^2 + \theta^2} - \cdots \infty \right)$

(881) $4\pi \left(\dfrac{1}{\pi^2 + 4\theta^2} - \dfrac{3}{9\pi^2 + 4\theta^2} + \dfrac{5}{25\pi^2 + 4\theta^2} - \cdots \infty \right)$

(882) $\dfrac{1}{\theta} + 2\theta \left(\dfrac{1}{\pi^2 + \theta^2} + \dfrac{1}{4\pi^2 + \theta^2} + \dfrac{1}{9\pi^2 + \theta^2} + \ldots \right)$

(883) $\displaystyle\sum_{1}^{\infty} \frac{(3^n - 3)\{1 - (-1)^n\}}{8n!} \theta^n$

(884) $\displaystyle\sum_{1}^{\infty} \frac{(3^n + 3)\{1 + (-1)^n\}}{8n!} \theta^n$

† For values of B_n, see No. (1129).
‡ No. (877) has been omitted because it duplicates a previous series.—Ed.

$= \tanh \theta$ where $\theta^2 < \dfrac{\pi}{4}$ H. 498

$= \cosh m\pi$ C. 421

$= \tanh^{-1} \theta$ where $|\theta| < 1$ H. 475

$= \pi\sqrt{2} \cosh \dfrac{\pi\sqrt{3}}{4} \operatorname{sech} \dfrac{\pi\sqrt{3}}{2}$ A. 314

$= \theta \coth \theta$ C. 343

$= \theta \operatorname{cosech} \theta$ where $\theta^2 < \pi^2$ C. 343

$= \operatorname{cosech} \theta$ Q. 136

$= \operatorname{sech} \theta$ Q. 136

$= \coth \theta$ Q. 136

$= \sinh^3 \theta$ Y. 80

$= \cosh^3 \theta$ Y. 80

Series No.

(885) $\dfrac{b}{a^2 + b^2} - \dfrac{b}{(2a)^2 + b^2} + \dfrac{b}{(3a)^2 + b^2} - \ldots \infty$

$$= \int_0^\infty \frac{\sin b\theta \; d\theta}{\epsilon^{a\theta} + 1}$$

(886) $\dfrac{b}{a^2 + b^2} + \dfrac{b}{(2a)^2 + b^2} + \dfrac{b}{(3a)^2 + b^2} + \ldots \infty$

$$= \int_0^\infty \frac{\sin b\theta \; d\theta}{\epsilon^{a\theta} - 1}$$

(887) $1 - \dfrac{\theta^2}{3!} + \dfrac{14\theta^4}{6!} - \ldots \infty$

(888) $\pi - 2\left(\theta - \dfrac{\theta^3}{3} + \dfrac{\theta^5}{5} - \ldots\right)$

(889) $1 + \dfrac{1^2 + 1^2}{2!} \sin^2 \theta + \dfrac{(1^2 + 1^2)(1^2 + 3^2)}{4!} \sin^4 \theta + \ldots \infty$

(890) $\dfrac{1^2}{1} \sin \theta + \dfrac{(1^2 + 2^2)}{3!} \sin^3 \theta$

$$+ \dfrac{(1^2 + 2^2)(1^2 + 4^2)}{5!} \sin^5 \theta + \ldots \infty$$

(891) $1 + \dfrac{\theta^2}{2} - \dfrac{11\theta^4}{24} + \ldots \infty$

(892) $\theta - \dfrac{\theta^3}{3} - \dfrac{\theta^5}{5} - \ldots \infty$

(893) $1 - \dfrac{2^2\theta^4}{4!} + \dfrac{2^4\theta^8}{8!} - \ldots \infty$

(894) $\dfrac{2^2\theta^2}{2!} - \dfrac{2^4\theta^6}{6!} + \dfrac{2^6\theta^{10}}{10!} - \ldots \infty$

(895) $\theta + \dfrac{2\theta^3}{3!} - \dfrac{2^2\theta^5}{5!} - \dfrac{2^3\,\theta^7}{7!} + \dfrac{2^4\,\theta^9}{9!} + \ldots \infty$

(896) $\theta - \dfrac{2\theta^3}{3!} - \dfrac{2^2\theta^5}{5!} + \dfrac{2^3\theta^7}{7!} + \ldots \infty$

$$= \frac{1}{2} \left[\frac{1}{b} - \frac{\pi}{a \sinh \frac{\pi b}{a}} \right]$$
A. 501

$$= \frac{\pi}{a} \left[\frac{1}{\epsilon^{2\pi b/a} - 1} - \frac{a}{2\pi b} + \frac{1}{2} \right]$$
A. 501

$$= \frac{\theta}{\sinh \theta}$$
H. 498

$$= \cos^{-1} (\tanh \operatorname{logh} \theta)$$
L. 80

$$= \frac{\cosh \theta}{\cos \theta}$$
L. 81

$$= \frac{\sinh \theta}{\cos \theta}$$
L. 81

$$= \cosh (\theta \cos \theta)$$
L. 80

$$= \sinh (\theta \cos \theta)$$
L. 80

$$= \cosh \theta . \cos \theta$$
H. 497

$$= 2 \sinh \theta . \sin \theta$$
T. 127

$$= \cosh \theta . \sin \theta$$
H. 497

$$= \sinh \theta . \cos \theta$$
H. 497

Series No.

(897)　$1 - \dfrac{\theta^2}{2} + \dfrac{5}{24}\theta^4 - \dfrac{61}{720}\theta^6 + \ldots \infty = 1 + \displaystyle\sum_1^\infty (-1)^n \dfrac{E_n^*}{(2n)!}\theta^{2n}$

For E_n^* see No. (1131).

(898)　$\displaystyle\sum_0^\infty (-1)^n \dfrac{(2n)!}{2^{2n}(n!)^2(2n+1)}\theta^{2n+1}$

$$= \operatorname{logh} 2\theta + \sum_0^\infty (-1)^n \dfrac{(2n)!}{2^{2n}(n!)^2 2n}\theta^{-2n}$$

(899)　$\operatorname{logh} 2\theta - \displaystyle\sum_0^\infty \dfrac{(2n)!}{2^{2n}(n!)^2 2n}\theta^{-2n}$

$$= \operatorname{logh} 2\theta - \dfrac{1}{2}\cdot\dfrac{1}{2\theta^2} - \dfrac{1\cdot 3}{2\cdot 4}\cdot\dfrac{1}{4\theta^4} - \ldots \infty$$

(900)　$\displaystyle\sum_0^\infty (-1)^n \dfrac{(2n)!}{2^{2n}(n!)^2(2n+1)}\theta^{-2n-1}$

$$= \dfrac{1}{\theta} - \dfrac{1}{2}\cdot\dfrac{1}{3\theta^3} + \dfrac{1\cdot 3}{2\cdot 4}\cdot\dfrac{1}{5\theta^5} - \ldots \infty$$

(901)　$\dfrac{\theta^2}{2} + \dfrac{2}{3}\cdot\dfrac{\theta^4}{4} + \dfrac{2\cdot 4}{3\cdot 5}\cdot\dfrac{\theta^6}{6} - \ldots \infty$

For values of the coefficients in Nos. (902) through (938), see No. (1142).

(902)　$2a\left(x - \dfrac{1}{2}\right) + \dfrac{(2a)^3}{2!}A_3(x) + \dfrac{(2a)^5}{4!}A_5(x) + \ldots \infty$

(903)　$(2a)^2 B_2(x) + \dfrac{(2a)^4}{3!}B_4(x) + \dfrac{(2a)^6}{5!}B_6(x) + \ldots \infty$

(904)　$1 + (2a)^2 A_2(x) + \dfrac{(2a)^4}{3!}A_4(x) + \dfrac{(2a)^6}{5!}A_6(x) + \ldots \infty$

(905)　$(2a)^2 B_2\left(\dfrac{1}{4}\right) + \dfrac{(2a)^4}{3!}B_4\left(\dfrac{1}{4}\right) + \ldots \infty$

$$= \operatorname{sech} \theta \quad \text{where } \theta^2 < \frac{\pi}{4}$$

$$\text{where } \theta^2 < 1$$

$$= \sinh^{-1} \theta \quad \text{where } \theta^2 > 1$$

$$= \cosh^{-1} \theta \quad \text{where } \theta^2 > 1$$

$$= \sinh^{-1} \frac{1}{\theta} = \operatorname{cosech}^{-1} \theta \quad \text{where } \theta^2 > 1$$

$$= \frac{(\sinh^{-1} \theta)^2}{2!}$$

$$= \frac{a \sinh a(2x - 1)}{\sinh a}$$

$$= \frac{a \cosh a(2x - 1) - a \cosh a}{\sinh a}$$

$$= \frac{a \cosh a(2x - 1)}{\sinh a}$$

$$= \frac{- 2a \sinh \tfrac{1}{4}a \sinh \tfrac{3}{4}a}{\sinh a}$$

(906) $-\dfrac{1}{3}a + \dfrac{(2a)^3}{2!}B_3\left(\dfrac{1}{3}\right) + \dfrac{(2a)^5}{4!}B_5\left(\dfrac{1}{3}\right) + \ldots \infty$

(907) $1 + (2a)^2 A_2\left(\dfrac{1}{4}\right) + \dfrac{(2a)^4}{3!}A_4\left(\dfrac{1}{4}\right) + \ldots \infty$

(908) $a - \dfrac{(4a)^3}{2!}B_3\left(\dfrac{1}{4}\right) - \dfrac{(4a)^5}{4!}B_5\left(\dfrac{1}{4}\right) - \ldots \infty$

(909) $\dfrac{1}{2}a - \dfrac{(3a)^3}{2!}B_3\left(\dfrac{1}{3}\right) - \dfrac{(3a)^5}{4!}B_5\left(\dfrac{1}{3}\right) - \ldots \infty$

(910) $2a - \dfrac{(6a)^3}{2!}B_3\left(\dfrac{1}{6}\right) - \dfrac{(6a)^5}{4!}B_5\left(\dfrac{1}{6}\right) - \ldots \infty$

(911) $\dfrac{3a}{2} - \dfrac{(6a)^3}{2!}\left\{B_3\left(\dfrac{1}{6}\right) - \dfrac{1}{2^3}B_3\left(\dfrac{1}{3}\right)\right\}$
$$- \dfrac{(6a)^5}{4!}\left\{B_5\left(\dfrac{1}{6}\right) - \dfrac{1}{2^5}B_5\left(\dfrac{1}{3}\right)\right\} - \ldots \infty$$

(912) $a - \dfrac{(6a)^3}{2!}B_3\left(\dfrac{1}{3}\right) - \dfrac{(6a)^5}{4!}B_5\left(\dfrac{1}{3}\right) - \ldots \infty$

(913) $H_0 - \dfrac{H_1}{2!}(2a)^2 + \dfrac{H_2}{4!}(2a)^4 - \ldots \infty$

(914) $2 - \dfrac{a^2}{2!}\left\{8^3 B_3\left(\dfrac{1}{8}\right) - 4^3 B_3\left(\dfrac{1}{4}\right)\right\}$
$$- \dfrac{a^4}{4!}\left\{8^5 B_5\left(\dfrac{1}{8}\right) - 4^5 B_5\left(\dfrac{1}{4}\right)\right\} - \ldots \infty$$

(915) $1 + (2a)^2 A_2\left(\dfrac{1}{4}\right) + \dfrac{(2a)^4}{3!}A_4\left(\dfrac{1}{4}\right) + \ldots \infty$

(916) $\dfrac{1}{3} + (2-1)(3-1)B_1\dfrac{a^2}{2!} - (2^3-1)(3^3-1)B_2\dfrac{a^4}{4!}$
$$+ (2^5-1)(3^5-1)B_3\dfrac{a^6}{6!} + \ldots$$

(917) $\dfrac{1}{3} - 2(3-1)B_1\dfrac{a^2}{2!} + 2^3(3^3-1)B_2\dfrac{a^4}{4!}$
$$- 2^5(3^5-1)B_3\dfrac{a^6}{6!} + \ldots$$

$$= - \frac{a \sinh \frac{1}{3}a}{\sinh a}$$

AE. 35

$$= \frac{a}{2 \sinh \frac{1}{2}a}$$

AE. 33

$$= \frac{a}{\cosh a}$$

AE. 32

$$- \frac{3a \sinh \frac{1}{2}a}{2 \ \sinh \frac{3}{2}a}$$

AE. 51

$$= \frac{3a \sinh 2a}{\sinh 3a}$$

AE. 43

$$= \frac{3a \cosh \frac{1}{2}a}{2 \ \cosh \frac{3}{2}a}$$

AE. 51

$$= \frac{3a \sinh a}{\sinh 3a}$$

AE. 35

$$= \frac{3 \cosh a}{2 \cosh 3a}$$

AE. 49

$$= \frac{2 \cosh a}{\cosh 2a}$$

AE. 60

$$= \frac{a}{2} \operatorname{cosech} \frac{a}{2}$$

AE. 33

$$= \frac{a \cosh 2a}{\sinh 3a}$$

AE. 47

$$= \frac{a \cosh a}{\sinh 3a}$$

AE. 47

Series No.

(918) $1 + (2a)^2 A_2\left(\dfrac{1}{2}\right) + \dfrac{(2a)^4}{3!} A_4\left(\dfrac{1}{2}\right) + \dfrac{(2a)^6}{5!} A_6\left(\dfrac{1}{2}\right) + \ldots$

(919) $a - \dfrac{(4a)^3}{2!} B_3\left(\dfrac{1}{4}\right) - \dfrac{(4a)^5}{4!} B_5\left(\dfrac{1}{4}\right) - \ldots$

(920) $(2a)^2 B_2\left(\dfrac{1}{2}\right) + \dfrac{(2a)^4}{3!} B_4\left(\dfrac{1}{2}\right) + \dfrac{(2a)^6}{5!} B_6\left(\dfrac{1}{2}\right) + \ldots$

(921) $1 + B_1 \dfrac{a^2}{2!} - B_2 \dfrac{a^4}{4!} + B_3 \dfrac{a^6}{6!} - \ldots$

(922) $I_0 - \dfrac{I_1}{2!} a^2 + \dfrac{I_2}{4!} a^4 - \dfrac{I_3}{6!} a^6 + \ldots$

(923) $(8a)^2 B_2\left(\dfrac{1}{4}\right) + \dfrac{(8a)^4}{3!} B_4\left(\dfrac{1}{4}\right) + \ldots$

(924) $\dfrac{1}{2} a - \dfrac{(3a)^3}{2!} B_3\left(\dfrac{1}{3}\right) - \dfrac{(3a)^5}{4!} B_5\left(\dfrac{1}{3}\right) - \ldots$

(925) $\dfrac{3}{2} a - \dfrac{a^3}{2!}\left\{ 6^3 B_6\left(\dfrac{1}{6}\right) - 3^3 B_3\left(\dfrac{1}{3}\right)\right\}$

$\qquad\qquad\qquad - \dfrac{a^5}{4!}\left\{ 6^5 B_5\left(\dfrac{1}{6}\right) - 3^5 B_5\left(\dfrac{1}{3}\right)\right\} - \ldots \infty$

(926) $(12a)^2 B_2\left(\dfrac{1}{6}\right) + \dfrac{(12a)^4}{3!} B_4\left(\dfrac{1}{6}\right) + \dfrac{(12a)^6}{5!} B_6\left(\dfrac{1}{6}\right) + \ldots \infty$

(927) $- (12a) B_2\left(\dfrac{1}{6}\right) - \dfrac{(12a)^3}{3!} B_4\left(\dfrac{1}{6}\right) - \dfrac{(12a)^5}{5!} B_6\left(\dfrac{1}{6}\right) - \ldots \infty$

(928) $\dfrac{1}{2} a - \dfrac{(2a)^3}{2!} B_3\left(\dfrac{1}{4}\right) - \dfrac{(2a)^5}{4!} B_5\left(\dfrac{1}{4}\right) - \ldots \infty$

(929) $\dfrac{1}{2} a - \dfrac{(3a)^3}{2!} B_3\left(\dfrac{1}{3}\right) - \dfrac{(3a)^5}{4!} B_5\left(\dfrac{1}{3}\right) - \ldots \infty$

(930) $\dfrac{3}{4} a - \dfrac{(2a)^3}{2!} B_3\left(\dfrac{1}{8}\right) - \dfrac{(2a)^5}{4!} B_5\left(\dfrac{1}{8}\right) - \ldots \infty$

(931) $(2a)^2 B_2\left(\dfrac{1}{3}\right) + \dfrac{(2a)^4}{3!} B_4\left(\dfrac{1}{3}\right) + \ldots \infty$

$= a \operatorname{cosech} a$ AE. 30

$= a \operatorname{sech} a$ AE. 32

$= - a \tanh \frac{1}{2} a$ AE. 30

$= \frac{1}{2} a \coth \frac{1}{2} a$ AE. 47

$= \frac{3(\sinh 2a - \sinh a)}{2 \sinh 3a}$ AE. 45

$= - \frac{8a \sinh a \sinh 3a}{\sinh 4a}$ AE. 33

$= \frac{3a}{2(1 + 2 \cosh a)}$ AE. 37

$= \frac{3a}{2(2 \cosh a - 1)}$ AE. 48

$= \frac{- 12a \sinh a \sinh 5a}{\sinh 6a}$ AE. 46

$= \frac{\sinh 5a}{2(\cosh a + \cosh 3a + \cosh 5a)}$ AE. 46

$= \frac{a \sinh \frac{1}{2}a}{\sinh a}$ AE. 60

$= \frac{3a \sinh \frac{1}{2}a}{2 \sinh \frac{3}{2}a}$ AE. 48

$= \frac{a \sinh \frac{3}{4}a}{\sinh a}$ AE. 60

$= - \frac{2a \sinh \frac{1}{3}a \sinh \frac{2}{3}a}{\sinh a}$ AE. 40

Series No.

(932) $-\dfrac{2}{3}a + \dfrac{(2a)^3}{2!}B_3\!\left(\dfrac{1}{6}\right) + \dfrac{(2a)^5}{4!}B_5\!\left(\dfrac{1}{6}\right) + \ldots \infty$

(933) $-\dfrac{1}{3}a + \dfrac{(2a)^3}{2!}B_3\!\left(\dfrac{1}{3}\right) + \dfrac{(2a)^5}{4!}B_5\!\left(\dfrac{1}{3}\right) + \ldots \infty$

(934)† $t_2 a^2 - t_4 a^4 + t_6 a^6 - \ldots \infty$

(935) $(2a)^2 B_2\!\left(\dfrac{1}{4}\right) + \dfrac{(2a)^4}{3!}B_4\!\left(\dfrac{1}{4}\right) + \ldots \infty$

(936) $2a\!\left(x - \dfrac{1}{2}\right) + \dfrac{(2a)^3}{2!}A_3(x) + \dfrac{(2a)^5}{4!}A_5(x) + \ldots \infty$

(937) $1 + (2a)^2 A_2(x) + \dfrac{(2a)^4}{3!}A_4(x) + \dfrac{(2a)^6}{5!}A_6(x) + \ldots \infty$

(938)† $p_1 a - p_3 a^3 + p_5 a^5 - \ldots \infty$

(939) $\log h\,\dfrac{2}{\theta} - \displaystyle\sum_0^\infty \dfrac{(2n)!}{2^{2n}(n!)^2 2n}\,\theta^{2n}$

$$= \log h\,\dfrac{2}{\theta} - \dfrac{1}{2}\cdot\dfrac{\theta^2}{2} - \dfrac{1\cdot 3}{2\cdot 4}\cdot\dfrac{\theta^4}{4} - \ldots \infty$$

(940) $\log h\,\dfrac{2}{\theta} + \displaystyle\sum_0^\infty (-1)^n \dfrac{(2n)!}{2^{2n}(n!)^2 2n}\,\theta^{2n}$

$$= \log h\,\dfrac{2}{\theta} + \dfrac{1}{2}\cdot\dfrac{\theta^2}{2} - \dfrac{1\cdot 3}{2\cdot 4}\cdot\dfrac{\theta^4}{4} \ldots \infty$$

(941) $\displaystyle\sum_0^\infty \dfrac{\theta^{-2n-1}}{2n+1} = \dfrac{1}{\theta} + \dfrac{1}{3\theta^3} + \dfrac{1}{5\theta^5} + \ldots \infty$

(942) $\displaystyle\sum_0^\infty \epsilon^{-\theta(2n+1)}$

† For values of p and t, see No. (330).

$$= -\frac{a \sinh \tfrac{2}{3}a}{\sinh a}$$

AE. 43

$$= -\frac{a \sinh \tfrac{1}{3}a}{\sinh a}$$

AE. 35

$$= \frac{\pi a}{\sqrt{3}}\,\frac{\sinh \dfrac{\pi a}{6}}{2 \cosh \dfrac{\pi a}{3} - 1}$$

AE. 75

$$= -\frac{2a \sinh \tfrac{1}{4}a \sinh \tfrac{3}{4}a}{\sinh a}$$

AE. 33

$$= \frac{a \sinh a(2x - 1)}{\sinh a}$$

AE. 19

$$= \frac{a \cosh a(2x - 1)}{\sinh a}$$

AE. 19

$$= \frac{\pi a}{2\sqrt{2}} \cdot \frac{\cosh \dfrac{\pi a}{4}}{\cosh \dfrac{\pi a}{2}}$$

AE. 60

$$= \cosh^{-1}\frac{1}{\theta} = \operatorname{sech}^{-1}\theta \quad \text{where } \theta^2 < 1$$

T. 128

$$= \sinh^{-1}\frac{1}{\theta} = \operatorname{cosech}^{-1}\theta \quad \text{where } \theta^2 < 1$$

T. 128

$$= \tanh^{-1}\frac{1}{\theta} = \coth^{-1}\theta \quad \text{where } \theta^2 > 1$$

T. 128

$$= \frac{1}{2 \sinh \theta}$$

T. 129

Series No.

(943) $\displaystyle\sum_{0}^{\infty} (-1)^n \epsilon^{-\theta(2n+1)}$

(944) $\displaystyle\sum_{1}^{\infty} (-1)^n \epsilon^{-2n\theta}$

(945) $\displaystyle\sum_{0}^{\infty} \frac{1}{2n+1} \epsilon^{-\theta(2n+1)}$

(946) $\displaystyle\sum_{1}^{\infty} \left\{ \frac{1}{(2n\pi - a)^2 + \theta^2} + \frac{1}{(2n\pi + a)^2 + \theta^2} \right\}$

(947) $1 + \dfrac{2}{1 + 1^2} + \dfrac{2}{1 + 2^2} + \dfrac{2}{1 + 3^2} + \ldots \infty$

(948) $1 + \dfrac{2}{1 + 2^2} + \dfrac{2}{1 + 4^2} + \dfrac{2}{1 + 6^2} + \ldots \infty$

(949) $\dfrac{1}{2^2 + 1^2} + \dfrac{1}{2^2 + 3^2} + \dfrac{1}{2^2 + 5^2} + \ldots \infty$

(950) $\dfrac{1}{1 + 1^2} + \dfrac{1}{1 + 3^2} + \dfrac{1}{1 + 5^2} + \ldots \infty$

(951) $\dfrac{1}{2} + \theta^2 \displaystyle\sum_{1}^{\infty} \frac{1}{\theta^2 + n^2\pi^2}$

(952) $\displaystyle\sum_{-\infty}^{\infty} \frac{1}{(n + \theta)^2 + y^2}$

(953) $\dfrac{\theta^2}{6} - \dfrac{\theta^4}{180} + \ldots \infty$

$$= B_1 {}^* \frac{2^2 \cdot \theta^2}{2 \cdot 2!} - B_3 {}^* \frac{2^4 \cdot \theta^4}{4 \cdot 4!} + B_5 {}^* \frac{2^6 \cdot \theta^6}{6 \cdot 6!} - \ldots \infty$$

(954) $1 + \dfrac{n\theta^2}{2!} + \dfrac{n(3n - 2)}{4!} \theta^4 + \ldots \infty$

(956)† $\theta - \dfrac{2}{3} \theta^3 + \dfrac{2 \cdot 4}{3 \cdot 5} \theta^5 - \ldots$

† No. (955) has been omitted because it duplicates a previous series.—Ed.

$$= \frac{1}{2 \cosh \theta}$$ T. 129

$$= \frac{1}{2} (\tanh \theta - 1)$$ T. 129

$$= -\frac{1}{2} \operatorname{logh} \tanh \frac{\theta}{2}$$ T. 129

$$= \frac{1}{2\theta} \cdot \frac{\sinh \theta}{\cosh \theta - \cos a} - \frac{1}{a^2 + \theta^2}$$ A. 314

$$= \pi \coth \pi$$ Y. 55

$$= \frac{\pi}{2} \coth \frac{\pi}{2}$$ Y. 55

$$= \frac{\pi}{8} \tanh \pi$$ Y. 55

$$= \frac{\pi}{4} \tanh \frac{\pi}{2}$$ Y. 55

$$= \frac{\theta}{2} \coth \theta$$ Y. 55

$$= \frac{\pi}{y} \frac{\sinh 2\pi y}{\cosh 2\pi y - \cos 2\pi\theta}$$ A. 314

$$= \operatorname{logh} \frac{\sinh \theta}{\theta}$$ Y. 109

$$= \cosh^n \theta$$ Y. 80

$$= \frac{\sinh^{-1} \theta}{\sqrt{1 + \theta^2}}$$ Y. 90

Series No.

XVIII. Taylor's and Maclaurin's Theorem

(957) $\phi(a) + x\phi'(a) + \dfrac{x^2}{2!}\,\phi''(a)\;\ldots\;\dfrac{x^n}{n!}\,\phi^n(a) + \ldots\;\infty$

(958) $\phi(0) + x\phi'(0) + \dfrac{x^2}{2!}\,\phi''(0) + \ldots\;\dfrac{x^n}{n!}\,\phi^n(0) + \ldots\;\infty$

XIX. Bessel Functions

(959) $\displaystyle\sum_{r=0}^{\infty} \dfrac{(-1)^r x^{n+2r}}{2^{n+2r} r!\,(n+r)!}$

(960) $1 - \dfrac{x^2}{2\cdot 2} + \dfrac{x^4}{2^2\cdot 4^2} - \dfrac{x^6}{2^2\cdot 4^2\cdot 6^2} + \ldots\;\infty$

(961) $\dfrac{x}{2} - \dfrac{x^3}{2^2\cdot 4} + \dfrac{x^5}{2^2\cdot 4^2\cdot 6} - \dfrac{x^7}{2^2\cdot 4^2\cdot 6^2\cdot 8} + \ldots\;\infty$

(962) $\dfrac{x^n}{2^n\cdot n!}\left\{1 - \dfrac{x^2}{2^2\cdot 1\cdot(n+1)} + \dfrac{x^4}{2^4\cdot 1\cdot 2(n+1)(n+2)} - \ldots\;\infty\right\}$

(963) $\displaystyle\sum_{r=0}^{\infty} \dfrac{(-1)^r x^{n+2r}}{2^{n+2r} r!\,\Gamma(n+r+1)}$

(964) $\sqrt{\dfrac{2x}{\pi}}\left\{1 - \dfrac{x^2}{2\cdot 3} + \dfrac{x^4}{2\cdot 3\cdot 4\cdot 5} - \ldots\;\infty\right\}$

(965) $\left(\dfrac{2}{\pi x}\right)^{1/2}\cos x$

(966) $\dfrac{x^n \epsilon^{n\sqrt{1-x^2}}}{\sqrt{2\pi n}\,(1-x^2)^{1/4}\{1 + \sqrt{1-x^2}\}^n}$

XX. Elliptic Functions

(967) $\dfrac{\pi}{2}\left[1 + \left(\dfrac{1}{2}\right)^2 k^2 + \left(\dfrac{1\cdot 3}{2\cdot 4}\right)^2 k^4 + \ldots\;\infty\right]$

(968) $\dfrac{\pi}{2}\left[1 - \left(\dfrac{1}{2}\right)^2 \dfrac{k^2}{1} - \left(\dfrac{1\cdot 3}{2\cdot 4}\right)^2 \dfrac{k^4}{3} - \ldots\;\infty\right]$

$= \phi(a + x)$ H. 481

$= \phi(x)$ H. 480

$= J_n(x)$ Q. 355

$= J_0(x)$ Q. 355

$= J_1(x)$ Q. 355

$= J_n(x)$ Q. 355

$= J_n(x)$ when n is any general value   Q. 359

$= \left(\dfrac{2}{\pi x}\right)^{1/2} \sin x = J_{1/2}(x)$ Q. 364

$= J_{-1/2}(x)$ Q. 364

$\approx J_n(nx)$ when n is large and $0 < x < 1$ Q. 369

$= \displaystyle\int_0^{\pi/2} \dfrac{d\theta}{\sqrt{1 - k^2 \sin^2 \theta}} \ \Big\}$ where $0 < k < 1$ A. 190

$= \displaystyle\int_0^{\pi/2} \sqrt{1 - k^2 \sin^2 \theta}\ d\theta$ where $0 < k < 1$ A. 190

Series No.

XXI. Various Integrals

(969) $\dfrac{n-1}{n}\cdot\dfrac{n-3}{n-2}\cdots\dfrac{1}{2}\cdot\dfrac{\pi}{2}$

(970) $x \log h\, 2 + \dfrac{1}{2}\left\{\dfrac{\sin 2x}{1^2} + \dfrac{\sin 4x}{2^2} + \dfrac{\sin 6x}{3^2} + \ldots \infty\right\}$

(971) $x \log h\, 2 - \dfrac{1}{2}\left\{\dfrac{\sin 2x}{1^2} - \dfrac{\sin 4x}{2^2} + \dfrac{\sin 6x}{3^2} + \ldots \infty\right\}$

(972) $\dfrac{\sin 2x}{1^2} + \dfrac{\sin 6x}{3^2} + \dfrac{\sin 10x}{5^2} + \ldots \infty$

(973) $x - \dfrac{1}{3}x^3 + \dfrac{x^5}{5\cdot 2!} - \dfrac{x^7}{7\cdot 3!} + \ldots \infty = \displaystyle\sum_0^{\infty} \dfrac{(-1)^k}{k!(2k+1)}x^{2k+1}$

(974) $x - \dfrac{x^5}{5\cdot 2!} + \dfrac{x^9}{9\cdot 4!} - \dfrac{x^{13}}{13\cdot 6!} + \ldots \infty$

$$= \displaystyle\sum_0^{\infty} \dfrac{(-1)^k}{(2k)!(4k+1)}x^{4k+1}$$

(975) $\dfrac{1}{a} - \dfrac{1}{a+b} + \dfrac{1}{a+2b} - \dfrac{1}{a+3b} + \ldots \infty$

(976) $\dfrac{1}{\epsilon}(1 - 2! + 3! - \ldots \infty) = \dfrac{0.4036526}{\epsilon}$

(977) $\log h\, x + \dfrac{ax}{1} + \dfrac{a^2x^2}{1\cdot 2^2} + \dfrac{a^3x^3}{1\cdot 2\cdot 3^2} + \ldots \infty$

(978) $\epsilon^{-ab}\left[\log h\,(b+x) + \dfrac{a(b+x)}{1\cdot 1} + \dfrac{a^2(b+x)^2}{2\cdot 2!} + \ldots \infty\right]$

(979) $\log h\, x + x \log h\, a + \dfrac{(x \log h\, a)^2}{2\cdot 2!} + \ldots \infty$

(980) $\dfrac{a^x x^n}{\log h\, a} - \dfrac{na^x x^{n-1}}{(\log h\, a)^2} + \dfrac{n(n-1)a^x x^{n-2}}{(\log h\, a)^3} + \ldots$

$$\pm \dfrac{n(n-1)(n-2)\ldots 2\cdot 1\cdot a^x}{(\log h\, a)^{n+1}}$$

$$= \int_0^{\pi/2} \cos^n \theta \, d\theta = \int_0^{\pi/2} \sin^n \theta \, d\theta \quad \text{where } n \text{ is even}$$

J. 48

$$= - \int_0^x \text{logh sin } x \, dx \quad \text{where } 0 < x < \pi$$

X. 142

$$= - \int_0^x \text{logh cos } x \, dx \quad \text{where } -\frac{\pi}{2} < x < \frac{\pi}{2}$$

X. 142

$$= - \int_0^x \text{logh tan } x \, dx \quad \text{where } 0 < x < \frac{\pi}{2}$$

X. 142

$$= \int_0^x \epsilon^{-x^2} \, dx \quad \text{where } x^2 < \infty$$

T. 133
See also
A. 336
T. 134

$$= \int_0^x \cos(x^2) \, dx \quad \text{where } x^2 < \infty$$

$$= \int_0^1 \frac{x^{a-1} dx}{1 + x^b}$$

T. 134

$$= \int_1^\infty \frac{\epsilon^{-t}}{t} \, dt = \int_0^1 \frac{\epsilon^{-1/y}}{y} \, dy$$

A. 336

$$= \int \frac{\epsilon^{ax} \, dx}{x}$$

$$= \int \frac{\epsilon^{ax} \, dx}{b + x}$$

$$= \int \frac{a^x \, dx}{x}$$

$$= \int x^n a^x \, dx$$

Series No.

(981) $x + \dfrac{x^3}{3 \cdot 3!} + \dfrac{7x^5}{3 \cdot 5 \cdot 5!} + \dfrac{31x^7}{3 \cdot 7 \cdot 7!} + \dfrac{127x^9}{3 \cdot 5 \cdot 9!} + \ldots \; \infty$

(982) $1 + \dfrac{x}{2^p} + \dfrac{x^2}{3^p} + \dfrac{x^3}{4^p} + \ldots \; \infty$

(983) $\dfrac{1}{1 + 1^2} + \dfrac{x}{1 + 2^2} + \dfrac{x^2}{1 + 3^2} + \ldots \; \infty$

(985)† $\operatorname{logh} \theta + \theta + \dfrac{\theta^2}{2 \cdot 2!} + \dfrac{\theta^3}{3 \cdot 3!} + \ldots \; \infty$

(986) $\dfrac{n - 1}{n} \cdot \dfrac{n - 3}{n - 2} \cdots \dfrac{2}{3}$

(987) $\theta - \dfrac{\theta^3}{3 \cdot 3!} + \dfrac{\theta^5}{5 \cdot 5!} - \dfrac{\theta^7}{7 \cdot 7!} + \ldots \; \infty$

(988) $\operatorname{logh} \theta - \dfrac{\theta^2}{2 \cdot 2!} + \dfrac{\theta^4}{4 \cdot 4!} - \ldots \; \infty$

(989) $\dfrac{\pi}{2} \operatorname{logh} 2 = 2 \displaystyle\sum_{1}^{\infty} (-1)^{n-1} \dfrac{\pi}{4n}$

(990) $2 \displaystyle\sum_{0}^{\infty} \dfrac{(-1)^n}{(2n + 1)^2}$

(991) $\dfrac{\pi^2}{4} - 2 \left[(1 + a)\epsilon^{-a} + \dfrac{1}{3^2}(1 + 3a)\epsilon^{-3a} \right.$

$\left. + \dfrac{1}{5^2}(1 + 5a)\epsilon^{-5a} + \ldots \; \infty \right]$

(992) $- C - \operatorname{logh} |x| + x - \dfrac{1}{2} \cdot \dfrac{x^2}{2!} + \dfrac{1}{3} \cdot \dfrac{x^3}{3!} - \dfrac{1}{4} \cdot \dfrac{x^4}{4!} + \ldots \; \infty$

C = Euler's constant; see No. (1132).

† No. (984) has been omitted because it duplicates a previous series.—Ed.

$$= \int \frac{x \, dx}{\sin x}$$

$$= \frac{1}{\Gamma(p)} \int_0^1 \frac{\left[\text{logh} \frac{1}{\zeta} \right]^{p-1}}{1 - x\zeta} \, d\zeta \quad \text{where } p > 0$$

$$= \int_0^1 \frac{\sin \left[\text{logh} \frac{1}{\zeta} \right]}{1 - x\zeta} \, d\zeta$$

$$= \int \frac{\epsilon^\theta}{\theta} \, d\theta$$

$$= \int_0^{\pi/2} \cos^n \theta \, d\theta = \int_0^{\pi/2} \sin^n \theta \, d\theta \quad \text{where } n \text{ is odd}$$

$$= \int \frac{\sin \theta}{\theta} \, d\theta$$

$$= \int \frac{\cos \theta}{\theta} \, d\theta$$

$$= \int_0^{\pi/2} \theta \cot \theta \, d\theta$$

$$= \int_0^{\pi/2} \frac{\theta \, d\theta}{\sin \theta} \quad \text{See also No. (308).}$$

$$= \int_0^{\pi/2} \tan^{-1} (\sinh a \sin \theta) d\theta = \int_0^a \frac{\theta \, d\theta}{\sinh \theta} \quad \text{where } a \text{ is positive}$$

$$= \int_x^\infty \frac{\epsilon^{-t}}{t} \, dt$$

Series No.

(993) $\dfrac{1}{x} - \dfrac{1}{1!}\dfrac{1}{x+1} + \dfrac{1}{2!}\dfrac{1}{x+2} - \dfrac{1}{3!}\dfrac{1}{x+3} + \ldots \infty$

(994) $\displaystyle\sum_{0}^{\infty} \dfrac{1\cdot 3\ldots 2n-1}{2\cdot 4\ldots 2n}\cdot\dfrac{1}{(2n+1)^2}$

(995) $\displaystyle\sum_{0}^{\infty} (-1)^n \dfrac{1}{(2n+1)^2}$　　　See also No. (308).

(996) $\dfrac{x^2}{1\cdot 2} - \dfrac{x^3}{2\cdot 3} + \dfrac{x^4}{3\cdot 4} - \ldots \infty$

(997) $-\displaystyle\sum_{1}^{\infty} \dfrac{x^n}{n^2}$

(998) $\displaystyle\sum_{1}^{\infty} (-1)^{n-1} \dfrac{x^n}{n^2}$

(999) $2\displaystyle\sum_{1}^{\infty} \dfrac{x^{2n-1}}{(2n-1)^2}$

(1000) $\dfrac{1}{a} - \dfrac{1}{a+1} + \dfrac{1}{a+2} - \ldots \infty$

(1001) $\dfrac{1}{(n-1)!}\cdot\dfrac{\pi}{2^n}\left[n^{n-1} - n(n-2)^{n-1}\right.$

$$\left. + \dfrac{n(n-1)}{2!}(n-4)^{n-1} + \ldots\right]$$

The number of terms in the brackets is $\tfrac{1}{2}n$ or $\tfrac{1}{2}(n+1)$.

(1002) $1 - \dfrac{x}{2^2} + \dfrac{x^2}{3^3} - \dfrac{x^3}{4^4} + \dfrac{x^4}{5^5} - \ldots \infty$

(1003) $\epsilon^\theta \displaystyle\sum_{r=0}^{r=n} (-1)^r \dfrac{n!}{(n-r)!}\,\theta^{n-r}2^{-(r+1)/2}\sin\left\{\theta - \dfrac{(r+1)\pi}{4}\right\}$

(1004) $\dfrac{1}{\epsilon}\left\{1 + \dfrac{1}{3\cdot 1!} + \dfrac{1}{5\cdot 2!} + \dfrac{1}{7\cdot 3!} + \ldots \infty\right\}$

$$= \int_0^1 \epsilon^{-t} t^{x-1} \, dt \quad \text{where } x > 1$$
Q. 260

$$= \int_0^1 \frac{\sin^{-1} x}{x} \, dx \quad \text{where } |x| < 1$$
AB. 165

$$= \int_0^1 \frac{\tan^{-1} x}{x} \, dx \quad \text{where } |x| < 1$$
AB. 165

$$= \int_0^x \text{logh} \, (1 + x) \, dx \quad \text{where } |x| < 1$$
AB. 166

$$= \int_0^x \text{logh} \, (1 - x) \frac{dx}{x} \quad \text{where } 0 < x < 1$$
AB. 166

$$= \int_0^x \text{logh} \, (1 + x) \frac{dx}{x} \quad \text{where } 0 < x < 1$$
AB. 166

$$= \int_0^x \text{logh} \, \frac{1 + x}{1 - x} \cdot \frac{dx}{x} \quad \text{where } 0 < x < 1$$
AB. 166

$$= \int_0^1 \frac{x^{a-1}}{1 + x} \, dx \quad \text{where } a > 0$$
A. 189

$$= \int_0^\infty \left(\frac{\sin \theta}{\theta} \right)^n d\theta$$
A. 518

$$= \int_0^1 \nu^{\nu x} \, d\nu$$
1Z. 135

$$= \int \theta^n \epsilon^\theta \sin \theta \, d\theta$$
1Z. 135

$$= \int_0^{\pi/2} \epsilon^{-\sin 2\theta} \cos \theta \, d\theta$$
1Z. 638

Series No.

(1005) $1^2 + \left(\dfrac{1}{1!}\right)^2 + \left(\dfrac{1}{2!}\right)^2 + \left(\dfrac{1}{3!}\right)^2 + \ldots \infty$

(1006) $8\left[-\dfrac{a}{1\cdot1\cdot3} + \dfrac{a^3}{1\cdot3\cdot5} + \dfrac{a^5}{3\cdot5\cdot7} + \dfrac{a^7}{5\cdot7\cdot9} + \ldots \infty\right]$

(1007) $\dfrac{\pi}{2^n}\dfrac{\epsilon^{-ar}}{(n-1)!}\left[r^{n-1}a^{-n} + \dfrac{n(n-1)}{2}r^{n-2}a^{-(n+1)}\right.$

$\left. + \dfrac{(n+1)n(n-1)(n-2)}{2\cdot4}r^{n-3}a^{-(n+2)} + \ldots n \text{ terms}\right]$

XXII. Beta and Gamma Functions. See also (1101).

(1008) $\displaystyle\int_0^1 x^{l-1}(1-x)^{m-1}\,dx$

$\displaystyle\int_0^\infty \epsilon^{-x}x^{n-1}\,dx$

$B(l,m)$

$\Gamma(n+1)$

$\Gamma\left(\dfrac{1}{n}\right)\Gamma\left(\dfrac{2}{n}\right)\Gamma\left(\dfrac{3}{n}\right)\ldots\Gamma\left(\dfrac{n-1}{n}\right)$

$\Gamma(x)\Gamma\left(x+\dfrac{1}{n}\right)\Gamma\left(x+\dfrac{2}{n}\right)\ldots\Gamma\left(x+\dfrac{n-1}{n}\right)$

$\Gamma\left(\dfrac{1}{2}\right) = \sqrt{\pi}$

(1009) $\displaystyle\sum_0^\infty \dfrac{2n!}{2^{2n}(n!)^2}\dfrac{1}{x+n}$

(1010) $\displaystyle\sum_0^\infty (-1)^n\dfrac{a(a-1)(a-2)\ldots(a-n)}{n!}\dfrac{1}{x+n}$

(1011) $\epsilon^{-x}x^{x-1/2}(2\pi)^{1/2}\left\{1 + \dfrac{1}{12x} + \dfrac{1}{288x^2}\right.$

$\left. - \dfrac{139}{51840x^3} - \dfrac{571}{2488320x^4} + 0\,\dfrac{1}{x^5}\right\}$

$$= \frac{2}{\pi} \int_0^\pi \epsilon^{2 \cos \theta} \cos^2 (\sin \theta) \, d\theta \; - \; 1 \qquad\qquad \text{2Z. 296}$$

$$= \int_0^\pi \sin 2\theta \, \text{logh} \, (1 \, - \, 2a \cos \theta \, + \, a^2) \, d\theta \quad \text{where } a^2 < 1 \quad \text{2Z. 308}$$

$$= \int_0^\infty \frac{\cos rx}{(a^2 \, + \, x^2)^n} \, dx \qquad\qquad \text{2Z. 227}$$

$$= B(l, m) \quad \text{(Beta function)}$$

$$= \Gamma(n) \quad \text{(Gamma function)}$$

$$= \frac{\Gamma(l)\Gamma(m)}{\Gamma(l + m)}$$

$$= n\Gamma(n) = n! \quad \text{where } n \text{ is a positive integer}$$

$$= (2\pi)^{(n-1)/2} \, n^{-1/2} \qquad\qquad \text{2Z. 62}$$

$$= \Gamma(nx)(2\pi)^{(n-1)/2}n^{1/2-nx} \qquad\qquad \text{2Z. 94}$$

$$\Gamma(0) = \infty \qquad\qquad \text{2Z. 59}$$

$$= \frac{\Gamma(x)\Gamma(\frac{1}{2})}{\Gamma(x + \frac{1}{2})} \qquad\qquad \text{Q. 259}$$

$$= \frac{\Gamma(x)\Gamma(a + 1)}{\Gamma(x + a)} \quad \text{where } a \text{ is positive} \qquad \text{Q. 260}$$

$$= \Gamma(x) \qquad\qquad \text{Q. 253}$$

Series No.

(1012) $\dfrac{1}{x} + \dfrac{1^2}{4} \cdot \dfrac{1}{x(x+1)} + \dfrac{1^2 \cdot 3^2}{4 \cdot 8} \dfrac{1}{x(x+1)(x+2)} + \ldots \infty$

(1013) $\dfrac{1}{x} - \dfrac{a-1}{x+1} + \dfrac{(a-1)(a-2)}{2!(x+2)}$

$$- \dfrac{(a-1)(a-2)(a-3)}{3!(x+3)} + \ldots \infty$$

(1014) $1 + \dfrac{a}{b}(x) + \dfrac{a(a+1)}{b(b+1)} x^2 + \dfrac{a(a+1)(a+2)}{b(b+1)(b+2)} x^3 + \ldots \infty$

(1015) If in No. (1014), $b = 1$

$$1 + ax + \dfrac{a(a+1)}{2!} x^2 + \ldots \infty$$

XXIII. Infinite Products

(1016) $\theta\left(1 - \dfrac{\theta^2}{\pi^2}\right)\left(1 - \dfrac{\theta^2}{2^2\pi^2}\right)\left(1 - \dfrac{\theta^2}{3^2\pi^2}\right) \ldots \infty$

(1017) $\left(1 - \dfrac{4\theta^2}{\pi^2}\right)\left(1 - \dfrac{4\theta^2}{3^2\pi^2}\right)\left(1 - \dfrac{4\theta^2}{5^2\pi^2}\right) \ldots \infty$

(1018) $2^{n-1}\left\{\cosh\phi - \cos\theta\right\}\left\{\cosh\phi - \cos\left(\theta + \dfrac{2\pi}{n}\right)\right\}$

$$\ldots\left\{\cosh\phi - \cos\left(\theta + \dfrac{2n-2}{n}\pi\right)\right\}$$

$$= 2^{n-1} \prod_{r=0}^{r=n-1} \left\{\cosh\phi - \cos\left(\theta + \dfrac{2r\pi}{n}\right)\right\}$$

(1019) $\displaystyle\prod_{r=0}^{r=\frac{n-2}{2}} \left(x^2 - 2x\cos\dfrac{2r+1}{n}\pi + 1\right)$

(1020) $(x+1) \displaystyle\prod_{r=0}^{r=\frac{n-3}{2}} \left\{x^2 - 2x\cos\dfrac{2r+1}{n}\pi + 1\right\}$

(1021) $2^{(n-1)/2} \sin\dfrac{2\pi}{2n} \sin\dfrac{4\pi}{2n} \ldots \sin\dfrac{n-2}{2n}\pi$

$$= \left[\frac{\Gamma(x)}{\Gamma(x + \frac{1}{2})}\right]^2 \quad \text{where } x \text{ is positive} \qquad \text{A. 524}$$

$$= \frac{\Gamma(x)\Gamma(a)}{\Gamma(x + a)} \quad \text{where } x \text{ and } a \text{ are positive} \qquad \text{A. 524}$$

$$= \frac{\Gamma(b)}{\Gamma(a)\Gamma(b - a)} \int_0^1 \frac{t^{a-1}(1 - t)^{b-a-1}}{1 - xt} \, dt \quad \text{where } b > a > 0 \qquad \begin{matrix} \text{A. 294} \\ (1907) \end{matrix}$$

$$= (1 - x)^{-a}$$

$$= \sin \theta \qquad \text{A. 213}$$

$$= \cos \theta \qquad \text{A. 214}$$

$$= \cosh n\phi - \cos n\theta \qquad \text{E. 143}$$

$$= x^n + 1 \quad \text{where } n \text{ is even} \qquad \text{E. 143}$$

$$= x^n + 1 \quad \text{where } n \text{ is odd} \qquad \text{E. 143}$$

$$= \sqrt{n} \quad \text{where } n \text{ is even} \qquad \text{E. 144}$$

Series No.

(1022) $2^{(n-1)/2} \cos \dfrac{2\pi}{2n} \cos \dfrac{4\pi}{2n} \ldots \cos \dfrac{n-1}{2n} \pi$

(1023) $\cos \theta \cos \left(\theta + \dfrac{2\pi}{n} \right) \ldots \cos \left\{ \theta + (n-1) \dfrac{2\pi}{n} \right\}$

(1024) $\sin \theta \sin \left(\theta + \dfrac{2\pi}{n} \right) \ldots \sin \left\{ \theta + (n-1) \dfrac{2\pi}{n} \right\}$

(1025) $\tan \dfrac{\pi}{n} \tan \dfrac{2\pi}{n} \ldots \tan \dfrac{\frac{1}{2}(n-1)\pi}{n}$

(1026) $2^{n-1} \left(\cos \theta - \cos \dfrac{\pi}{2n} \right) \left(\cos \theta - \cos \dfrac{3\pi}{2n} \right) \ldots$
$$\left(\cos \theta - \cos \dfrac{2n-1}{2n} \pi \right)$$

(1027) $2^{(n-1)/2} \sin \dfrac{\pi}{2n} \sin \dfrac{3\pi}{2n} \ldots \sin \dfrac{n-2}{2n} \pi$
$$= 2^{(n-1)/2} \cos \dfrac{2\pi}{2n} \cos \dfrac{4\pi}{2n} \ldots \cos \dfrac{n-1}{2n} \pi$$

(1028) $(1-x)\left(1 + \dfrac{1}{2}x\right)\left(1 - \dfrac{1}{3}x\right)\left(1 + \dfrac{1}{4}x\right) \ldots \infty$

(1029) $(1-x)\left(1 + \dfrac{1}{3}x\right)\left(1 - \dfrac{1}{5}x\right)\left(1 + \dfrac{1}{7}x\right) \ldots \infty$

(1030) $\pi x \left(1 + \dfrac{x}{1}\right)\left(1 + \dfrac{x}{2}\right)\left(1 + \dfrac{x}{3}\right)\left(1 - \dfrac{x}{1}\right)$
$$\times \left(1 + \dfrac{x}{4}\right)\left(1 + \dfrac{x}{5}\right)\left(1 + \dfrac{x}{6}\right)\left(1 - \dfrac{x}{2}\right) \ldots$$

(1031) $\displaystyle\prod_{-\infty}^{+\infty} \left\{ \epsilon^{\theta/n\pi} \left(1 - \dfrac{\theta}{n\pi}\right) \right\}$

$= 1$ where n is odd $\qquad\qquad\qquad$ E. 144

$= \dfrac{1}{2^{n-1}} \cos n\theta$ where n is odd

$= \dfrac{1}{2^{n-1}} [(-1)^{n/2} - \cos n\theta]$ where n is even $\qquad$ E. 73

$= (-1)^{(n-1)/2} \dfrac{1}{2^{n-1}} \sin n\theta$ where n is odd

$= (-1)^{n/2} \dfrac{1}{2^{n-1}} (1 - \cos n\theta)$ where n is even $\qquad$ E. 73

$= \sqrt{n}$ where n is odd $\qquad\qquad\qquad$ E. 145

$= \cos n\theta \qquad\qquad\qquad\qquad\qquad\qquad$ E. 145

$= 1$ where n is odd $\qquad\qquad\qquad$ E. 145

$= \dfrac{\Gamma(\frac{1}{2})}{\Gamma(1 + \frac{1}{2}x)\Gamma(\frac{1}{2} - \frac{1}{2}x)} \qquad\qquad$ A. 115

$= \cos \dfrac{\pi x}{4} - \sin \dfrac{\pi x}{4} \qquad\qquad\qquad$ A. 224

$= e^{x \log_h 3} \sin \pi x \qquad\qquad\qquad\qquad$ AG.40

$= \dfrac{\sin \theta}{\theta}$ omitting $n = 0$ $\qquad\qquad\qquad$ A. 215

Series No.

(1032) $\displaystyle\prod_{n=1}^{n=\infty} \left\{ \left(1 - \frac{\theta}{n\pi}\right) \epsilon^{\theta/n\pi} \left(1 + \frac{\theta}{n\pi}\right) \epsilon^{-\theta/n\pi} \right\}$

(1033) $\displaystyle\prod_{-\infty}^{+\infty} \left\{ \epsilon^{2\theta/(2n+1)\pi} \left(1 - \frac{2\theta}{(2n+1)\pi}\right) \right\}$

(1034) $\displaystyle\prod_{2}^{\infty} \frac{n^3 - 1}{n^3 + 1}$

(1035) $\displaystyle\prod_{1}^{\infty} \frac{\left(1 + \dfrac{1}{r}\right)^x}{1 + \dfrac{x}{r}}$

(1036) $\displaystyle x! \left(x - \frac{1}{n}\right)! \left(x - \frac{2}{n}\right)! \dots \left(x - \frac{n-1}{n}\right)!$

(1037) $\displaystyle \left\{ \left(1 + \frac{k}{\theta}\right)^2 \right\} \left\{ 1 + \left(\frac{k}{2\pi - \theta}\right)^2 \right\}$

$\displaystyle \qquad \left\{ 1 + \left(\frac{k}{2\pi + \theta}\right)^2 \right\} \left\{ 1 + \left(\frac{k}{4\pi - \theta}\right)^2 \right\} \left\{ 1 + \left(\frac{k}{4\pi + \theta}\right)^2 \right\} \dots \infty$

(1038) $\displaystyle \cos \frac{\theta}{2} \cdot \cos \frac{\theta}{2^2} \cdot \cos \frac{\theta}{2^3} \dots \infty$

(1039) $\displaystyle \theta \left(1 - \frac{\theta}{\pi}\right) \left(1 - \frac{\theta}{2\pi}\right) \left(1 + \frac{\theta}{\pi}\right) \left(1 - \frac{\theta}{3\pi}\right)$

$\displaystyle \qquad\qquad\qquad \times \left(1 - \frac{\theta}{4\pi}\right) \left(1 + \frac{\theta}{2\pi}\right) - \dots \infty$

(1040) $\displaystyle \left(1 - \frac{\sin^2 \theta}{\sin^2 \beta}\right) \left(1 - \frac{\sin^2 \theta}{\sin^2 3\beta}\right) \dots \left(1 - \frac{\sin^2 \theta}{\sin^2 (n-1)\beta}\right)$

(1041) $\displaystyle 2^{n-1} \prod_{0}^{n=1} \sin(\theta + ra)$

(1042) $\displaystyle \operatorname*{Lt}_{n=\infty} \left[\tan \frac{\pi}{2n} \cdot \tan \frac{2\pi}{2n} \dots \frac{\tan n\pi}{2n} \right]^{1/n}$

$$= \frac{\sin \theta}{\theta}$$

Q. 137

$$= \cos \theta$$

A. 216

$$= \frac{2}{3}$$

$$= x!$$

AD. 10

$$= \sqrt{\frac{(2\pi)^{n-1}}{n}} \frac{(n \cdot x) \ !}{n^{nx}}$$

AD. 18

$$= \frac{\cosh k - \cos \theta}{1 - \cos \theta}$$

Q. 137

$$= \frac{\sin \theta}{\theta}$$

A. 114

$$= \epsilon^{-(\theta/\pi) \ \log h \ 2} \sin \theta$$

Q. 35

$$= \cos n\theta \quad (n \text{ even}) \quad \beta = \frac{\pi}{2n}$$

A. 211

$$= \sin n\theta \quad \text{where } 0 < \theta < a$$

A. 211

$$= 1$$

1Z. 355

Series No.

(1043) $\underset{n=\infty}{\text{Lt}} \left[\left(1 + \frac{1}{n} \right)\left(1 + \frac{2}{n} \right)^{1/2}\left(1 + \frac{3}{n} \right)^{1/3} \ldots \left(1 + \frac{n}{n} \right)^{1/n} \right]$

(1044) $\dfrac{x + c}{c} \displaystyle\prod_{-\infty}^{+\infty} \left(1 + \frac{x}{n + c} \right) \epsilon^{-x/n}$

(1045) $2^{n-1} \displaystyle\prod_{r=0}^{r=n-1} \sin \left(\theta + \frac{r\pi}{n} \right)$

(1046) $2^{n-1} \sin \left(\theta + \dfrac{\pi}{2n} \right) \sin \left(\theta + \dfrac{3\pi}{n} \right) \ldots \sin \left(\theta + \dfrac{2n - 1}{2n}\, \pi \right)$

(1047) $2^{n-1} \cos \theta \cos \left(\theta + \dfrac{\pi}{n} \right) \cos \left(\theta + \dfrac{2\pi}{n} \right) \ldots \left(\theta + \dfrac{n - 1}{n}\, \pi \right)$

(1048) $2^{n-1} \cos \dfrac{\pi}{2n} \cos \dfrac{3\pi}{2n} \cos \dfrac{5\pi}{2n} \ldots \cos \dfrac{2n - 1}{2n}\, \pi$

(1049) $2^{n-1} \sin \dfrac{\pi}{2n} \sin \dfrac{3\pi}{2n} \ldots \sin \dfrac{2n - 1}{2n}\, \pi$

(1050) $\cos \dfrac{\pi}{n} \cos \dfrac{2\pi}{n} \ldots \cos \left(\dfrac{2n - 1}{n} \right)\pi$

(1051) $\left(1 - \dfrac{\theta}{a} \right)\left(1 + \dfrac{\theta}{\pi - a} \right)\left(1 - \dfrac{\theta}{\pi + a} \right)$
$\left(1 + \dfrac{\theta}{2\pi - a} \right)\left(1 - \dfrac{\theta}{2\pi + a} \right) \ldots \infty$

(1052) $\displaystyle\prod_{0}^{\infty} \left\{ 1 + \frac{\theta}{a + r\pi} \right\}$

(1053) $\displaystyle\prod_{0}^{\infty} \left\{ 1 + \frac{2\theta}{2a + r\pi} \right\}$

(1054) $\displaystyle\prod_{0}^{\infty} \left\{ 1 - \frac{2\theta}{2a + r\pi} \right\}$

$$= \epsilon^{\pi^2/12}$$ 1Z. 355

$$= \frac{\sin \pi(x + c)}{\sin \pi c}$$ A. 224

$$= \sin n\theta$$ E. 145

$$= \cos n\theta$$ E. 145

$$= (-1)^{n/2} \sin n\theta \quad \text{where } n \text{ is even}$$

$$= (-1)^{(n-1)/2} \cos n\theta \quad \text{where } n \text{ is odd}$$ E. 145

$$= \cos \frac{n\pi}{2}$$ E. 146

$$= 1$$ E. 146

$$= \frac{(-1)^n - 1}{2^{2n-1}}$$ E. 146

$$= \frac{\sin (a - \theta)}{\sin a}$$ E. 159

$$= \frac{\sin (a + \theta)}{\sin a} \quad \text{when } r \text{ is a positive or negative integer or zero}$$
                                                                  E. 159

$$= \frac{\cos (a + \theta)}{\cos a} \quad \text{when } r \text{ is an odd integer, positive or negative}$$
                                                                  E. 159

$$= \frac{\cos (a - \theta)}{\cos a} \quad \text{when } r \text{ is an odd integer, positive or negative}$$
                                                                  E. 159

Series No.

(1055) $\left\{1 - \left(\dfrac{\theta}{\pi + a}\right)^2\right\}\left\{1 - \left(\dfrac{\theta}{\pi - a}\right)^2\right\}\left\{1 - \left(\dfrac{\theta}{3\pi + a}\right)^2\right\}$

$$\times \left\{1 - \left(\dfrac{\theta}{3\pi - a}\right)^2\right\}\dots \infty$$

(1056) $\left(1 - \dfrac{\theta^2}{a^2}\right)\left\{1 - \left(\dfrac{\theta}{2\pi + a}\right)^2\right\}\left\{1 - \left(\dfrac{\theta}{2\pi - a}\right)^2\right\}\dots \infty$

(1057) $\left(1 - \dfrac{\theta}{a}\right)\left(1 - \dfrac{\theta}{\pi - a}\right)\left(1 + \dfrac{\theta}{\pi + a}\right)$

$$\times \left(1 + \dfrac{\theta}{2\pi - a}\right)\left(1 - \dfrac{\theta}{2\pi + a}\right)\dots \infty$$

(1058) $\left(\dfrac{3^2}{3^2 - 1}\right)\left(\dfrac{5^2 - 1}{5^2}\right)\left(\dfrac{7^2}{7^2 - 1}\right)\left(\dfrac{9^2 - 1}{9^2}\right)\dots \infty$

(1059) $\left(1 - \dfrac{1}{3^2}\right)\left(1 - \dfrac{1}{5^2}\right)\left(1 - \dfrac{1}{7^2}\right)\dots \infty$

(1060) $\displaystyle\prod_1^\infty \dfrac{n^3 - x^3}{n^3 + x^3}$

(1061) $\displaystyle\prod_1^\infty \dfrac{n(n + a + b)}{(n + a)(n + b)}$

(1062) $4\cos^2 \dfrac{a}{2}\left\{1 + \left(\dfrac{\theta}{\pi + a}\right)^2\right\}\left\{1 + \left(\dfrac{\theta}{a - \pi}\right)^2\right\}\dots \infty$

(1063) $\left(1 + \dfrac{1}{1^2}\right)\left(1 + \dfrac{1}{2^2}\right)\left(1 + \dfrac{1}{3^2}\right)\dots \infty$

(1064) $\displaystyle\prod_{m=1}^{m=\infty} \left\{1 - \dfrac{x^2}{m^2 - a^2}\right\}$

(1065) $\left(1 + \dfrac{1}{1}\right)\left(1 - \dfrac{1}{2}\right)\left(1 + \dfrac{1}{3}\right)\left(1 - \dfrac{1}{4}\right)\dots \infty$

$$= \frac{\cos\theta + \cos a}{1 + \cos a}$$ E. 159

$$= \frac{\cos\theta - \cos a}{1 - \cos a}$$ E. 159

$$= \frac{\sin a - \sin\theta}{\sin a}$$ E. 160

$$= \frac{\{\Gamma(\frac{1}{4})\}^4}{16\pi^2}$$ Q. 259

$$= \frac{\pi}{4}$$ A. 106

$$= \frac{\Gamma(1 + x)\Gamma(1 + tx)\Gamma(1 + t^2x)}{\Gamma(1 - x)\Gamma(1 - tx)\Gamma(1 - t^2x)}$$

when $t = \frac{1}{2}(-1 + i\sqrt{3})$

or $t^3 = 1$ A. 313

$$= \frac{\Gamma(1 + a)\Gamma(1 + b)}{\Gamma(1 + a + b)}$$ A. 115

$$= 2\cosh\theta + 2\cos a$$ E. 160

$$= \frac{1}{\pi}\sinh\pi$$ E. 160

$$= \frac{a}{\sqrt{a^2 + x^2}} \frac{\sin\{\pi\sqrt{a^2 + x^2}\}}{\sin\pi a}$$ E. 161

$$= 1$$ A. 108

Series No.

(1066) $\left(1 + \frac{1}{1}\right)\left(1 + \frac{1}{2}\right)\left(1 + \frac{1}{3}\right)\ldots \infty$

(1067) $\left(1 - \frac{1}{2}\right)\left(1 - \frac{1}{3}\right)\ldots \infty$

(1068) $\left(1 - \frac{1}{2^2}\right)\left(1 - \frac{1}{3^2}\right)\left(1 - \frac{1}{4^2}\right)\ldots \infty$

(1069) $\left(1 - \frac{1}{2}\right)\left(1 - \frac{1}{4}\right)\left(1 - \frac{1}{6}\right)\ldots \infty$

(1070) $\left(1 + \frac{1}{1\cdot 3}\right)\left(1 + \frac{1}{3\cdot 5}\right)$

(1071) $2(1 + 2^2)\left\{1 + \left(\frac{2}{3}\right)^2\right\}\left\{1 + \left(\frac{2}{5}\right)^2\right\}\ldots \infty$

(1072) $\left(1 + \frac{1}{\sqrt{2}}\right)\left(1 - \frac{1}{\sqrt{3}}\right)\left(1 + \frac{1}{\sqrt{4}}\right)\ldots \infty$

$\qquad = \left(1 - \frac{1}{\sqrt{2}}\right)\left(1 + \frac{1}{\sqrt{3}}\right)\left(1 - \frac{1}{\sqrt{4}}\right)\ldots \infty$

(1073)† $n\left(1 - \frac{\sin^2 \theta}{\sin^2 \alpha}\right)\left(1 - \frac{\sin^2 \theta}{\sin^2 2\alpha}\right)\ldots\left\{1 - \frac{\sin^2 \theta}{\sin^2 \frac{1}{2}(n - 1)\alpha}\right\}$

(1074)† $n\left(1 - \frac{\sin^2 \theta}{\sin^2 \alpha}\right)\left(1 - \frac{\sin^2 \theta}{\sin^2 2\alpha}\right)\ldots\left\{\frac{\sin^2 \theta}{1 \sin^2 \frac{1}{2}(n - 2)\alpha}\right\}$

(1075)‡ $\left(1 - \frac{\sin^2 \theta}{\sin^2 \beta}\right)\left(1 - \frac{\sin^2 \theta}{\sin^2 3\beta}\right)\ldots\left\{1 - \frac{\sin^2 \theta}{\sin^2 (n - 2)\beta}\right\}$

(1075a)‡ $\left(1 - \frac{\sin^2 \theta}{\sin^2 \beta}\right)\left(1 - \frac{\sin^2 \theta}{\sin^2 3\beta}\right)\ldots\left\{1 - \frac{\sin^2 \theta}{\sin^2 (n - 1)\beta}\right\}$

(1076) $2^{n-1} \prod_{0}^{n-1} \left\{\cos \theta - \cos\left(\beta + \frac{2\kappa\pi}{n}\right)\right\}$

$\qquad$ † $\alpha = \frac{\pi}{n}.$ $\qquad\qquad$ ‡ $\beta = \frac{\pi}{2n}.$

$= \infty$ A. 106

$= 0$ C. 159

$= \dfrac{1}{2}$ A. 106

$= 0$ E. 155

$= \dfrac{\pi}{2}$ A. 213

$= \epsilon^{\pi} + \epsilon^{-\pi}$ E. 190

$= 0$ A. 111

$= \dfrac{\sin n\theta}{\sin \theta}$ where n is odd   A. 210

$= \dfrac{\sin n\theta}{\sin \theta \cos \theta}$ where n is even   A. 210

$= \dfrac{\cos n\theta}{\cos \theta}$ where n is odd   A. 211

$= \cos n\theta$ where n is even   A. 211

$= \cos n\theta - \cos n\beta$ T. 84

Series No.

(1077) $\displaystyle\prod_0^{n-1} \left\{ a^2 - 2ab \cos\left(\theta + \frac{2\kappa\pi}{n}\right) + b^2 \right\}$

(1078) $\theta \displaystyle\prod_1^{\infty} \left(1 + \frac{\theta^2}{n^2\pi^2}\right)$

(1079) $\displaystyle\prod_0^{\infty} \left\{ 1 + \frac{4\theta^2}{(2n+1)^2\pi^2} \right\}$

(1080) $\displaystyle\prod_1^{\infty} \cos\frac{\theta}{2^n}$

(1081) $\displaystyle\prod_0^{\infty} (1 + x^{2n})$

(1082) $\displaystyle\prod_{-\infty}^{\infty} \left[1 - \frac{x^2}{(n+c)^2} \right]$

(1083) $\displaystyle\prod_{-\infty}^{\infty} \left[1 - \frac{4x^2}{(n\pi + x)^2} \right]$

(1084) $\displaystyle\prod_{-\infty}^{\infty} \left[e^{\theta/n\pi}\left(1 - \frac{\theta}{n\pi}\right) \right]$

XXIV. Fourier's Series

(1085) $\dfrac{f'(2\pi) - f'(0)}{n^2} - \dfrac{f'''(2\pi) - f'''(0)}{n^4} + \ldots \infty$

(1086) $\dfrac{1}{2}f(0) + f\left(\dfrac{2\pi}{n}\right) + f\left(\dfrac{4\pi}{n}\right) + \ldots + \dfrac{1}{2}f(2\pi)$

(1087) $\dfrac{2\pi}{n}\left\{ \dfrac{1}{2}f(0) + f\left(\dfrac{2\pi}{n}\right) + \ldots + \dfrac{1}{2}f(2\pi) \right\}$

$\qquad - 2\dfrac{f'(2\pi) - f'(0)}{n^2}\cdot\dfrac{\pi^2}{6} + 2\dfrac{f'''(2\pi) - f'''(0)}{n^4}\cdot\dfrac{\pi^4}{90} \ldots \infty$

$= a^{2n} - 2a^n b^n \cos n\theta + b^{2n}$ T. 84

$= \sinh \theta$ T. 130

$= \cosh \theta$ T. 130

$= \dfrac{\sin \theta}{\theta}$ T. 130

$= \dfrac{1}{1 - x}$ where $x^2 < 1$ T. 130

$= 1 - \dfrac{\sin^2 \pi x}{\sin^2 \pi c}$ A. 224

$= -\dfrac{\sin 3x}{\sin x}$ A. 224

$= \dfrac{\sin \theta}{\theta}$ $n = 0$ omitted   A. 215

$= \displaystyle\int_0^{2\pi} f(t) \cos nt \, dt$ if all differential coefficients are finite and

the series is convergent   X. 140

$= \dfrac{n}{2\pi} \displaystyle\int_0^{2\pi} f(t) \, dt + \dfrac{n}{\pi} \int_0^{2\pi} f(t) \cos nt \, dt$

$+ \dfrac{n}{\pi} \displaystyle\int_0^{2\pi} f(t) \cos 2nt \, dt + \dots \infty$ X. 140

$= \displaystyle\int_0^{2\pi} f(t) \, dt$ where $\dfrac{\pi^2}{6} = 1 + \dfrac{1}{2^2} + \dfrac{1}{3^2} + \dots \infty$

and $\dfrac{\pi^4}{90} = 1 + \dfrac{1}{2^4} + \dfrac{1}{3^4} + \dots \infty$, etc.   X. 140

Series No.

(1088) $h\left\{\dfrac{1}{2}f(0) + f(h) + f(2h) + \ldots \dfrac{1}{2}f(nh)\right\}$

$$- \dfrac{h^2}{2 \cdot 3!}\{f^1(nh) - f^1(0)\} + \dfrac{h^4}{6 \cdot 5!}\{f^3(nh) - f^3(0)\}$$

$$- \dfrac{h^6}{6 \cdot 7!}\{f^5(nh) - f^5(0)\} + \dfrac{3h^8}{10 \cdot 9!}\{f^7(nh) - f^7(0)\}$$

$$- \dfrac{5h^{10}}{6 \cdot 11!}\{f^9(nh) - f^9(0)\} + \ldots \infty$$

Series to be convergent

(1089) $h\left\{\dfrac{1}{2}f(x) + f(x + h) + f(x + 2h) + \ldots\right\} + \dfrac{h^2}{2 \cdot 3!}f^1(x)$

$$- \dfrac{h^4}{6 \cdot 5!}f^3(x) + \dfrac{h^6}{6 \cdot 7!}f^5(x) - \dfrac{3h^8}{10 \cdot 9!}f^7(x) + \ldots \infty$$

Series to be convergent

XXV. Hypergeometric Functions

(1090) $1 + \dfrac{ab}{1 \cdot c}x + \dfrac{a(a + 1)b(b + 1)}{2!c(c + 1)}x^2$

$$+ \dfrac{a(a + 1)(a + 2)b(b + 1)(b + 2)}{3!c(c + 1)(c + 2)}x^3 + \ldots \infty$$

(1091) $\dfrac{\Gamma(c)\Gamma(c - a - b)}{\Gamma(c - a)\Gamma(c - b)}$

(1092) $F(A, 1; C, x)$

(1093) $\dfrac{x^{m+1}}{m + 1}\left\{1 + \dfrac{m + 2}{m + 3}x^2 + \ldots \dfrac{(m + 2)\ldots(m + 2n - 2)}{(m + 3)\ldots(m + 2n - 1)}x^{2n-2}\right\}$

$$+ (1 - x^2)^{-1/2}\dfrac{(m + 2)(m + 4)\ldots(m + 2n)}{(m + 1)(m + 3)\ldots(m + 2n - 1)}$$

$$\times \int_0^x t^{m+2n}(1 - t^2) - \dfrac{1}{2}dt$$

$$= \int_0^{nh} f(t)\, dt \qquad\qquad\qquad \text{X. 140}$$

$$= \int_x^{\infty} f(t)\, dt \qquad\qquad\qquad \text{X. 141}$$

$$= F(a, b; c, x) \quad \text{where } |x| < | \qquad\qquad \text{Q. 281}$$

$$= F(a, b; c, 1) \qquad\qquad\qquad \text{Q. 282}$$

$$= \frac{1}{1-x} F\!\left(C - A, 1; C, \frac{x}{x-1}\right) \qquad\qquad \text{Q. 286}$$

$$= (1 - x^2)^{-1/2} \int_0^x t^m (1 - t^2)^{-1/2}\, dt \quad \text{where } x \text{ and } 1 - x \text{ are not}$$

negative real numbers   Q. 109

Series No.

XXVI. Relations between Products and Series

(1094) $(1 + xz)(1 + x^3z)\ldots(1 + x^{2m-1}z)$

(1095) $\log h \{(1 - x)(1 - x^2)(1 - x^3)\ldots \infty\}$

(1096) $\displaystyle\prod_1^\infty \left(1 + \frac{x}{p_n}\right)$

(1097) $\displaystyle\prod_1^m (1 + x^nz)$

(1098) $\displaystyle\prod_1^\infty (1 + x^nz)$

(1099) In the following relations between series and products, all p are prime and may be related to the p_n, q_n, r_n, and t_n of series Nos. (315) to (318).

Series (315) $1 + \dfrac{1}{5^n} - \dfrac{1}{7^n} - \dfrac{1}{11^n} + \dfrac{1}{13^n} \ldots = r_n$

Series (316) $1 - \dfrac{1}{5^n} - \dfrac{1}{7^n} + \dfrac{1}{11^n} + \dfrac{1}{13^n} \ldots = t_n$

Series (317) $1 + \dfrac{1}{3^n} - \dfrac{1}{5^n} - \dfrac{1}{7^n} + \dfrac{1}{11^n} \ldots = p_n$

Series (318) $1 - \dfrac{1}{3^n} - \dfrac{1}{5^n} + \dfrac{1}{7^n} - \dfrac{1}{11^n} \ldots = q_n$

$$= 1 + \sum_{n=1}^{m} \frac{(1 - x^{2m})(1 - x^{2m-2})\ldots(1 - x^{2m-2n+2})x^{n^2}z^n}{(1 - x^2)(1 - x^4)\ldots(1 - x^{2n})}$$ C. 344

$$= - \sum_{1}^{\infty} f(n)\frac{x^n}{n}$$ where $|x| < 1$ and $f(n)$ denotes the sum of all

the divisors of the positive integer n; for example, $f(4) = 1 + 2 + 4$ C. 345

$$= 1 + \sum_{1}^{\infty} \frac{x(x + p_1)(x + p_2)\ldots(x + p_{n-1})}{p_1 p_2 p_3 \cdots p_n}$$ if the product

converges to a definite limit   C. 420

$$= 1 + \sum_{1}^{m} \frac{(1 - x^m)(1 - x^{m-1})\ldots(1 - x^{m-n+1})}{(1 - x)(1 - x^2)\ldots(1 - x^n)} x^{\{m(n+1)\}/2} z^n$$

C. 340

$$= 1 + \sum_{1}^{\infty} \frac{x^{\{n(n+1)\}/2}z^n}{(1 - x)(1 - x^2)\ldots(1 - x^n)}$$ where $|x| < 1$ C. 341

AE. 87

$$= \frac{1}{\left(1 - \frac{1}{5^n}\right)\left(1 + \frac{1}{7^n}\right)\left(1 + \frac{1}{11^n}\right)\left(1 - \frac{1}{13^n}\right)\cdots}$$

$$= \frac{1}{\left(1 + \frac{1}{5^n}\right)\left(1 + \frac{1}{7^n}\right)\left(1 - \frac{1}{11^n}\right)\left(1 - \frac{1}{13^n}\right)\cdots}$$

$$= \frac{1}{\left(1 - \frac{1}{3^n}\right)\left(1 + \frac{1}{5^n}\right)\left(1 + \frac{1}{7^n}\right)\left(1 - \frac{1}{11^n}\right)}\cdots \text{ omitting non-primes}$$

$$= \frac{1}{\left(1 + \frac{1}{3^n}\right)\left(1 + \frac{1}{5^n}\right)\left(1 - \frac{1}{7^n}\right)\left(1 + \frac{1}{11^n}\right)}\cdots \text{ omitting non-primes}$$

Series No.

$$(1100) \quad \prod_1^\infty (1 + v_n)$$

XXVII. Special Functions

$$(1101) \quad \psi(x) = \frac{\Gamma'(x)}{\Gamma(x)} = \frac{d}{dx} \text{logh } \Gamma(x)$$

$C = $ Euler's constant; see No. (1132).

$$\psi(x) = -\frac{1}{x} - \frac{1}{x+1} - \frac{1}{x+2} - \cdots$$

$$-\frac{1}{x+n} + \psi(x+n+1)$$

$$\sum_0^\infty \left(\frac{1}{x+n} - \frac{1}{n+1} \right)$$

$$\sum_0^\infty \left(\frac{1}{y+n} - \frac{1}{x+n} \right)$$

$$\sum_1^\infty \left(\frac{1}{n} - \frac{1}{x+n} \right)$$

$$\sum_0^\infty \frac{(-1)^n}{x+n}$$

$$\text{logh } n + \sum_0^{n-1} \frac{1}{n} \psi\left(1 + \frac{r}{n} \right)$$

$$\psi(x+1) = \frac{1}{x} + \psi(x)$$

$$\psi(1-x) = \psi(x) + \pi \cot \pi x$$

$$\psi(0) = -\infty$$

$$= 1 + \sum_1^\infty u_n \quad \text{where} \frac{v_n}{u_n} = \frac{1}{1 + u_1 + u_2 + \ldots u_{n-1}}$$

and the series is convergent

$$= - C + \int_0^1 \frac{1 - t^{x-1}}{1 - t} dt \quad \text{where } x \text{ is a real and positive integer}$$

$$= - C + \frac{1}{1} \cdot \frac{x - 1}{x} + \ldots \frac{1}{n} \frac{x - 1}{x + n - 1} \ldots \infty$$

$$= - C - \psi(x)$$

$$= \psi(x) - \psi(y)$$

$$= \psi(x) + C + \frac{1}{x}$$

$$= \frac{1}{2}\left\{ \psi\left(\frac{x+1}{2}\right) - \psi\left(\frac{x}{2}\right) \right\} = \beta(x)$$

$$= \int_0^1 \frac{t^x - 1}{t + 1} dt$$

$$= \psi(n)$$

$$\psi\left(\frac{1}{2}\right) = - C - 2 \log h \ 2$$

$$\psi\left(\frac{3}{2}\right) = 2 - C - 2 \log h \ 2$$

$$\psi\left(\frac{5}{2}\right) = \frac{8}{3} - C - 2 \log h \ 2$$

Series No.

$$\psi(1) = -C$$

$$\psi(2) = 1 - C$$

$$\psi(3) = \frac{3}{2} - C$$

$$\psi(4) = \left(1 + \frac{1}{2} + \frac{1}{3}\right) - C$$

$$\psi(n) = \left(1 + \frac{1}{2} + \frac{1}{3} + \dots \frac{1}{n}\right) - C$$

$$\beta(x + 1) + \beta(x) = \frac{1}{x}$$

$$\beta(x) + \beta(1 - x) = \frac{\pi}{\sin \pi x}$$

$$\beta(1) = \text{logh } 2$$

$$\beta(2) = 1 - \text{logh } 2$$

$$\beta(3) = -\frac{1}{2} + \text{logh } 2$$

$$\beta(4) = \frac{1}{3} + \frac{1}{2} - \text{logh } 2$$

$$\beta\left(\frac{1}{2}\right) = \frac{\pi}{2} \qquad\qquad \beta\left(\frac{1}{3}\right) = \text{logh } 2 + \frac{1}{3}\pi\sqrt{3}$$

$$\beta\left(\frac{3}{2}\right) = 2 - \frac{\pi}{2} \qquad\qquad \beta\left(\frac{2}{3}\right) = -\text{logh } 2 + \frac{1}{3}\pi\sqrt{3}$$

$$\beta\left(\frac{5}{2}\right) = \frac{2}{3} - 2 + \frac{\pi}{2}$$

$$\text{If } \frac{d^2}{dx^2} \text{logh } \Gamma(x) = \psi'(x)$$

$$\psi\left(\frac{1}{3}\right) = -\,C - \frac{3}{2}\log h\,3$$
$$-\frac{\pi}{2\sqrt{3}}$$

$$\psi\left(\frac{2}{3}\right) = -\,C - \frac{3}{2}\log h\,3$$
$$+\frac{\pi}{2\sqrt{3}}$$

$$\psi\left(\frac{3}{4}\right) = \frac{\pi}{2} - C - 3\log 2$$

$$\psi\left(\frac{1}{4}\right) = -\frac{\pi}{2} - C - 3\log 2$$

$$= \sum_{0}^{\infty} \frac{1}{(x + n)^2}$$

Series No.

$$\psi'(0)$$

$$\psi'\left(\frac{1}{2}\right) = 4\left(\frac{1}{1^2} + \frac{1}{3^2} + \frac{1}{5^2} + \ldots\right)$$

$$\psi'(1) = \frac{1}{1^2} + \frac{1}{2^2} + \frac{1}{3^2} + \ldots$$

$$\psi'\left(\frac{3}{2}\right) = 4\left(\frac{1}{3^2} + \frac{1}{5^2} + \ldots\right)$$

$$\psi'(2) = \frac{1}{2^2} + \frac{1}{3^2} + \frac{1}{4^2} + \ldots$$

$$\psi'\left(\frac{5}{2}\right) = 4\left(\frac{1}{5^2} + \frac{1}{7^2} + \ldots\right)$$

$$\psi'(3) = \frac{1}{3^2} + \frac{1}{4^2} + \frac{1}{5^2} + \ldots$$

$$\psi'(\infty)$$

(1102) If $\dfrac{a!}{b!(a-b)!'} = \dbinom{a}{b} = {}_aC_b$

$$\sum_0^{\frac{r}{2}-p} \binom{r}{2p+2n}\binom{p+n}{n}$$

$$\sum_0^{\frac{r-1}{2}-p} \binom{r}{2p+2n+1}\binom{p+n}{n}$$

$$1 + \binom{n}{1} + \binom{n}{2} + \ldots + \binom{n}{n}$$

$$1 - \binom{n}{1} + \binom{n}{2} - \ldots (-1)^n \binom{n}{n}$$

$$1 + \binom{n}{1}^2 + \binom{n}{2}^2 + \ldots \binom{n}{n}^2$$

$= \infty$

$= \dfrac{\pi^2}{2}$

$= \dfrac{\pi^2}{6}$

$= \dfrac{\pi^2}{2} - 4$

$= \dfrac{\pi^2}{6} - 1$

$= 4\left(\dfrac{\pi^2}{8} - \dfrac{1}{1^2} - \dfrac{1}{3^2}\right) = \dfrac{\pi^2}{2} - 4\cdot\dot{4}$

$= \dfrac{\pi^2}{6} - \dfrac{5}{4}$

$= 0$

$= \dfrac{a(a-1)(a-2)\ldots(a-b+1)}{b!}$ T. 19

$= \dfrac{r}{2(r-p)}\dbinom{r-p}{p}2^{r-2p}$

$= \dbinom{r-p-1}{p}2^{r-2p-1}$

$= 2^n$ T. 19

$= 0$ T. 19

$= \dbinom{2n}{n}$ T. 19

Series No.

$$\binom{k}{k} + \binom{k+1}{k} + \binom{k+2}{k} + \ldots \binom{n}{k}$$

$$1 - \binom{n}{1} + \binom{n}{2} - \ldots (-1)^k \binom{n}{k}$$

See also No. (189), etc.

Table of Binomial Coefficients $\binom{n}{1} = n^{c_1} = n$

$\binom{n}{1}$	$\binom{n}{2}$	$\binom{n}{3}$	$\binom{n}{4}$	$\binom{n}{5}$	$\binom{n}{6}$	$\binom{n}{7}$	$\binom{n}{8}$	$\binom{n}{9}$	$\binom{n}{10}$	$\binom{n}{11}$	$\binom{n}{12}$
1											
2	1										
3	3	1									
4	6	4	1								
5	10	10	5	1							
6	15	20	15	6	1						
7	21	35	35	21	7	1					
8	28	56	70	56	28	8	1				
9	36	84	126	126	84	36	9	1			
10	45	120	210	252	210	120	45	10	1		
11	55	165	330	462	462	330	165	55	11	1	
12	66	220	495	792	924	792	495	220	66	12	1

XXVIII. Zeta Functions

(1103) $\displaystyle\sum_{n=0}^{\infty} \frac{1}{(a+n)}s$

If s is a negative integer $= -m$

$\zeta(-2m)$

$\zeta(1-2m)$

$\zeta(0)$

$$= \binom{n+1}{k+1}$$

$$= (-1)^k \binom{n-1}{k}$$

$$= \zeta(s, a)$$

$$= \frac{1}{\Gamma(s)} \int_0^\infty \frac{x^{s-1} \epsilon^{-ax}}{1 - \epsilon^{-x}} \, dx$$

$$= 0$$

$$= \frac{(-1)^m B_m}{2m} \quad \text{where } m = 1, 2, 3, \text{ etc.}$$

$$= -\frac{1}{2}$$

Series No.

XXIX. Legendre Polynomials

(1104) If $P_0(x) + hP_1(x) + h^2P_2(x) + \dots$

where $P_0(x) = 1, \quad P_1(x) = x, \quad P_2(x) = \frac{1}{2}(3x^2 - 1)$

$$P_3(x) = \frac{1}{2}(5x^3 - 3x), \quad P_4(x) = \frac{1}{8}(35x^4 - 30x^2 + 3)$$

$$P_5(x) = \frac{1}{8}(63x^5 - 70x^3 + 15x)$$

and

$$P_n(x) = \frac{(2n)!}{2^n(n!)^2}\left[x^n - \frac{n(n-1)}{2(2n-1)}x^{n-2}\right.$$
$$\left. + \frac{n(n-1)(n-2)(n-3)}{2\cdot4(2n-1)(2n-3)}x^{n-4}\dots\right]$$

then

$$\sum_{r=0}^{m}(-1)^r\frac{(2n-2r)!}{2^nr!(n-r)!(n-2r)!}x^{n-2r}$$

Also

$$P_n(1) = 1 \quad P_n(-1) = (-1)^n \quad P_{2n+1}(0) = 0$$
$$P_{2n}(0) = (-1)^n\frac{1\cdot3\dots(2n-1)}{2\cdot4\dots(2n)}$$

Finally, $P_n(x) = \omega$ is a solution of

$$P_n(x) = F\left(n+1, -n; 1; \frac{1}{2} - \frac{1}{2}x\right) = P_{-n-1}(x)$$

XXX. Special Products

(1105) If $q_0 = \prod_{1}^{\infty}(1 - q^{2n})$

$$q_1 = \prod_{1}^{\infty}(1 + q^{2n})$$

$= (1 - 2xh + h^2)^{-1/2}$ where $|2xh - h^2| < 1$ Q. 302

$= P_n(x)$ where $m = \dfrac{n}{2}$ or $\dfrac{n-1}{2}$ whichever is an integer

$(1 - z^2)\dfrac{d^2\omega}{dx^2} - 2x\dfrac{d\omega}{dx} + n(n+1)\omega = 0$ Q. 304

$= \displaystyle\sum_{r=0}^{\infty} \dfrac{(n+1)(n+2)\ldots(n+r)(-n)(1-n)\ldots(r-1-n)}{(r!)^2}$

$\times \left(\dfrac{1}{2} - \dfrac{1}{2}x\right)^r$ Q. 312

Then $q_0 q_3 = \displaystyle\prod_{1}^{\infty} (1 - q^n)$ where $|q| < 1$ A. 116

$q_1 q_2 = \displaystyle\prod_{1}^{\infty} (1 + q^n)$ where $n = 1, 2, 3$, etc.

Series No.

$$q_2 = \prod_1^\infty (1 + q^{2n-1})$$

$$q_3 = \prod_1^\infty (1 - q^{2n-1})$$

The four products q_0, q_1, q_2, and q_3 are absolutely convergent.

For example, $$\frac{1}{(1 - q)(1 - q^3)(1 - q^5)\ldots \infty}$$

$$q_0 q_2^2 = 1 + 2q + 2q^4 + 2q^9 + \ldots \infty$$

$$q_0 q_1^2 = 1 + q^2 + q^6 + q^{12} + \ldots q^{n(n+1)} + \ldots \infty$$

$$\frac{q_0}{q_1} = 1 - 2q^2 + 2q^8 - 2q^{18} + \ldots + 2q^{2n^2} + \ldots \infty$$

$$q_0 q_3 = 1 - (q + q^2) + (q^5 + q^7) - (q^{12} + q^{15}) + \ldots \infty$$

$$q_2^8 = q_3^8 + 16 q q_1^8$$

$$q_0^3 = 1 - 3q^2 + 5q^6 - 7q^{12} + 9q^{20} \ldots$$

XXXI. General Forms

(1106) $$\sum_1^\infty \frac{\phi(n)x^n}{(n + a)(n + b)\ldots(n + k)}$$

If the degree of $\phi(n)$ is less than that of the denominator, resolve into partial fractions and use

$$\sum_1^\infty \frac{x^n}{a + n} = - x^{-a}\left\{\frac{x}{1} + \frac{x^2}{2} + \ldots + \frac{x^a}{a} + \log h\,(1 - x)\right\}$$

See also No. (370).

$$q_1 q_2 q_3 = 1$$

$$= (1 + q)(1 + q^2)(1 + q^3) \ldots \infty$$

$$q_0 q_3^2 = 1 - 2q + 2q^4 - 2q^9 + \ldots \infty$$

$$q_0^3 = 1 - 3q^2 + 5q^6 - 7q^{12} + 9q^{20} - \ldots \infty$$

$$\frac{q_0}{q_3} = 1 + q + q^3 + q^6 + q^{10} + \ldots + q^{\{m(m+1)\}/2} + \ldots \infty$$

indices being alternately of the form $\frac{1}{2} n(3n \pm 1)$

This can always be summed if convergent.   C. 246
$a, b, \ldots k$ are positive or negative, unequal integers and $\phi(n)$ is
an integral function of n.

If degree of $\phi(n)$ is greater than that of the denominator, it may
be written

$$\psi(n)x^n + \frac{\chi(n)x^n}{(n + a)(n + b)\ldots(n + k)}$$

where the degree of $\chi(n)$ is less than that of the denominator and

$$\sum \psi(n)x^n$$

may be found by partial fractions and (370)

Series No.

(1107) $\displaystyle\sum_{1}^{\infty} \frac{\phi(n)}{(n + a)(n + b)\ldots(n + k)}$

If in No. (1106) $x = 1$, the series is not convergent unless the degree of $\phi(n)$ is less than the degree of $(n + a)\ldots(n + k)$.

(1108) $\displaystyle\sum_{1}^{\infty} (-1)^{n-1} \frac{\phi(n)}{(n + a)(n + b)\ldots(n + k)}$

If absolutely convergent,   Sum S_1

If semi-convergent,   Sum S_2

In the above two, the series is absolutely convergent if the degree of $\phi(n)$ is less than $(n + a)\ldots(n + k)$ by two units, and semi-convergent if it is less than $(n + a)\ldots(n + k)$ by one unit.

(1109) $\displaystyle\sum_{0}^{\infty} \phi_r(n) \frac{x^n}{n!}$ can be summed

The identity can be established

$\phi_r(n)$

Then $\displaystyle\sum_{0}^{\infty} \frac{\phi_r(n)x^n}{n!}$

$$= - \sum_{a, b, c, \ldots k} \frac{\phi(-a)\left\{\frac{1}{1} + \frac{1}{2} + \frac{1}{3} + \ldots \frac{1}{a}\right\}}{(b - a)(c - a)\ldots(k - a)}$$

where $\displaystyle\sum_{a, b, c \ldots k}$ means the summation with respect to

a, b, $c\ldots k$, and a, $b\ldots k$ are positive and unequal integers, and $\phi(n)$ is an integral function of n

a, $b\ldots k$ are all positive integers and $\phi(n)$ is an integral function of n.   C. 253

$$= \sum_{a, b, c \ldots k} \frac{\phi(-a)\left\{\frac{1}{a} - \frac{1}{a - 1} + \ldots(-1)^{a-1}\frac{1}{1}\right.}{(b - a)(c - a)\ldots(k - a)}$$

$$= S_1 + \log h\, 2 \sum_{a, b, c \ldots k} \frac{(-1)^a\phi(-a)}{(b - a)(c - a)\ldots(k - a)}$$

if $\phi_r(n)$ is an integral function of n of the rth degree   C. 234

(and see Part I, p. 107)

$$= A_0 + A_1 n + A_2 n(n - 1) + \ldots A_r n(n - 1)\ldots(n - r + 1)$$

$$= A_0 \sum_0^\infty \frac{x^n}{n!} + A_1 x \sum_1^\infty \frac{x^{n-1}}{(n - 1)!} + A_2 x^2 \sum_2^\infty \frac{x^{n-2}}{(n - 2)!} + \ldots$$

$$+ A_r x^r \sum_r^\infty \frac{x^{n-r}}{(x - r)!}$$

$$= (A_0 + A_1 x + A_2 x^2 + \ldots A_r x^r)e^x$$

Series No.

To determine the constants A_0, etc.,

divide $\phi_r(n)$ by n $\phi_r(n)$

divide $\phi_{r-1}(n)$ by $n - 1$ $\phi_{r-1}(n)$

$\phi_1(n)$

(1110) $\sum_0^\infty \phi_r(n) \, _mC_n \, x^n$

The identity can be established as in (1109)

$\phi_r(n)$

Then the general term in the series is

$$\phi_r(n) \, _mC_n \, x^n + A_0 \, _mC_n \, x^n + A_1 n \, _mC_n \, x^n + \ldots$$
$$+ A_r n(n - 1)\ldots(n - r + 1) \, _mC_n \, x^n$$

Therefore

$$\sum_0^\infty \phi_r(n) \, _mC_n \, x^n = A_0 \sum_0^\infty \, _mC_n \, x^n$$

$$+ mA_1 x \sum_1^\infty \, _{m-1}C_{n-1} \, x^{n-1} + \ldots$$

$$+ m(m - 1)\ldots(m - r + 1)A_r x^r \sum_r^\infty \, _{m-r}C_{n-r} \, x^{n-r}$$

The constants A_0, etc., may be evaluated as in No. (1109).

(1111) $\dfrac{\sum_0^\infty \phi_r(n) \, _mC_n \, x^n}{(n + a)(n + b)\ldots(n + k)}$

This can in general be reduced to

$$\sum^\infty \frac{\psi(n) \, _{n+k}C_{m+k} \, x^{n+k}}{(m + 1)(m + 2)\ldots(m + k)x^k}$$

$$= \phi_{r-1}(n)n + A_0$$
$$= \phi_{r-2}(n)(n - 1) + A_1$$
$$= A_r(n - r) + A_{r-1}$$

where $\phi_r(n)$ is any integral function of n of the rth degree   C. 195

$$= A_0 + A_1 n + A_2 n(n - 1) + \ldots + A_r n(n - 1) \ldots (n - r + 1)$$

$$\equiv A_0 \,_m C_n \, x^n + m A_1 x \,_{m-1} C_{n-1} \, x^{n-1}$$
$$+ \, m(m - 1) A_2 x^2 \,_{m-2} C_{n-2} \, x^{n-2} + \ldots$$
$$+ \, m(m - 1) \ldots (m - r + 1) A_r x^r \,_{m-r} C_{n-r} \, x^{n-r}$$

$$= A_0(1 + x)^m + m A_1 x(1 + x)^{m-1} + \ldots$$
$$+ \, m(m - 1) \ldots (m - r + 1) A_r x^r (1 + x)^{m-r}$$

$$= \left\{ A_0 + \frac{m A_1 x}{1 + x} + \frac{m(m - 1) A_2 x^2}{(1 + x)^2} + \ldots \right.$$
$$\left. + \, m(m - 1) \ldots (m - r + 1) \frac{A_r x^r}{(1 + x)} r \right\} (1 + x)^m$$

where $a, b \ldots k$ are unequal positive integers in ascending order of magnitude.

where $\psi(n)$ is an integral function of n viz. $\phi_r(n)$ multiplied by all the factors which are not absorbed by $_{m+k} C_{n+k}$.

                                                              C. 196

Series No.

(1112) $\sum a^x \phi(x)$

The series within the brackets stops at the nth difference of $\phi(x)$, supposing $\phi(x)$ to be of the nth degree.

$\phi(x)$ is rational and integral

(1113) Sum of a series whose nth term is r^n times an integral function of n of the Sth degree, such as

$$\sum_{}^{n} \{a_0 n^S + a_1 n^{S-1} + \ldots a_r\} r^n$$

Multiply by $(1 - r)^{S+1}$. For example,

$$(1 - r)^3 \sum_{1}^{n} (1^2 r + 2^2 r^2 + \ldots n^2 r^n)$$

whence by addition

$$\sum (1^2 r + 2^2 r^2 + \ldots n^2 r^n)$$

(1114)† $\sum u_x$ (Approximate summation)

The constant K is to be determined in each case by substituting a known value of x.

(1115) If the sum $f(r)$ of a finite or infinite series
$f(r) = a_0 + a_1 r + a_2 r^2 + \ldots$ is known, then
$a_0 \cos x + a_1 r \cos (x + y) + a_2 r^2 \cos (x + 2y) \ldots$

$a_0 \sin x + a_1 r \sin (x + y) + a_2 r^2 \sin (x + 2y) \ldots$

† For values of $B_n{}^*$, see No. (1129).

$$= C + \frac{a^x}{a - 1}\left\{\phi(x) - \frac{a}{a - 1}\,\Delta\phi(x)\right.$$

$$\left. + \frac{a^2}{(a - 1)^2}\,\Delta^2\phi(x) - \frac{a^3}{(a - 1)^3}\,\Delta^3\phi(x)\dots\right\}$$

W. 53

where $\Delta\phi(x) = \phi(x + h) - \phi(x)$

$$= 1^2 r + 2^2 r^2 + 3^2 r^3 + \dots n^2 r^n$$
$$- 3r^2 - 3\cdot 2^2 r^3 \dots$$
$$+ 3\cdot 1^2 r^3 + \dots$$
$$- 1^2 r^4 \dots - n^2 r^{n+3}$$

$$= \frac{r + r^2 - (n + 1)^2 r^{n+1} + (2n^2 + 2n - 1)r^{n+2} - n^2 r^{n+3}}{(1 - r)^3}$$

$$= K + \int u_x\,dx - \frac{1}{2}u_x$$

$$+ \frac{B_1{}^*}{2!}\frac{du_x}{dx} - \frac{B_3{}^*}{4!}\frac{d^3 u_x}{dx^3} + \frac{B_5{}^*}{6!}\frac{d^5 u_x}{dx^5} + \dots \infty$$

2Z. 117

$$= \frac{1}{2}\{e^{ix}f(re^{iy}) + e^{-ix}f(re^{-iy})\}$$

$$= -\frac{i}{2}\{e^{ix}f(re^{iy}) - e^{-ix}f(re^{-iy})\}$$

T. 81

Series No.

(1116) Euler's Summation Formula

$$\sum f(x) = f(1) + f(2) + \ldots + f(x)$$

When $f(x)$ is a rational algebraic fraction or a transcendental function, this cannot necessarily be used, and the right-hand side becomes an infinite series which may not converge. (See Bromwich, Chap. XII, for a number of applications of this summation.)

(1117) If $I_a\ I_a'\ I_a''$, etc., are the magnitudes of the differences of the discontinuities of the function and its various differential coefficients at point a, and similarly for points b, then

$$-\frac{1}{n}\sum I_a \sin na - \frac{1}{n^2}\sum I_a' \cos na + \frac{1}{n^3}\sum I_a'' \sin na$$

$$+\frac{1}{n^4}\sum I_a''' \cos na - \ldots \infty$$

$$\frac{1}{n}\sum I_a \cos na - \frac{1}{n^2}\sum I_a' \sin na - \frac{1}{n^3}\sum I_a'' \cos na$$

$$+\frac{1}{n^4}\sum I_a''' \sin na + \ldots \infty$$

XXXII. Double and Treble Series

(1118) $$\sum_0^\infty \sum_0^\infty \frac{(m+n)}{m!n!}\left(\frac{x}{2}\right)^{m+n}$$

(1119) $$\sum_0^\infty \sum_0^\infty \sum_0^\infty \frac{(m+n+p)!}{m!n!p!}\left(\frac{x}{3}\right)^{m+n+p}$$

$$= \int f(x)\, dx + \frac{1}{2} f(x) + \frac{1}{2!} B_1 f'(x) - \frac{1}{4!} B_2 f'''(x) + \ldots \qquad \text{A. 304}$$

where $f(x)$ is a polynomial and there is no term on the right-hand side (in its final form) which is not divisible by x.

$$= \pi a_n$$

(Fourier's nth harmonic amplitudes)

$$= \pi b_n \qquad\qquad\qquad\qquad\qquad\qquad\qquad\qquad \text{X. 57}$$

where $a_n = \dfrac{1}{\pi} \displaystyle\int_0^{2\pi} f(t) \cos nt\, dt$ and $b_n = \dfrac{1}{\pi} \displaystyle\int_0^{2\pi} /(t) \sin nt\, dt$

and $f(t) = \dfrac{a_0}{2} + a_1 \cos t + a_2 \cos 2t + a_3 \cos 3t + \ldots$
$$+ b_1 \sin t + b_2 \sin 2t + b_3 \sin 3t + \ldots$$

$$= \frac{1}{1-x} \quad \text{where } -2 < x < 1 \qquad\qquad \text{A. 194}$$

$$= \frac{1}{1-x} \quad \text{where } -3 < x < 1 \qquad\qquad \text{A. 194}$$

Series No.

(1120) $\displaystyle\sum_{r=2}^{\infty} \sum_{s=2}^{\infty} \frac{1}{(p+s)}r$

(1121) $\displaystyle\sum_{r=1}^{\infty} \sum_{s=1}^{\infty} \frac{1}{(4s-1)^{2r+1}}$

(1122) $\displaystyle\sum_{r=1}^{\infty} \sum_{s=1}^{\infty} \frac{1}{(4s-2)^{2r}}$

(1123) $\displaystyle\sum_{r=2}^{\infty} \sum_{s=1}^{\infty} \frac{1}{(2s)}r$

(1124) $\displaystyle\sum_{r=1}^{\infty} \sum_{s=1}^{\infty} \frac{1}{(4s-1)^{2r}}$

(1125) $\displaystyle\operatorname*{Lim}_{r=\infty} \left[\sum_{m=-r}^{r} \sum_{n=-r}^{r} \frac{1}{(x-m)(x-n)} \right]$

(1126)† $\displaystyle\sum_{n-1}^{n=\infty} \left[\sum_{m-1}^{m=\infty} \frac{\cos 2m\pi x \cdot \cos 2n\pi y}{m^2 - n^2} \right]$

(1127) $\displaystyle\sum_{m=-\infty}^{+\infty} \sum_{n=-\infty}^{\infty} \frac{1}{(m^2+a^2)(n^2+b^2)}$

XXXIII. Bernoulli's Functions

(1128) Bernoulli Functions.

Values of $\phi_n(x)$

$\phi_n(x)$

See also No. (1129).

† See No. (1128) for values of $\phi_2(y)$.

$$= \frac{1}{p + 1}$$ A. 194

$$= \frac{\pi}{8} - \frac{1}{2} \log h\, 2$$ A. 194

$$= \frac{\pi}{8}$$ A. 194

$$= \log h\, 2$$ A. 194

$$= \frac{1}{4} \log h\, 2$$ A. 194

$$= -\pi^2 \quad \text{all values } m = n \text{ are excluded}$$ A. 225

$$= \pi^2 \left[\frac{3}{4} \{\phi_2(y) - \phi_2(x)\} + \frac{1}{4} \left(y - \frac{1}{2} \right) \right] \quad \text{omit } m = n$$ A. 391

$$= 0 \quad \text{if} \quad x = y \quad \text{where } 0 \leqslant y < x \leqslant \frac{1}{2}$$

$$= \frac{\pi^2}{ab} \coth \pi a \coth \pi b$$ Q. 136

$$= x^n - \frac{n}{2} x^{n-1} + \frac{n(n - 1)}{2!} B_1 x^{n-2} - \frac{n(n - 1)(n - 2)(n - 3)}{4!} B_2 x^{n-4}$$
A. 300

terminating either in x or x^2.

Therefore

$\phi_1(x) = x$

$\phi_2(x) = x^2 - x$

$\phi_3(x) = x^3 - \dfrac{3}{2} x^2 + \dfrac{1}{2} x$

$\phi_4(x) = x^4 - 2x^3 + x^2$

$\phi_5(x) = x^5 - \dfrac{5}{2} x^4 + \dfrac{5}{3} x^3 - \dfrac{1}{6} x$

$\phi_6(x) = x^6 - 3x^5 + \dfrac{5}{2} x^4 - \dfrac{1}{2} x^2$

$\phi_n(x + 1) - \phi_n(x) = nx^{n-1}$

$\phi_2(x + 1) = x^2 + x$

etc.

This function is related to that in No. (1135) by $nB_n(x) = \phi_n(x)$.

(1129) Bernoulli's numbers can be calculated from the expression

$$\frac{2(2n)!}{(2\pi)^{2n}} \left\{ \frac{1}{1^{2n}} + \frac{1}{2^{2n}} + \frac{1}{3^{2n}} + \cdots \infty \right\}$$

A similar confusion arises in the case of Euler's numbers, No. (1131). Some authorities, for the same value of n, quote the values of B_n, and others B_{2n-1}. In the tables following and in this book B_n values are used.

For example, in AC. 42, A. 297, C. 231 and AE. 3, etc.

$$B_1 = \frac{1}{6}, \quad B_2 = \frac{1}{30}, \quad B_3 = \frac{1}{42}, \text{ etc.}$$

whereas in Y. 503, etc.

$$B_1{}^* = \frac{1}{6}, \quad B_3{}^* = \frac{1}{30}, \quad B_5{}^* = \frac{1}{42}, \text{ etc.}$$

where $B_n = B_{2n-1}{}^*$.

Reference

$\phi_n(x)$ is the coefficient of $t_n/n!$ in the expansion of $t\,\dfrac{e^{xt}-1}{e^t-1}$ A. 300

C. 231
C. 363
A. 297
Y. 503

$$= \frac{2(2n)!}{[1-(\tfrac{1}{2})^{2n}](2\pi)^{2n}}\left\{\frac{1}{1^{2n}}+\frac{1}{3^{2n}}+\frac{1}{5^{2n}}+\ldots\infty\right\}$$

$$= B_n = B_{2n-1}{}^{*}$$

Extract from British Association Report, 1877 (Adams)

Table of Bernoulli's Numbers expressed in Vulgar Fractions

Numerator	$B_0 = -1$	Denominator	No.
	1	6	1
	1	30	2
	1	42	3
	1	30	4
	5	66	5
	691	2730	6
	7	6	7
	3617	510	8
	43867	798	9
	1 74611	330	10
	8 54513	138	11
	2363 64091	2730	12
	85 53103	6	13
	2 37494 61029	870	14
	861 58412 76005	14322	15
	770 93210 41217	510	16
	257 76878 58367	6	17
	26315 27155 30534 77373	1919190	18
	2 92999 39138 41559	6	19
	2 61082 71849 64491 22051	13530	20
	15 20097 64391 80708 02691	1806	21
	278 33269 57930 10242 35023	690	22
	5964 51111 59391 21632 77961	282	23
	560 94033 68997 81768 62491 27547	46410	24
	49 50572 05241 07964 82124 77525	66	25

Table of Bernoulli's Numbers expressed in Integers and Repeating Decimals

No.

1	0.16̇
2	0.03̇
3	0.02̇380 95̇
4	0.03̇
5	0.075̇
6	0.25̇311 35̇
7	1.16̇
8	7.09̇215 68627 45098 03̇
9	54.97̇117 79448 62155 3884̇
10	529.124̇
11	6192.12̇318 84057 97101 44927 536̇
12	86580.25̇311 35̇
13	14 25517.16̇
14	272 98231.06̇781 60919 54022 98850 57471 2643̇
15	6015 80873.90̇064 23683 84303 86817 48359 16771 4̇
16	1 51163 15767.09̇215 68627 45098 03̇
17	42 96146 43061.16̇
18	1371 16552 05088.33̇277 21590 87948 5616̇
19	48833 23189 73593.16̇
20	19 29657 93419 40068.14̇863 26681 4̇
21	841 69304 75736 82615.00̇055 37098 56035 43743 07862 67995 57032 11517 165̇
22	40338 07185 40594 55413.07̇681 15942 02898 55072 463̇
23	21 15074 86380 81991 60560.14̇539 00709 21985 81560 28368 79432 62411 34751 77304 96̇
24	1208 66265 22296 52593 46027.31̇193 70825 25317 81943 54664 94290 02370 17884 07670 7606̇
25	75008 66746 07696 43668 55720.075̇

In the "Report of the British Association for the Advancement of Science, 1877," page 10, etc., Bernoulli's numbers are calculated up to $n = 62$. Further, the method by which they are calculated is also described.

Series No.

Values of Constants used in Series Nos. (305) to (318)

(1130)

n	0	1	2	3	4	5
B_n	-1	1/6	1/30	1/42	1/30	5/66
α_n	0	1	1	3	17	155
β_n	1	1/3	7/15	31/21	127/15	2555/33
γ_n	0	1	2	13	164	3355
δ_n	2	1	13/5	121/7	1093/5	49205/11
ϵ_n	-1	1	91/5	3751/7	1 38811/5	251 43755/11
ζ_n	0	1	13	363	18581	15 25355
η_n	0	1	14	403	20828	17 14405
θ_n	0	1	10	273	13940	11 44055
E_n	$\lbrace 1$	1	1	2	5	16
$E_n{}^*$	1^*	1^*	5^*	61^*	1385^*	50521^*
R_n	1	7	305	33367	68 15585	22374 23527
S_n	1	5	205	22265	45 44185	14916 32525
I_n	1/2	1/3	1	7	809/9	1847
H_n	3/2	3	33	903	46113	37 84503
J_n	2	10/3	34	910	4 15826/9	37 86350
T_n	0	1	23	1681	2 57543	676 37281
P_n	1	3	57	2763	2 50737	365 81523
Q_n	0	1	11	361	24611	28 73041

For the theory of Bernoulli polynomials, etc., including very many practically useful recurrence formulae, see Glaisher 1898a, c, and Lehmer 1935, 1936.

The numbers B_n, I_n, T_n, P_n, and Q_n are fundamental and are not expressible simply in terms of the others. It is to be noted that the odd Eulerian numbers are not calculable directly and are fundamental. See Edwards *Differential Calculus*, p. 502.

See No. (1131) for explanation of E_n and $E_n{}^*$.

Reference

AC. 42

Series No.

α_n

β_n

γ_n

δ_n

ϵ_n

η_n

ζ_n

θ_n

H_n

J_n

$E_n{}^*$

H_n

I_n

J_n

P_n

Q_n

See No. (330) for q_n.

† For a connection between $B_{2n+1}\left(\dfrac{1}{\kappa}\right)$, etc., see No. (1142).

$$= 2(2^{2n} - 1)B_n$$
AC. 41, 42, and 48

$$= (2^{2n} - 2)B_n$$

$$= \frac{3}{4}(3^{2n} - 1)B_n$$

$$= (3^{2n} - 3)B_n$$

$$= \frac{1}{2}(2^{2n} - 2)(3^{2n} - 3)B_n$$

$$= \frac{3}{8}(2^{2n} - 2)(3^{2n} - 1)B_n$$

$$= \frac{1}{3}(2^{2n} - 1)(3^{2n} - 3)B_n$$

$$= \frac{1}{4}(2^{2n} - 1)(3^{2n} - 1)B_n$$

$$= (2^{2n+1} + 1)I_n$$

$$= 2(r^{2n} + 1)I_n$$

$$= H_n + I_n$$

$$= (-1)^{n+1}4^{2n+1}B_{2n+1}\left(\frac{1}{4}\right)^{\dagger}$$
AE. 51

$$= (-1)^{n+1}\left\{6^{2n+1}B_{2n+1}\left(\frac{1}{6}\right) - 3^{2n+1}B_{2n+1}\left(\frac{1}{3}\right)\right\}$$
AE. 51

$$= (-1)^{n+1}3^{2n+1}B_{2n+1}\left(\frac{1}{3}\right)$$
AE. 51

$$= (-1)^{n+1}6^{2n+1}B_{2n+1}\left(\frac{1}{6}\right)$$
AE. 51

$$= 2^{2n}E_n{}^* - (2n)_2 2^{2n-2}E_{n-1}{}^* \ldots (-1)^{n-1}(2n)_2 2^2 E_1{}^* + (-1)^n E_0{}^*$$

$$= \frac{1}{2}\left[(-1)^{n+1}8^{2n+1}B_{2n+1}\left(\frac{1}{8}\right) - E_n{}^*\right]$$
AE. 62

$$= \frac{q_n}{\sqrt{2}}(2n - 1)!\left(\frac{4}{\pi}\right)^{2n}$$
AE. 64

Series No.

R_n

S_n

T_n

(1131) Euler's Numbers are calculated from the equation

$$2(2n)! \left(\frac{2}{\pi}\right)^{2n+1} \left\{ \frac{1}{1^{2n+1}} - \frac{1}{3^{2n+1}} + \frac{1}{5^{2n+1}} - \dots \infty \right\}$$

$$= 2(2n)! \left(\frac{2}{\pi}\right)^{2n+1} \left(1 + \frac{1}{3^{2n+1}}\right)\left(1 - \frac{1}{5^{2n+1}}\right)\left(1 + \frac{1}{7^{2n+1}}\right) \dots$$

In the list below of Euler's numbers odd values of E_n have been included for completeness. These have sometimes been called "Prepared Bernoulli Numbers," and have been omitted from many lists, and only the even numbers included. This has led to confusion because in some cases the even numbers were then called "Euler's Numbers E_n."

In 2Z. 243 and Y. 501 Eulers' numbers are as shown in the long list below; but in AE., AC. 42, T. 141, and C. 342 and 365, the numbers are shown as E_n^* where $E_n^* = E_{2n}$

$$n = 0 \quad 1 \quad 2 \quad 3 \quad 4 \quad 5$$
$$E_n^* = 1 \quad 1 \quad 5 \quad 61 \quad 1385 \quad 50521 \quad \text{etc.}$$

and throughout this collection E_n and E_n^* have been used to distinguish between them.

$$E_1 = 1 \quad E_2 = 1 \quad E_3 = 2 \quad E_4 = 5 \quad E_5 = 16$$
$$E_6 = 61 \quad E_7 = 272 \quad E_8 = 1385 \quad E_9 = 7936 \quad E_{10} = 50521$$

(1132) Euler's Constant

$$C = 0.57721\ 56649\ 01532\ 86060\dots$$

$$= \frac{1}{4}(3^{2n+1} + 1)E_n{}^*$$ AC. 50

$$= \frac{1}{2}(3^{2n} + 1)E_n{}^*$$ AC. 50

$$3S_n = 2R_n + E_n{}^*$$

$$= \frac{t_{2n}}{2\sqrt{3}} \cdot (2n - 1)! \left(\frac{6}{\pi}\right)^{2n}$$ AE. 75

C. 342
C. 365
Y. 502

$$= E_n{}^* = E_{2n}$$

$E_{12} = 270\,2765 \quad E_{14} = 1993\,60981 \quad E_{16} = 1\,93915\,12145$

$E_{18} = 240\,48796\,75441 \quad E_{20} = 37037\,11882\,37525$

2Z. 245

2Z. 87

Series No.

(1133) Sum of Power Series

$$\mathcal{S}_n = \frac{1}{1^n} + \frac{1}{2^n} + \frac{1}{3^n} + \ldots \infty$$

Values of $\mathcal{S}_n$ to sixteen places of decimals are given in the table.

n	$\mathcal{S}_n$ to sixteen places of decimals
1	0.57721 56649 01532 9 ... + log ∞ (Euler's Const. + ∞)
2	1.64493 40668 48226 4
3	1.20205 69031 59594 3
4	1.08232 32337 11138 2
5	1.03692 77551 43370 0
6	1.01734 30619 84449 1
7	1.00834 92773 81922 7
8	1.00407 73561 97944 3
9	1.00200 83928 26082 2
10	1.00099 45751 27818 0
11	1.00049 41886 04119 4
12	1.00024 60865 53308 0
13	1.00012 27133 47578 5
14	1.00006 12481 35058 7
15	1.00003 05882 36307 0
16	1.00001 52822 59408 6
17	1.00000 76371 97637 9
18	1.00000 38172 93265 0
19	1.00000 19082 12716 6
20	1.00000 09539 62033 9
21	1.00000 04769 32986 8
22	1.00000 02384 50502 7
23	1.00000 01192 19926 0
24	1.00000 00596 08189 1
25	1.00000 00298 03503 5
26	1.00000 00149 01554 8
27	1.00000 00074 50711 8

The sixteenth decimal place is not always the sixteenth occurring, but the nearest in consideration of terms to follow, e.g. C has for its 16th, 17th, etc.... figures 8606....

$\text{Log}_e 10 = 2.30258\ 50929$
$\phantom{\text{Log}_e 10 = 2.30258\ } 94045\ 6840...$

Euler's Const. $= C = 0.57721$
$\phantom{\text{Euler's Const. } = C = } 56649\ 01532\ 8606...$

$\mu = 0.43429\ 44819...$

Reference

2Z. 144

Series No.

n	S_n to sixteen places of decimals
28	1.00000 00037 25334 0
29	1.00000 00018 62659 7
30	1.00000 00009 31327 4
31	1.00000 00004 65662 9
32	1.00000 00002 32831 2
33	1.00000 00001 16415 5
34	1.00000 00000 58207 7
35	1.00000 00000 29103 8

Relations between Bernoulli's Numbers

(1134) $1^{n-1} + 2^{n-1} + 3^{n-1} + \ldots (x - 1)^{n-1}$

(1135) $\dfrac{x^n}{n} - \dfrac{1}{2} x^{n-1} + \dfrac{n - 1}{2!} B_1 x^{n-2}$

$$- \dfrac{(n - 1)(n - 2)(n - 3)}{4!} B_2 x^{n-4} + \ldots$$

The last term is

The last term is

(1136) $B_{2n+1}(1 - x)$

$B_{2n}(1 - x)$

$B_n(0)$

$B_n(1)$

(1137) $B_n(x) - (n - 1)xB_{n-1}(x) + (n - 1)_2 x^2 B_{n-2}(x)$

$$+ \ldots (-1)^{n-2} x^{n-2} B_2(x) + (-1)^{n-1} x^n$$

$(n)_r = \dfrac{n(n - 1)(n - 2)\ldots(n - r + 1)}{r!}$

(1138) $1^{2n} + 2^{2n} + 3^{2n} + \ldots (2x)^{2n}$

$1^{2n} + 3^{2n} + \ldots (2x - 1)^{2n}$

$2^{2n} + 4^{2n} + \ldots + (2x)^{2n}$

$= B_n(x)$ where x is a positive integer   AE. 8

    A. 304

$= B_n(x)$

$(-1)^{n/2} \dfrac{n-1}{2} B_{n/2-1} x^2$ where n is even

$(-1)^{(n-1)/2} B_{(n-1)/2} x$ where n is odd   AE. 7

$= - B_{2n+1}(x)$ AE. 4

$= B_{2n}(x)$

$= 0$

$= 0$

$= - B_n(-x)$ AE. 11

$= {}_nC_r = \left(\dfrac{n}{r}\right)$

$= B_{2n+1}(2x + 1)$

$= B_{2n+1}(2x + 1) - 2^{2n} B_{2n+1}(x + 1)$ AE. 15

$= 2^{2n} B_{2n+1}(x + 1)$

Series No.

(1139) $nA_n(x)$

$A_{2n}(x)$

$A_n(1 - x)$

$A_{2n+1}(0)$

$A_{2n}(0)$

(1140) k is a positive integer

$$B_n(x) + B_n\left(x + \frac{1}{k}\right) + \ldots B_n\left(x + \frac{k-1}{k}\right)$$

(1141) $B_n\left(\dfrac{1}{k}\right) + B_n\left(\dfrac{2}{k}\right) + \ldots B_n\left(\dfrac{k-1}{k}\right)$

(1142) $B_{2n}\left(\dfrac{1}{6}\right)$

$B_{2n}\left(\dfrac{1}{4}\right)$

$B_{2n}\left(\dfrac{1}{3}\right)$

$B_{2n}\left(\dfrac{1}{2}\right)$

$B_{2n+1}\left(\dfrac{1}{12}\right)$

$B_{2n+1}\left(\dfrac{1}{8}\right) - B_{2n+1}\left(\dfrac{3}{8}\right)$

$$= x^n - \frac{1}{2} nx^{n-1} + (n)_2 B_1 x^{n-2} - (n)_4 B_2 x^{n-4}, \text{ etc., the series being}$$

continued so long as the exponents are not negative   AE. 19

$$= B_{2n}(x) + (-1)^{n-1} \frac{B_n}{2n}$$ AE. 18 and 20

$$= (-1)^n A_n(x)$$

$$= A_{2n+1}(1) = 0$$

$$= A_{2n}(1) = (-1)^{n-2} \frac{B_n}{2n}$$

$$= \frac{1}{k^{n-1}} B_n(kx) \quad \text{where } n \text{ is odd}$$ AE. 9

$$= \frac{1}{k^{n-1}} B_n(kx) + (-1)^{n/2} \frac{k^n - 1}{k^{n-1}} \frac{B_{n/2}}{n} \quad \text{where } n \text{ is even}$$

$$= 0 \quad \text{where } n \text{ is odd}$$ AE. 9

$$= (-1)^{n/2} \frac{k^n - 1}{k^{n-1}} \frac{B_{n/2}}{n} \quad \text{where } n \text{ is even}$$

$$= (-1)^n \left\{ 1 + \frac{1}{2^{2n-1}} + \frac{1}{3^{2n-1}} - \frac{1}{6^{2n-1}} \right\} \frac{B_n}{4n}$$ AE. 43

$$= (-1)^n \left\{ 2 + \frac{1}{2^{2n-1}} - \frac{1}{4^{2n-1}} \right\} \frac{B_n}{4n}$$ AE. 31

$$= (-1)^n \frac{3^{2n} - 1}{3^{2n-1}} \frac{B_n}{4n}$$ AE. 36

$$= (-1)^n \frac{2^{2n} - 1}{2^{2n}} \frac{B_n}{n}$$ AE. 26

$$= \frac{1}{2} \left(1 + \frac{1}{3^{2n}} \right) B_{2n+1}\left(\frac{1}{4}\right) + \frac{1}{2^{2n+1}} B_{2n+1}\left(\frac{1}{6}\right)$$ AE. 74

$$= \frac{1}{2^{2n}} B_{2n+1}\left(\frac{1}{4}\right)$$ AE. 63

Series No.

$$B_{2n+1}\left(\frac{1}{6}\right)$$

$$6^{2n+1}B_{2n+1}\left(\frac{1}{6}\right) - 3^{2n+1}B_{2n+1}\left(\frac{1}{3}\right)$$

$$B_{2n+1}\left(\frac{1}{4}\right)$$

$$B_{2n+1}\left(\frac{1}{3}\right)$$

$$B_{2n+1}\left(\frac{1}{2}\right)$$

$$B_{2n+1}\left(\frac{3}{4}\right)$$

$$A_{2n}\left(\frac{1}{12}\right) + A_{2n}\left(\frac{5}{12}\right)$$

$$A_{2n}\left(\frac{1}{8}\right) + A_{2n}\left(\frac{3}{8}\right)$$

$$A_{2n}\left(\frac{1}{6}\right)$$

$$A_{2n}\left(\frac{1}{4}\right)$$

$$A_{2n}\left(\frac{1}{3}\right)$$

$$A_{2n}\left(\frac{1}{2}\right)$$

$$(2n + 1)4^{2n+1}B_{2n+1}\left(\frac{1}{4}\right)$$

$$= \left(1 + \frac{1}{2^{2n}}\right) B_{2n+1}\left(\frac{1}{3}\right)$$ AE.52

$$= (-1)^{n+1} H_n$$ AE. 51

$$= A_{2n+1}\left(\frac{1}{4}\right) = (-1)^{n+1} \frac{E_n^*}{4^{2n+1}}$$ AE. 31

$$= A_{2n+1}\left(\frac{1}{3}\right) = \frac{(-1)^{n+1}}{3^{2n+1}} I_n$$ AE. 35

$$= A_{2n+1}\left(\frac{1}{2}\right) = 0$$ AE. 26

$$= - B_{2n+1}\left(\frac{1}{4}\right)$$ AE. 63

$$= \frac{1}{2^{2n-1}} A_n\left(\frac{1}{6}\right)$$ AE. 77

$$= \frac{1}{2^{2n-1}} A_{2n}\left(\frac{1}{4}\right)$$ AE. 66

$$= (-1)^n \left\{\frac{1}{2^{2n-1}} - \frac{1}{6^{2n-1}}\right\} \frac{B_n}{4n} - A_{2n}\left(\frac{1}{3}\right)$$ AE. 42

$$= (-1)^n \left\{\frac{1}{2^{2n-1}} - \frac{1}{4^{2n-1}}\right\} \frac{B_n}{4n}$$ AE. 31

$$= (-1)^n \left\{1 - \frac{1}{3^{2n-1}}\right\} \frac{B_n}{4n}$$ AE. 36

$$= (-1)^n \frac{2^{2n-1} - 1}{2^{2n}} \frac{B_n}{n}$$ AE. 26

$$= - 1 + (2n + 1)_2 4^2\left(1 - \frac{1}{2}\right) B_1$$ AE. 57

$$- (2n + 1)_4 4^4\left(1 - \frac{1}{2^3}\right) B_2$$

$$+ \ldots + (-1)^{n-1}(2n + 1) 4^{2n}\left(1 - \frac{1}{2^{2n-1}}\right) B_n$$

Series No.

$$(2n + 1)6^{2n+1}B_{2n+1}\left(\frac{1}{3}\right)$$

The derivation of some of these numbers is from such series as No. (576) and No. (577) by putting $\theta = \frac{1}{4}, \frac{1}{3}, \frac{1}{2}$, etc.; but the original article in AE. should be consulted for a full description of the derivation.

(1143) $\dfrac{2}{3}\left\{I_0 - \dfrac{I_1}{2!}a^2 + \dfrac{I_2}{4!}a^4 - \ldots \infty\right\}$

(1144) $\dfrac{3}{2}I_n - (2n)_2I_{n-1} + (2n)_4I_{n-2} + \ldots$
$$+ (-1)^{n-1}(2n)_2I_1 + (-1)^nI_0$$

(1145) $E_n{}^* - (2n)_2E_{n-1}{}^* + (2n)_4E_{n-2}{}^* + \ldots$
$$+ (-1)^{n-1}(2n)_2E_1{}^* + (-1)^nE_0{}^*$$

In No. (1142), see No. (1130) for values of I, E^*, and H. n_r is the binomial coefficient

$$\frac{n(n - 1)\ldots(n - r + 1)}{r!}$$

(1146) $2^2B_2\left(\dfrac{1}{2}\right) = -\dfrac{1}{2}$

$2^4B_4\left(\dfrac{1}{2}\right) = \dfrac{1}{4}$

$2^6B_6\left(\dfrac{1}{2}\right) = -\dfrac{1}{2}$

$2^8B_8\left(\dfrac{1}{2}\right) = \dfrac{51}{24}$

$$= -1 + (2n+1)_2 6^2\left(1 - \frac{1}{2}\right) B_1$$

$$- (2n+1)_4 6^4\left(1 - \frac{1}{2^3}\right) B_2$$

$$+ \ldots + (-1)^{n-1}(2n+1)6^{2n}\left(1 - \frac{1}{2^{2n-1}}\right) B_n$$

$$= \frac{1}{1 + e^a + e^{-a}}$$

$$= 0$$

$$= 0$$

$$2^2 A_2\left(\frac{1}{2}\right) = -\frac{1}{6}$$

$$2^4 A_4\left(\frac{1}{2}\right) = \frac{7}{60}$$

$$2^6 A_6\left(\frac{1}{2}\right) = -\frac{31}{126}$$

$$2^8 A_8\left(\frac{1}{2}\right) = \frac{127}{120}$$

Series No.

$$3^2 B_2\left(\frac{1}{3}\right) = -1$$

$$3^4 B_4\left(\frac{1}{3}\right) = 1$$

$$3^6 B_6\left(\frac{1}{3}\right) = -\frac{13}{3}$$

$$3^8 B_8\left(\frac{1}{3}\right) = 41$$

$$4^2 B_2\left(\frac{1}{4}\right) = -\frac{3}{2}$$

$$4^4 B_4\left(\frac{1}{4}\right) = \frac{9}{4}$$

$$4^6 B_6\left(\frac{1}{4}\right) = -\frac{33}{2}$$

$$4^8 B_8\left(\frac{1}{4}\right) = \frac{6579}{24}$$

$$B_3\left(\frac{1}{8}\right) = \frac{7}{8^3}$$

$$B_5\left(\frac{1}{8}\right) = -\frac{119}{8^5}$$

$$3^2 A_2\left(\frac{1}{3}\right) = -\frac{1}{4}$$

AE. 36

$$3^4 A_4\left(\frac{1}{3}\right) = \frac{13}{40}$$

$$3^6 A_6\left(\frac{1}{3}\right) = -\frac{121}{84}$$

$$3^8 A_8\left(\frac{1}{3}\right) = \frac{1093}{80}$$

$$4^2 A_2\left(\frac{1}{4}\right) = -\frac{1}{6}$$

AE. 31

$$4^4 A_4\left(\frac{1}{4}\right) = \frac{7}{60}$$

$$4^6 A_6\left(\frac{1}{4}\right) = -\frac{31}{126}$$

$$4^8 A_8\left(\frac{1}{4}\right) = \frac{127}{120}$$

AE. 61

AE. 61

A CATALOGUE OF SELECTED DOVER BOOKS
IN ALL FIELDS OF INTEREST

A CATALOGUE OF SELECTED DOVER BOOKS
IN ALL FIELDS OF INTEREST

AMERICA'S OLD MASTERS, James T. Flexner. Four men emerged unexpectedly from provincial 18th century America to leadership in European art: Benjamin West, J. S. Copley, C. R. Peale, Gilbert Stuart. Brilliant coverage of lives and contributions. Revised, 1967 edition. 69 plates. 365pp. of text.

21806-6 Paperbound $3.00

FIRST FLOWERS OF OUR WILDERNESS: AMERICAN PAINTING, THE COLONIAL PERIOD, James T. Flexner. Painters, and regional painting traditions from earliest Colonial times up to the emergence of Copley, West and Peale Sr., Foster, Gustavus Hesselius, Feke, John Smibert and many anonymous painters in the primitive manner. Engaging presentation, with 162 illustrations. xxii + 368pp.

22180-6 Paperbound $3.50

THE LIGHT OF DISTANT SKIES: AMERICAN PAINTING, 1760-1835, James T. Flexner. The great generation of early American painters goes to Europe to learn and to teach: West, Copley, Gilbert Stuart and others. Allston, Trumbull, Morse; also contemporary American painters—primitives, derivatives, academics—who remained in America. 102 illustrations. xiii + 306pp.

22179-2 Paperbound $3.00

A HISTORY OF THE RISE AND PROGRESS OF THE ARTS OF DESIGN IN THE UNITED STATES, William Dunlap. Much the richest mine of information on early American painters, sculptors, architects, engravers, miniaturists, etc. The only source of information for scores of artists, the major primary source for many others. Unabridged reprint of rare original 1834 edition, with new introduction by James T. Flexner, and 394 new illustrations. Edited by Rita Weiss. 6⅝ x 9⅝.

21695-0, 21696-9, 21697-7 Three volumes, Paperbound $13.50

EPOCHS OF CHINESE AND JAPANESE ART, Ernest F. Fenollosa. From primitive Chinese art to the 20th century, thorough history, explanation of every important art period and form, including Japanese woodcuts; main stress on China and Japan, but Tibet, Korea also included. Still unexcelled for its detailed, rich coverage of cultural background, aesthetic elements, diffusion studies, particularly of the historical period. 2nd, 1913 edition. 242 illustrations. lii + 439pp. of text.

20364-6, 20365-4 Two volumes, Paperbound $6.00

THE GENTLE ART OF MAKING ENEMIES, James A. M. Whistler. Greatest wit of his day deflates Oscar Wilde, Ruskin, Swinburne; strikes back at inane critics, exhibitions, art journalism; aesthetics of impressionist revolution in most striking form. Highly readable classic by great painter. Reproduction of edition designed by Whistler. Introduction by Alfred Werner. xxxvi + 334pp.

21875-9 Paperbound $2.50

"ESSENTIAL GRAMMAR" SERIES

All you really need to know about modern, colloquial grammar. Many educational shortcuts help you learn faster, understand better. Detailed cognate lists teach you to recognize similarities between English and foreign words and roots—make learning vocabulary easy and interesting. Excellent for independent study or as a supplement to record courses.

ESSENTIAL FRENCH GRAMMAR, Seymour Resnick. 2500-item cognate list. 159pp.
(EBE) 20419-7 Paperbound $1.25

ESSENTIAL GERMAN GRAMMAR, Guy Stern and Everett F. Bleiler. Unusual shortcuts on noun declension, word order, compound verbs. 124pp.
(EBE) 20422-7 Paperbound $1.25

ESSENTIAL ITALIAN GRAMMAR, Olga Ragusa. 111pp.
(EBE) 20779-X Paperbound $1.25

ESSENTIAL JAPANESE GRAMMAR, Everett F. Bleiler. In Romaji transcription; no characters needed. Japanese grammar is regular and simple. 156pp.
21027-8 Paperbound $1.25

ESSENTIAL PORTUGUESE GRAMMAR, Alexander da R. Prista. vi + 114pp.
21650-0 Paperbound $1.35

ESSENTIAL SPANISH GRAMMAR, Seymour Resnick. 2500 word cognate list. 115pp.
(EBE) 20780-3 Paperbound $1.25

ESSENTIAL ENGLISH GRAMMAR, Philip Gucker. Combines best features of modern, functional and traditional approaches. For refresher, class use, home study. x + 177pp.
21649-7 Paperbound $1.25

A PHRASE AND SENTENCE DICTIONARY OF SPOKEN SPANISH. Prepared for U. S. War Department by U. S. linguists. As above, unit is idiom, phrase or sentence rather than word. English-Spanish and Spanish-English sections contain modern equivalents of over 18,000 sentences. Introduction and appendix as above. iv + 513pp.
20495-2 Paperbound $2.75

A PHRASE AND SENTENCE DICTIONARY OF SPOKEN RUSSIAN. Dictionary prepared for U. S. War Department by U. S. linguists. Basic unit is not the word, but the idiom, phrase or sentence. English-Russian and Russian-English sections contain modern equivalents for over 30,000 phrases. Grammatical introduction covers phonetics, writing, syntax. Appendix of word lists for food, numbers, geographical names, etc. vi + 573 pp. 6⅛ x 9¼.
20496-0 Paperbound $4.00

CONVERSATIONAL CHINESE FOR BEGINNERS, Morris Swadesh. Phonetic system, beginner's course in Pai Hua Mandarin Chinese covering most important, most useful speech patterns. Emphasis on modern colloquial usage. Formerly *Chinese in Your Pocket.* xvi + 158pp.
21123-1 Paperbound $1.75

ALPHABETS AND ORNAMENTS, Ernst Lehner. Well-known pictorial source for decorative alphabets, script examples, cartouches, frames, decorative title pages, calligraphic initials, borders, similar material. 14th to 19th century, mostly European. Useful in almost any graphic arts designing, varied styles. 750 illustrations. 256pp. 7 x 10. 21905-4 Paperbound $4.00

PAINTING: A CREATIVE APPROACH, Norman Colquhoun. For the beginner simple guide provides an instructive approach to painting: major stumbling blocks for beginner; overcoming them, technical points; paints and pigments; oil painting; watercolor and other media and color. New section on "plastic" paints. Glossary. Formerly *Paint Your Own Pictures*. 221pp. 22000-1 Paperbound $1.75

THE ENJOYMENT AND USE OF COLOR, Walter Sargent. Explanation of the relations between colors themselves and between colors in nature and art, including hundreds of little-known facts about color values, intensities, effects of high and low illumination, complementary colors. Many practical hints for painters, references to great masters. 7 color plates, 29 illustrations. x + 274pp.
20944-X Paperbound $2.50

THE NOTEBOOKS OF LEONARDO DA VINCI, compiled and edited by Jean Paul Richter. 1566 extracts from original manuscripts reveal the full range of Leonardo's versatile genius: all his writings on painting, sculpture, architecture, anatomy, astronomy, geography, topography, physiology, mining, music, etc., in both Italian and English, with 186 plates of manuscript pages and more than 500 additional drawings. Includes studies for the Last Supper, the lost Sforza monument, and other works. Total of xlvii + 866pp. $7\frac{7}{8}$ x $10\frac{3}{4}$.
22572-0, 22573-9 Two volumes, Paperbound $10.00

MONTGOMERY WARD CATALOGUE OF 1895. Tea gowns, yards of flannel and pillow-case lace, stereoscopes, books of gospel hymns, the New Improved Singer Sewing Machine, side saddles, milk skimmers, straight-edged razors, high-button shoes, spittoons, and on and on . . . listing some 25,000 items, practically all illustrated. Essential to the shoppers of the 1890's, it is our truest record of the spirit of the period. Unaltered reprint of Issue No. 57, Spring and Summer 1895. Introduction by Boris Emmet. Innumerable illustrations. xiii + 624pp. $8\frac{1}{2}$ x $11\frac{5}{8}$.
22377-9 Paperbound $6.95

THE CRYSTAL PALACE EXHIBITION ILLUSTRATED CATALOGUE (LONDON, 1851). One of the wonders of the modern world—the Crystal Palace Exhibition in which all the nations of the civilized world exhibited their achievements in the arts and sciences—presented in an equally important illustrated catalogue. More than 1700 items pictured with accompanying text—ceramics, textiles, cast-iron work, carpets, pianos, sleds, razors, wall-papers, billiard tables, beehives, silverware and hundreds of other artifacts—represent the focal point of Victorian culture in the Western World. Probably the largest collection of Victorian decorative art ever assembled—indispensable for antiquarians and designers. Unabridged republication of the Art-Journal Catalogue of the Great Exhibition of 1851, with all terminal essays. New introduction by John Gloag, F.S.A. xxxiv + 426pp. 9 x 12.
22503-8 Paperbound $4.50

THE ARCHITECTURE OF COUNTRY HOUSES, Andrew J. Downing. Together with Vaux's *Villas and Cottages* this is the basic book for Hudson River Gothic architecture of the middle Victorian period. Full, sound discussions of general aspects of housing, architecture, style, decoration, furnishing, together with scores of detailed house plans, illustrations of specific buildings, accompanied by full text. Perhaps the most influential single American architectural book. 1850 edition. Introduction by J. Stewart Johnson. 321 figures, 34 architectural designs. xvi + 560pp.
22003-6 Paperbound $4.00

LOST EXAMPLES OF COLONIAL ARCHITECTURE, John Mead Howells. Full-page photographs of buildings that have disappeared or been so altered as to be denatured, including many designed by major early American architects. 245 plates. xvii + 248pp. 7⅞ x 10¾. 21143-6 Paperbound $3.50

DOMESTIC ARCHITECTURE OF THE AMERICAN COLONIES AND OF THE EARLY REPUBLIC, Fiske Kimball. Foremost architect and restorer of Williamsburg and Monticello covers nearly 200 homes between 1620-1825. Architectural details, construction, style features, special fixtures, floor plans, etc. Generally considered finest work in its area. 219 illustrations of houses, doorways, windows, capital mantels. xx + 314pp. 7⅞ x 10¾. 21743-4 Paperbound $4.00

EARLY AMERICAN ROOMS: 1650-1858, edited by Russell Hawes Kettell. Tour of 12 rooms, each representative of a different era in American history and each furnished, decorated, designed and occupied in the style of the era. 72 plans and elevations, 8-page color section, etc., show fabrics, wall papers, arrangements, etc. Full descriptive text. xvii + 200pp. of text. 8⅜ x 11¼.
21633-0 Paperbound $5.00

THE FITZWILLIAM VIRGINAL BOOK, edited by J. Fuller Maitland and W. B. Squire. Full modern printing of famous early 17th-century ms. volume of 300 works by Morley, Byrd, Bull, Gibbons, etc. For piano or other modern keyboard instrument; easy to read format. xxxvi + 938pp. 8⅜ x 11.
21068-5, 21069-3 Two volumes, Paperbound $10.00

KEYBOARD MUSIC, Johann Sebastian Bach. Bach Gesellschaft edition. A rich selection of Bach's masterpieces for the harpsichord: the six English Suites, six French Suites, the six Partitas (Clavierübung part I), the Goldberg Variations (Clavierübung part IV), the fifteen Two-Part Inventions and the fifteen Three-Part Sinfonias. Clearly reproduced on large sheets with ample margins; eminently playable. vi + 312pp. 8⅛ x 11. 22360-4 Paperbound $5.00

THE MUSIC OF BACH: AN INTRODUCTION, Charles Sanford Terry. A fine, nontechnical introduction to Bach's music, both instrumental and vocal. Covers organ music, chamber music, passion music, other types. Analyzes themes, developments, innovations. x + 114pp. 21075-8 Paperbound $1.25

BEETHOVEN AND HIS NINE SYMPHONIES, Sir George Grove. Noted British musicologist provides best history, analysis, commentary on symphonies. Very thorough, rigorously accurate; necessary to both advanced student and amateur music lover. 436 musical passages. vii + 407 pp. 20334-4 Paperbound $2.75

ADVENTURES OF AN AFRICAN SLAVER, Theodore Canot. Edited by Brantz Mayer. A detailed portrayal of slavery and the slave trade, 1820-1840. Canot, an established trader along the African coast, describes the slave economy of the African kingdoms, the treatment of captured negroes, the extensive journeys in the interior to gather slaves, slave revolts and their suppression, harems, bribes, and much more. Full and unabridged republication of 1854 edition. Introduction by Malcom Cowley. 16 illustrations. xvii + 448pp. 22456-2 Paperbound $3.50

MY BONDAGE AND MY FREEDOM, Frederick Douglass. Born and brought up in slavery, Douglass witnessed its horrors and experienced its cruelties, but went on to become one of the most outspoken forces in the American anti-slavery movement. Considered the best of his autobiographies, this book graphically describes the in-human treatment of slaves, its effects on slave owners and slave families, and how Douglass's determination led him to a new life. Unaltered reprint of 1st (1855) edition. xxxii + 464pp. 22457-0 Paperbound $2.50

THE INDIANS' BOOK, recorded and edited by Natalie Curtis. Lore, music, narratives, dozens of drawings by Indians themselves from an authoritative and important survey of native culture among Plains, Southwestern, Lake and Pueblo Indians. Standard work in popular ethnomusicology. 149 songs in full notation. 23 draw-ings, 23 photos. xxxi + 584pp. 6⅝ x 9⅜. 21939-9 Paperbound $4.50

DICTIONARY OF AMERICAN PORTRAITS, edited by Hayward and Blanche Cirker. 4024 portraits of 4000 most important Americans, colonial days to 1905 (with a few important categories, like Presidents, to present). Pioneers, explorers, colonial figures, U. S. officials, politicians, writers, military and naval men, scientists, inven-tors, manufacturers, jurists, actors, historians, educators, notorious figures, Indian chiefs, etc. All authentic contemporary likenesses. The only work of its kind in existence; supplements all biographical sources for libraries. Indispensable to any-one working with American history. 8,000-item classified index, finding lists, other aids. xiv + 756pp. 9¼ x 12¾. 21823-6 Clothbound $30.00

TRITTON'S GUIDE TO BETTER WINE AND BEER MAKING FOR BEGINNERS, S. M. Tritton. All you need to know to make family-sized quantities of over 100 types of grape, fruit, herb and vegetable wines; as well as beers, mead, cider, etc. Com-plete recipes, advice as to equipment, procedures such as fermenting, bottling, and storing wines. Recipes given in British, U. S., and metric measures. Accompanying booklet lists sources in U. S. A. where ingredients may be bought, and additional information. 11 illustrations. 157pp. 5⅝ x 8⅛.
(USO) 22090-7 Clothbound $3.50

GARDENING WITH HERBS FOR FLAVOR AND FRAGRANCE, Helen M. Fox. How to grow herbs in your own garden, how to use them in your cooking (over 55 recipes included), legends and myths associated with each species, uses in medicine, per-fumes, etc.—these are elements of one of the few books written especially for Amer-ican herb fanciers. Guides you step-by-step from soil preparation to harvesting and storage for each type of herb. 12 drawings by Louise Mansfield. xiv + 334pp.
22540-2 Paperbound $2.50

INCIDENTS OF TRAVEL IN YUCATAN, John L. Stephens. Classic (1843) exploration of jungles of Yucatan, looking for evidences of Maya civilization. Stephens found many ruins; comments on travel adventures, Mexican and Indian culture. 127 striking illustrations by F. Catherwood. Total of 669 pp.

20926-1, 20927-X Two volumes, Paperbound $5.00

INCIDENTS OF TRAVEL IN CENTRAL AMERICA, CHIAPAS, AND YUCATAN, John L. Stephens. An exciting travel journal and an important classic of archeology. Narrative relates his almost single-handed discovery of the Mayan culture, and exploration of the ruined cities of Copan, Palenque, Utatlan and others; the monuments they dug from the earth, the temples buried in the jungle, the customs of poverty-stricken Indians living a stone's throw from the ruined palaces. 115 drawings by F. Catherwood. Portrait of Stephens. xii + 812pp.

22404-X, 22405-8 Two volumes, Paperbound $6.00

A NEW VOYAGE ROUND THE WORLD, William Dampier. Late 17-century naturalist joined the pirates of the Spanish Main to gather information; remarkably vivid account of buccaneers, pirates; detailed, accurate account of botany, zoology, ethnography of lands visited. Probably the most important early English voyage, enormous implications for British exploration, trade, colonial policy. Also most interesting reading. Argonaut edition, introduction by Sir Albert Gray. New introduction by Percy Adams. 6 plates, 7 illustrations. xlvii + 376pp. 6½ x 9¼.

21900-3 Paperbound $3.00

INTERNATIONAL AIRLINE PHRASE BOOK IN SIX LANGUAGES, Joseph W. Bátor. Important phrases and sentences in English paralleled with French, German, Portuguese, Italian, Spanish equivalents, covering all possible airport-travel situations; created for airline personnel as well as tourist by Language Chief, Pan American Airlines. xiv + 204pp. 22017-6 Paperbound $2.00

STAGE COACH AND TAVERN DAYS, Alice Morse Earle. Detailed, lively account of the early days of taverns; their uses and importance in the social, political and military life; furnishings and decorations; locations; food and drink; tavern signs, etc. Second half covers every aspect of early travel; the roads, coaches, drivers, etc. Nostalgic, charming, packed with fascinating material. 157 illustrations, mostly photographs. xiv + 449pp. 22518-6 Paperbound $4.00

NORSE DISCOVERIES AND EXPLORATIONS IN NORTH AMERICA, Hjalmar R. Holand. The perplexing Kensington Stone, found in Minnesota at the end of the 19th century. Is it a record of a Scandinavian expedition to North America in the 14th century? Or is it one of the most successful hoaxes in history. A scientific detective investigation. Formerly *Westward from Vinland.* 31 photographs, 17 figures. x + 354pp. 22014-1 Paperbound $2.75

A BOOK OF OLD MAPS, compiled and edited by Emerson D. Fite and Archibald Freeman. 74 old maps offer an unusual survey of the discovery, settlement and growth of America down to the close of the Revolutionary war: maps showing Norse settlements in Greenland, the explorations of Columbus, Verrazano, Cabot, Champlain, Joliet, Drake, Hudson, etc., campaigns of Revolutionary war battles, and much more. Each map is accompanied by a brief historical essay. xvi + 299pp. 11 x 13¾. 22084-2 Paperbound $6.00

EINSTEIN'S THEORY OF RELATIVITY, Max Born. Relativity theory analyzed, explained for intelligent layman or student with some physical, mathematical background. Includes Lorentz, Minkowski, and others. Excellent verbal account for teachers. Generally considered the finest non-technical account. vii + 376pp.
60769-0 Paperbound $2.75

PHYSICAL PRINCIPLES OF THE QUANTUM THEORY, Werner Heisenberg. Nobel Laureate discusses quantum theory, uncertainty principle, wave mechanics, work of Dirac, Schroedinger, Compton, Wilson, Einstein, etc. Middle, non-mathematical level for physicist, chemist not specializing in quantum; mathematical appendix for specialists. Translated by C. Eckart and F. Hoyt. 19 figures. viii + 184pp.
60113-7 Paperbound $2.00

PRINCIPLES OF QUANTUM MECHANICS, William V. Houston. For student with working knowledge of elementary mathematical physics; uses Schroedinger's wave mechanics. Evidence for quantum theory, postulates of quantum mechanics, applications in spectroscopy, collision problems, electrons, similar topics. 21 figures. 288pp.
60524-8 Paperbound $3.00

ATOMIC SPECTRA AND ATOMIC STRUCTURE, Gerhard Herzberg. One of the best introductions to atomic spectra and their relationship to structure; especially suited to specialists in other fields who require a comprehensive basic knowledge. Treatment is physical rather than mathematical. 2nd edition. Translated by J. W. T. Spinks. 80 illustrations. xiv + 257pp.
60115-3 Paperbound $2.00

ATOMIC PHYSICS: AN ATOMIC DESCRIPTION OF PHYSICAL PHENOMENA, Gaylord P. Harnwell and William E. Stephens. One of the best introductions to modern quantum ideas. Emphasis on the extension of classical physics into the realms of atomic phenomena and the evolution of quantum concepts. 156 problems. 173 figures and tables. xi + 401pp.
61584-7 Paperbound $3.00

ATOMS, MOLECULES AND QUANTA, Arthur E. Ruark and Harold C. Urey. 1964 edition of work that has been a favorite of students and teachers for 30 years. Origins and major experimental data of quantum theory, development of concepts of atomic and molecular structure prior to new mechanics, laws and basic ideas of quantum mechanics, wave mechanics, matrix mechanics, general theory of quantum dynamics. Very thorough, lucid presentation for advanced students. 230 figures. Total of xxiii + 810pp.
61106-X, 61107-8 Two volumes, Paperbound $6.00

INVESTIGATIONS ON THE THEORY OF THE BROWNIAN MOVEMENT, Albert Einstein. Five papers (1905-1908) investigating the dynamics of Brownian motion and evolving an elementary theory of interest to mathematicians, chemists and physical scientists. Notes by R. Fürth, the editor, discuss the history of study of Brownian movement, elucidate the text and analyze the significance of the papers. Translated by A. D. Cowper. 3 figures. iv + 122pp.
60304-0 Paperbound $1.50

JOHANN SEBASTIAN BACH, Philipp Spitta. One of the great classics of musicology, this definitive analysis of Bach's music (and life) has never been surpassed. Lucid, nontechnical analyses of hundreds of pieces (30 pages devoted to St. Matthew Passion, 26 to B Minor Mass). Also includes major analysis of 18th-century music. 450 musical examples. 40-page musical supplement. Total of xx + 1799pp.

(EUK) 22278-0, 22279-9 Two volumes, Clothbound $17.50

MOZART AND HIS PIANO CONCERTOS, Cuthbert Girdlestone. The only full-length study of an important area of Mozart's creativity. Provides detailed analyses of all 23 concertos, traces inspirational sources. 417 musical examples. Second edition. 509pp.
(USO) 21271-8 Paperbound $3.50

THE PERFECT WAGNERITE: A COMMENTARY ON THE NIBLUNG'S RING, George Bernard Shaw. Brilliant and still relevant criticism in remarkable essays on Wagner's Ring cycle, Shaw's ideas on political and social ideology behind the plots, role of Leitmotifs, vocal requisites, etc. Prefaces. xxi + 136pp.
21707-8 Paperbound $1.50

DON GIOVANNI, W. A. Mozart. Complete libretto, modern English translation; biographies of composer and librettist; accounts of early performances and critical reaction. Lavishly illustrated. All the material you need to understand and appreciate this great work. Dover Opera Guide and Libretto Series; translated and introduced by Ellen Bleiler. 92 illustrations. 209pp.
21134-7 Paperbound $2.00

HIGH FIDELITY SYSTEMS: A LAYMAN'S GUIDE, Roy F. Allison. All the basic information you need for setting up your own audio system: high fidelity and stereo record players, tape records, F.M. Connections, adjusting tone arm, cartridge, checking needle alignment, positioning speakers, phasing speakers, adjusting hums, trouble-shooting, maintenance, and similar topics. Enlarged 1965 edition. More than 50 charts, diagrams, photos. iv + 91pp.
21514-8 Paperbound $1.25

REPRODUCTION OF SOUND, Edgar Villchur. Thorough coverage for laymen of high fidelity systems, reproducing systems in general, needles, amplifiers, preamps, loudspeakers, feedback, explaining physical background. "A rare talent for making technicalities vividly comprehensible," R. Darrell, *High Fidelity*. 69 figures. iv + 92pp.
21515-6 Paperbound $1.25

HEAR ME TALKIN' TO YA: THE STORY OF JAZZ AS TOLD BY THE MEN WHO MADE IT, Nat Shapiro and Nat Hentoff. Louis Armstrong, Fats Waller, Jo Jones, Clarence Williams, Billy Holiday, Duke Ellington, Jelly Roll Morton and dozens of other jazz greats tell how it was in Chicago's South Side, New Orleans, depression Harlem and the modern West Coast as jazz was born and grew. xvi + 429pp.
21726-4 Paperbound $2.50

FABLES OF AESOP, translated by Sir Roger L'Estrange. A reproduction of the very rare 1931 Paris edition; a selection of the most interesting fables, together with 50 imaginative drawings by Alexander Calder. v + 128pp. 6½x9¼.
21780-9 Paperbound $1.50

INTRODUCTION TO THE DIFFERENTIAL EQUATIONS OF PHYSICS, Ludwig Hopf. No math background beyond elementary calculus is needed to follow this classroom or self-study introduction to ordinary and partial differential equations. Approach is through classical physics. Translated by Walter Nef. 48 figures. v + 154pp.

60120-X Paperbound $1.75

DIFFERENTIAL EQUATIONS FOR ENGINEERS, Philip Franklin. For engineers, physicists, applied mathematicians. Theory and application: solution of ordinary differential equations and partial derivatives, analytic functions. Fourier series, Abel's theorem, Cauchy Riemann differential equations, etc. Over 400 problems deal with electricity, vibratory systems, heat, radio; solutions. Formerly *Differential Equations for Electrical Engineers*. 41 illustrations. vii + 299pp.

60601-5 Paperbound $2.50

THEORY OF FUNCTIONS, PART II. Single- and multiple-valued functions; full presentation of the most characteristic and important types. Proofs fully worked out. Translated by Frederick Bagemihl. x + 150pp. 60157-9 Paperbound $1.50

PROBLEM BOOK IN THE THEORY OF FUNCTIONS, I. More than 300 elementary problems for independent use or for use with "Theory of Functions, I." 85pp. of detailed solutions. Translated by Lipman Bers. viii + 126pp.

60158-7 Paperbound $1.50

PROBLEM BOOK IN THE THEORY OF FUNCTIONS, II. More than 230 problems in the advanced theory. Designed to be used with "Theory of Functions, II" or with any comparable text. Full solutions. Translated by Frederick Bagemihl. 138pp.

60159-5 Paperbound $1.75

INTRODUCTION TO THE THEORY OF EQUATIONS, Florian Cajori. Classic introduction by leading historian of science covers the fundamental theories as reached by Gauss, Abel, Galois and Kronecker. Basics of equation study are followed by symmetric functions of roots, elimination, homographic and Tschirnhausen transformations, resolvents of Lagrange, cyclic equations, Abelian equations, the work of Galois, the algebraic solution of general equations, and much more. Numerous exercises include answers. ix + 239pp. 62184-7 Paperbound $2.75

LAPLACE TRANSFORMS AND THEIR APPLICATIONS TO DIFFERENTIAL EQUATIONS, N. W. McLachlan. Introduction to modern operational calculus, applying it to ordinary and partial differential equations. Laplace transform, theorems of operational calculus, solution of equations with constant coefficients, evaluation of integrals, derivation of transforms, of various functions, etc. For physics, engineering students. Formerly *Modern Operational Calculus*. xiv + 218pp.

60192-7 Paperbound $2.50

PARTIAL DIFFERENTIAL EQUATIONS OF MATHEMATICAL PHYSICS, Arthur G. Webster. Introduction to basic method and theory of partial differential equations, with full treatment of their applications to virtually every field. Full, clear chapters on Fourier series, integral and elliptic equations, spherical, cylindrical and ellipsoidal harmonics, Cauchy's method, boundary problems, method of Riemann-Volterra, many other basic topics. Edited by Samuel J. Plimpton. 97 figures. vii + 446pp. 60263-X Paperbound $3.00

PRINCIPLES OF STELLAR DYNAMICS, Subrahmanyan Chandrasekhar. Theory of stellar dynamics as a branch of classical dynamics; stellar encounter in terms of 2-body problem, Liouville's theorem and equations of continuity. Also two additional papers. 50 illustrations. x + 313pp. 5⅝ x 8⅜.
60659-7 Paperbound $3.00

CELESTIAL OBJECTS FOR COMMON TELESCOPES, T. W. Webb. The most used book in amateur astronomy: inestimable aid for locating and identifying hundreds of celestial objects. Volume 1 covers operation of telescope, telescope photography, precise information on sun, moon, planets, asteroids, meteor swarms, etc.; Volume 2, stars, constellations, double stars, clusters, variables, nebulae, etc. Nearly 4,000 objects noted. New edition edited, updated by Margaret W. Mayall. 77 illustrations. Total of xxxix + 606pp.
20917-2, 20918-0 Two volumes, Paperbound $5.50

A SHORT HISTORY OF ASTRONOMY, Arthur Berry. Earliest times through the 19th century. Individual chapters on Copernicus, Tycho Brahe, Galileo, Kepler, Newton, etc. Non-technical, but precise, thorough, and as useful to specialist as layman. 104 illustrations, 9 portraits, xxxi + 440 pp.
20210-0 Paperbound $3.00

ORDINARY DIFFERENTIAL EQUATIONS, Edward L. Ince. Explains and analyzes theory of ordinary differential equations in real and complex domains: elementary methods of integration, existence and nature of solutions, continuous transformation groups, linear differential equations, equations of first order, non-linear equations of higher order, oscillation theorems, etc. "Highly recommended," *Electronics Industries*. 18 figures. viii + 558pp.
60349-0 Paperbound $4.00

DICTIONARY OF CONFORMAL REPRESENTATIONS, H. Kober. Laplace's equation in two dimensions for many boundary conditions; scores of geometric forms and transformations for electrical engineers, Joukowski aerofoil for aerodynamists, Schwarz-Christoffel transformations, transcendental functions, etc. Twin diagrams for most transformations. 447 diagrams. xvi + 208pp. 6⅛ x 9¼.
60160-9 Paperbound $2.50

ALMOST PERIODIC FUNCTIONS, A. S. Besicovitch. Thorough summary of Bohr's theory of almost periodic functions citing new shorter proofs, extending the theory, and describing contributions of Wiener, Weyl, de la Vallée, Poussin, Stepanoff, Bochner and the author. xiii + 180pp.
60018-1 Paperbound $2.50

AN INTRODUCTION TO THE STUDY OF STELLAR STRUCTURE, S. Chandrasekhar. A rigorous examination, using both classical and modern mathematical methods, of the relationship between loss of energy, the mass, and the radius of stars in a steady state. 38 figures. 509pp.
60413-6 Paperbound $3.75

INTRODUCTION TO THE THEORY OF GROUP'S OF FINITE ORDER, Robert D. Carmichael. Progresses in easy steps from sets, groups, permutations, isomorphism through the important types of groups. No higher mathematics is necessary. 783 exercises and problems. xiv + 447pp.
60300-8 Paperbound $4.00

ELEMENTARY MATHEMATICS FROM AN ADVANCED STANDPOINT: VOLUME II—
GEOMETRY, Feliex Klein. Using analytical formulas, Klein clarifies the precise
formulation of geometric facts in chapters on manifolds, geometric and higher
point transformations, foundations. "Nothing comparable," *Mathematics Teacher.*
Translated by E. R. Hedrick and C. A. Noble. 141 figures. ix + 214pp.
(USO) 60151-X Paperbound $2.25

ENGINEERING MATHEMATICS, Kenneth S. Miller. Most useful mathematical techniques for graduate students in engineering, physics, covering linear differential
equations, series, random functions, integrals, Fourier series, Laplace transform,
network theory, etc. "Sound and teachable," Science. 89 figures. xii + 417pp.
6 x 8½.   61121-3 Paperbound $3.00

INTRODUCTION TO ASTROPHYSICS: THE STARS, Jean Dufay. Best guide to ob-
servational astrophysics in English. Bridges the gap between elementary populariza-
tions and advanced technical monographs. Covers stellar photometry, stellar spectra
and classification, Hertzsprung-Russell diagrams, Yerkes 2-dimensional classification, temperatures, diameters, masses and densities, evolution of the stars. Translated by Owen Gingerich. 51 figures, 11 tables. xii + 164pp.
60771-2 Paperbound $2.50

INTRODUCTION TO BESSEL FUNCTIONS, Frank Bowman. Full, clear introduction to
properties and applications of Bessel functions. Covers Bessel functions of zero
order, of any order; definite integrals; asymptotic expansions; Bessel's solution to
Kepler's problem; circular membranes; etc. Math above calculus and fundamentals
of differential equations developed within text. 636 problems. 28 figures. x +
135pp.   60462-4 Paperbound $1.75

DIFFERENTIAL AND INTEGRAL CALCULUS, Philip Franklin. A full and basic introduction, textbook for a two- or three-semester course, or self-study. Covers para-
metric functions, force components in polar coordinates, Duhamel's theorem,
methods and applications of integration, infinite series, Taylor's series, vectors and
surfaces in space, etc. Exercises follow each chapter with full solutions at back
of the book. Index. xi + 679pp.   62520-6 Paperbound $4.00

THE EXACT SCIENCES IN ANTIQUITY, O. Neugebauer. Modern overview chiefly
of mathematics and astronomy as developed by the Egyptians and Babylonians.
Reveals startling advancement of Babylonian mathematics (tables for numerical
computations, quadratic equations with two unknowns, implications that Pytha-
gorean theorem was known 1000 years before Pythagoras), and sophisticated
astronomy based on competent mathematics. Also covers transmission of this
knowledge to Hellenistic world. 14 plates, 52 figures. xvii + 240pp.
22332-9 Paperbound $2.50

THE THIRTEEN BOOKS OF EUCLID'S ELEMENTS, translated with introduction and
commentary by Sir Thomas Heath. Unabridged republication of definitive edition
based on the text of Heiberg. Translator's notes discuss textual and linguistic
matters, mathematical analysis, 2500 years of critical commentary on the Elements.
Do not confuse with abridged school editions. Total of xvii + 1414pp.
60088-2, 60089-0, 60090-4 Three volumes, Paperbound $9.50

ALGEBRAS AND THEIR ARITHMETICS, Leonard E. Dickson. Complete background for advanced study of abstract algebra. Clear rigorous exposition of the structures of many special algebras, from an elementary introduction to linear transformations, matrices and complex numbers to a generalization of the classic theory of integral algebraic numbers. Each definition and theorem illustrated by a simple example. xii + 241pp. 60616-3 Paperbound $1.50

ASTRONOMY AND COSMOGONY, Sir James Jeans. Modern classic of exposition, Jean's latest work. Descriptive astronomy, atrophysics, stellar dynamics, cosmology, presented on intermediate level. 16 illustrations. Preface by Lloyd Motz. xv + 428pp. 60923-5 Paperbound $3.50

EXPERIMENTAL SPECTROSCOPY, Ralph A. Sawyer. Discussion of techniques and principles of prism and grating spectrographs used in research. Full treatment of apparatus, construction, mounting, photographic process, spectrochemical analysis, theory. Mathematics kept to a minimum. Revised (1961) edition. 110 illustrations. x + 358pp. 61045-4 Paperbound $3.00

THEORY OF LIGHT, Richard von Mises. Introduction to fluid dynamics, explaining fully the physical phenomena and mathematical concepts of aeronautical engineering, general theory of stability, dynamics of incompressible fluids and wing theory. Still widely recommended for clarity, though limited to situations in which air compressibility effects are unimportant. New introduction by K. H. Hohenemser. 408 figures. xvi + 629pp. 60541-8 Paperbound $3.75

AIRPLANE STRUCTURAL ANALYSIS AND DESIGN, Ernest E. Sechler and Louis G. Dunn. Valuable source work to the aircraft and missile designer: applied and design loads, stress-strain, frame analysis, plates under normal pressure, engine mounts, landing gears, etc. 47 problems. 256 figures. xi + 420pp. 61043-8 Paperbound $2.50

PHOTOELASTICITY: PRINCIPLES AND METHODS, H. T. Jessop and F. C. Harris. An introduction to general and modern developments in 2- and 3-dimensional stress analysis techniques. More advanced mathematical treatment given in appendices. 164 figures. viii + 184pp. 6⅛ x 9¼. (USO) 60720-8 Paperbound $2.00

THE MEASUREMENT OF POWER SPECTRA FROM THE POINT OF VIEW OF COMMUNICATIONS ENGINEERING, Ralph B. Blackman and John W. Tukey. Techniques for measuring the power spectrum using elementary transmission theory and theory of statistical estimation. Methods of acquiring sound data, procedures for reducing data to meaningful estimates, ways of interpreting estimates. 36 figures and tables. Index. x + 190pp. 60507-8 Paperbound $2.50

GASEOUS CONDUCTORS: THEORY AND ENGINEERING APPLICATIONS, James D. Cobine. An indispensable reference for radio engineers, physicists and lighting engineers. Physical backgrounds, theory of space charges, applications in circuit interrupters, rectifiers, oscillographs, etc. 83 problems. Over 600 figures. xx + 606pp. 60442-X Paperbound $3.75

ALGEBRAS AND THEIR ARITHMETICS, Leonard E. Dickson. Complete background for advanced study of abstract algebra. Clear rigorous exposition of the structures of many special algebras, from an elementary introduction to linear transformations, matrices and complex numbers to a generalization of the classic theory of integral algebraic numbers. Each definition and theorem illustrated by a simple example. xii + 241pp. 60616-3 Paperbound $1.50

ASTRONOMY AND COSMOGONY, Sir James Jeans. Modern classic of exposition, Jean's latest work. Descriptive astronomy, atrophysics, stellar dynamics, cosmology, presented on intermediate level. 16 illustrations. Preface by Lloyd Motz. xv + 428pp. 60923-5 Paperbound $3.50

EXPERIMENTAL SPECTROSCOPY, Ralph A. Sawyer. Discussion of techniques and principles of prism and grating spectrographs used in research. Full treatment of apparatus, construction, mounting, photographic process, spectrochemical analysis, theory. Mathematics kept to a minimum. Revised (1961) edition. 110 illustrations. x + 358pp. 61045-4 Paperbound $3.00

THEORY OF LIGHT, Richard von Mises. Introduction to fluid dynamics, explaining fully the physical phenomena and mathematical concepts of aeronautical engineering, general theory of stability, dynamics of incompressible fluids and wing theory. Still widely recommended for clarity, though limited to situations in which air compressibility effects are unimportant. New introduction by K. H. Hohenemser. 408 figures. xvi + 629pp. 60541-8 Paperbound $3.75

AIRPLANE STRUCTURAL ANALYSIS AND DESIGN, Ernest E. Sechler and Louis G. Dunn. Valuable source work to the aircraft and missile designer: applied and design loads, stress-strain, frame analysis, plates under normal pressure, engine mounts, landing gears, etc. 47 problems. 256 figures. xi + 420pp. 61043-8 Paperbound $2.50

PHOTOELASTICITY: PRINCIPLES AND METHODS, H. T. Jessop and F. C. Harris. An introduction to general and modern developments in 2- and 3-dimensional stress analysis techniques. More advanced mathematical treatment given in appendices. 164 figures. viii + 184pp. 6⅛ x 9¼. (USO) 60720-8 Paperbound $2.00

THE MEASUREMENT OF POWER SPECTRA FROM THE POINT OF VIEW OF COMMUNICATIONS ENGINEERING, Ralph B. Blackman and John W. Tukey. Techniques for measuring the power spectrum using elementary transmission theory and theory of statistical estimation. Methods of acquiring sound data, procedures for reducing data to meaningful estimates, ways of interpreting estimates. 36 figures and tables. Index. x + 190pp. 60507-8 Paperbound $2.50

GASEOUS CONDUCTORS: THEORY AND ENGINEERING APPLICATIONS, James D. Cobine. An indispensable reference for radio engineers, physicists and lighting engineers. Physical backgrounds, theory of space charges, applications in circuit interrupters, rectifiers, oscillographs, etc. 83 problems. Over 600 figures. xx + 606pp. 60442-X Paperbound $3.75

ASTRONOMY AND COSMOGONY, Sir James Jeans. Modern classic of exposition, Jean's latest work. Descriptive astronomy, atrophysics, stellar dynamics, cosmology, presented on intermediate level. 16 illustrations. Preface by Lloyd Motz. xv + 428pp. 60923-5 Paperbound $3.50

EXPERIMENTAL SPECTROSCOPY, Ralph A. Sawyer. Discussion of techniques and principles of prism and grating spectrographs used in research. Full treatment of apparatus, construction, mounting, photographic process, spectrochemical analysis, theory. Mathematics kept to a minimum. Revised (1961) edition. 110 illustrations. x + 358pp. 61045-4 Paperbound $3.50

THEORY OF FLIGHT, Richard von Mises. Introduction to fluid dynamics, explaining fully the physical phenomena and mathematical concepts of aeronautical engineering, general theory of stability, dynamics of incompressible fluids and wing theory. Still widely recommended for clarity, though limited to situations in which air compressibility effects are unimportant. New introduction by K. H. Hohenemser. 408 figures. xvi + 629pp. 60541-8 Paperbound $5.00

AIRPLANE STRUCTURAL ANALYSIS AND DESIGN, Ernest E. Sechler and Louis G. Dunn. Valuable source work to the aircraft and missile designer: applied and design loads, stress-strain, frame analysis, plates under normal pressure, engine mounts; landing gears, etc. 47 problems. 256 figures. xi + 420pp.
61043-8 Paperbound $3.50

PHOTOELASTICITY: PRINCIPLES AND METHODS, H. T. Jessop and F. C. Harris. An introduction to general and modern developments in 2- and 3-dimensional stress analysis techniques. More advanced mathematical treatment given in appendices. 164 figures. viii + 184pp. 6⅛ x 9¼. (USO) 60720-8 Paperbound $2.50

THE MEASUREMENT OF POWER SPECTRA FROM THE POINT OF VIEW OF COMMUNICATIONS ENGINEERING, Ralph B. Blackman and John W. Tukey. Techniques for measuring the power spectrum using elementary transmission theory and theory of statistical estimation. Methods of acquiring sound data, procedures for reducing data to meaningful estimates, ways of interpreting estimates. 36 figures and tables. Index. x + 190pp. 60507-8 Paperbound $2.50

GASEOUS CONDUCTORS: THEORY AND ENGINEERING APPLICATIONS, James D. Cobine. An indispensable reference for radio engineers, physicists and lighting engineers. Physical backgrounds, theory of space charges, applications in circuit interrupters, rectifiers, oscillographs, etc. 83 problems. Over 600 figures. xx + 606pp. 60442-X Paperbound $3.75

Prices subject to change without notice.

Available at your book dealer or write for free catalogue to Dept. Sci, Dover Publications, Inc., 180 Varick St., N.Y., N.Y. 10014. Dover publishes more than 150 books each year on science, elementary and advanced mathematics, biology, music, art, literary history, social sciences and other areas

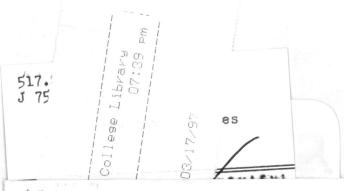